MAN. WALKS INTO A BAR

MAN WALKS INTO A BAR 3

THE ULTIMATE COLLECTION OF JOKES AND ONE-LINERS

JONATHAN SWAN

EBURY
PRESS

3 5 7 9 10 8 6 4

Published in 2010 by Ebury Press, an imprint of Ebury Publishing
A Random House Group company

The Random House Group Limited Reg. No. 954009

Addresses for companies within the Random House Group can be found at
www.randomhouse.co.uk

A CIP catalogue record for this book is available from the British Library

The Random House Group Limited supports the Forest Stewardship Council® (FSC®), the leading
international forest certification organisation. All our titles that are printed on Greenpeace approved
FSC® certified paper carry the FSC® logo. Our paper procurement policy can be found at
www.randomhouse.co.uk/environment

Designed and set by seagulls.net

Printed and bound in the UK by CPI Group (UK) Ltd, Croydon, CR0 4YY

ISBN 9780091937850

To buy books by your favourite authors and register for offers visit www.randomhouse.co.uk

CONTENTS

A

B

C

H

i

J

M

N

O

P

R

S

T

V

W

ACTORS

✳ How many actors does it take to screw in a light bulb? Depends on what it says in the script!

✳ What's the most dangerous thing in your average community theatre? An actor with a power tool.

✳ When an actress saw her first strands of grey hair she thought she'd dye.

✳ Soldiers in plays like to Shakespeares.

✳ A man walks into a daily newspaper looking for work. When asked about his special skills he replies: 'I actually have no particular interests or talents myself but enjoy belittling the artistic endeavours of others.' 'Fabulous!!' retorted the employment officer. 'We have an opening for a theatre critic.'

✳ The story goes that three people died one day and went to Heaven where they were greeted at the Pearly Gates by St Peter. 'How much do you make a year?' St Peter asked the first person. The man replied, '£500,000.' 'Go and stand over there with the surgeons and lawyers,' St Peter said. Then he asked the second person: 'And how much do you make a year?' 'About £200,000,' she replied and was promptly told to stand with the accountants. St Peter then turned to the third person. 'How much do you earn a year?' he asked. 'About £6,000,' admitted the man. St Peter stopped in his tracks, looked at the man keenly and said: 'And would I have seen you in anything?'

✳ An actor phones another actor friend whom he hasn't spoken to in a while to see how he's doing. 'I'm doing great!' his friend replies. 'In fact, I couldn't be better! My agent has been sending me out every day, I just finished shooting a national commercial and it looks like I'm a shoe-in for a regular on a new sitcom this autumn!' 'Oh gosh, I'm sorry,' says the first actor. 'I'll call you back when you don't have company.'

✳ An actor comes home one day to find his home ransacked … Just trashed … As he stands in the rubble, stunned, he hears moaning from the upstairs bedroom. He races upstairs to find his wife, obviously beaten and taken advantage of. Through his tears he asks, 'Who did this?' His wife whispers, 'Your agent.' The man brightens. 'My agent? He came to the house? Wow!'

✳ A great actor could no longer remember his lines. After many years he found a theatre where they were prepared to give him a chance to shine again. The director told him, 'This is the most important part, and it has only one line. You walk on to the stage at the opening carrying a rose. You hold the rose to your nose with just one finger and thumb, sniff the rose deeply and then say the line, "Ah, the sweet aroma of my mistress."'

The actor is thrilled. All day long before the play he's practising his line over and over again.

Finally, the time came. The curtain went up, the actor walked onto the stage, and with great passion delivered the line, 'Ah, the sweet aroma of my mistress.'

The theatre erupted, the audience was screaming with laughter and the director was steaming!

'You bloody fool!' he cried. 'You have ruined me!'

The actor was bewildered. 'What happened, did I forget my line?'

'No!' screamed the director. 'You forgot the rose!'

* Did you hear about the crowd that the ventriloquist hangs out with? They're a bunch of dummies.

* A director is screen-testing Sylvester Stallone and Arnold Schwarzenegger for a new film about classical composers. Not having figured out whom to give which part to, he asks Sly who he would like to be.

Stallone says, 'I like Mozart. I want to be Mozart.' So the director says, 'Very well, you can be Mozart.' Then he turns to Arnie and says, 'Arnie, who would you like to play?'

And Arnie says, 'Ah'll be Bach!'

* The astronomer became an actor because he always wanted to visit the stars.

✳ Sky have just won the rights to screen the first World Origami Championships from Tokyo.
Unfortunately it's only available on Paper View!

✳ 'Dad, guess what? I've just got my first part in a play. I play the part of a man who's been married for thirty years.'
'Well, keep at it, son. Maybe one day you'll get a speaking part.'

✳ Did you hear about the actor who auditioned for a part as a trumpet player? He blew it.

✳ An actor went to see a new agent one day and said, 'You must have a look at my act, it really is innovative.' So saying, he flew up to the ceiling, circled the room a few times and landed smoothly on the agent's desk. 'So you do bird impressions,' said the agent, 'what else can you do?'

✳ Neighbour: Haven't I seen you on TV?
Actor: Well, I do appear, on and off, you know. How do you like me?
Neighbour: Off.

✳ When the unemployed actor got a job with a demolition company he finally brought down the house.

✳ Who stars in cowboy films and is always broke? Skint Eastwood.

✳ Did you hear about the actor who got lead part after lead part?
He was on a role!

✳ I met a really conceited actor the other day.

Why do you say he's conceited?

Well, every time there was a thunderclap during the storm, he went to the window and took a bow.

😮 AEROPLANES AND FLYiNG

✳ Muhammad Ali was on a flight when the flight attendant came and asked him to buckle his seatbelt. He replied, 'Superman don't need no seatbelt.' She responded, 'Superman don't need no *plane.*'

✳ Old skydivers never die, they're just more down to earth.

✳ A BA 747 pilot had waited for take-off clearance for 45 minutes. A German 737 was cleared immediately. The BA pilot asked the tower why the German aircraft had been given clearance at once. Before the tower could reply, the German pilot came back with: 'Because I got up very early in the morning and put a towel on the runway!'

✳ Three men are on a plane. They open a window and one throws an orange out. The other throws out an apple. The third throws out a hand grenade. After getting off the plane, they see a boy crying. They ask what's wrong, and he replies, 'An apple hit me in the head!'

They see another boy crying. He says, 'An orange hit me in the head!'

Then they see a boy rolling on the sidewalk laughing.

They asked why he was laughing, and he replied, 'I farted and my house blew up!'

✳ You know you're on a no-frills airline when:
  You can't board the plane unless you have the exact change.
  Before you take off, the stewardess tells you to fasten your Velcro.
  The captain asks all the passengers to chip in a little for fuel.
  When they pull the steps away, the plane starts rocking.
  The captain yells at the ground crew to get the cows off the runway.
  You ask the captain how often their planes crash and he says,
  'Just once.'
  No movie. Don't need one. Your life keeps flashing before your eyes.
  You see a man with a gun, but he's demanding to be let off the plane.
  All the planes have both a bathroom and a chapel.
  There is an announcement: 'As you exit the plane, make sure to gather
  all of your belongings. Anything left behind will be distributed evenly
  among the flight attendants. Please do not leave children or spouses.'

✳ A man goes to a warehouse to apply for a job as a forklift operator.
  The manager asks him whether he knows how to operate a forklift.
  The man replies that he does. The manager then asks how long he's
  been driving a forklift. A year or so, answers the man. The manager
  then asks, 'How many loads have you dropped?' 'None. We weren't
  allowed to drop loads.' 'Where did you work?' asks the clearly
  incredulous manager. 'For the air force,' came the reply. 'What did you
  move?' 'Bombs.'

✳ Tower: 'Delta 351, you have traffic at 10 o'clock, six miles!'
  Delta 351: 'Give us another hint! We have digital watches!'

✳ At a software engineering management course, the participants were
  given an awkward question to answer. 'If you had just boarded an

airliner and discovered that your team of programmers had been responsible for the flight control software how many of you would disembark immediately?' Among the ensuing forest of raised hands, only the man from Microsoft sat motionless. When asked what he would do, he replied that he would be quite content to stay onboard. With his team's software, he said, the plane was unlikely to even taxi as far as the runway, let alone take off.

* Two wrongs don't make a right, but two Wrights make an aeroplane.

* Stay out of clouds. The silver lining everyone keeps talking about might be another aeroplane going in the opposite direction.

* Why was the skydiver arrested for taking pictures?
They were in-descent exposures.

* A plane crashed into a lumber yard. Emergency services found the scene remarkably smooth.

* Always try to keep the number of landings you make equal to the number of take-offs you've made.

* Remember, gravity is not just a good idea. It's the law. And it's not subject to appeal.

* There is a theory that the rings of Saturn are made entirely of lost luggage.

✳ It was a few days before Christmas. A man had been on a business trip that had gone badly, and he was ready to go back home. The airport had turned a tacky red and green, and loudspeakers blared annoying lift renditions of cherished Christmas carols.

Being someone who took Christmas very seriously, and being tired, he was not in a particularly good mood. Going to check in his luggage, he saw hanging mistletoe. Not real mistletoe, but very cheap plastic fake mistletoe.

With a considerable degree of irritation and nowhere else to vent it, he said to the attendant, 'Even if we were married, I would not want to kiss you under such a ghastly mockery of mistletoe.'

'Sir, look more closely at where the mistletoe is.'

'OK, I see that it's above the luggage scale which is the place you'd have to step forward for a kiss.'

'That's not why it's there.'

'OK, I give up. Why is it there?'

'It's there so you can kiss your luggage goodbye.'

✳ An elderly aunt loved to visit her nieces and nephews. However, her relatives lived all over the place. The problem was that no matter how much she enjoyed seeing them, she hated flying. No matter how safe people told her it was, she was always worried that someone would have a bomb on the plane. She read books about how safe it was and listened to the stewardess demonstrate all the safety features. But she still worried herself silly every time a visit was coming up. Finally, the family decided that maybe if she saw the statistics she'd be convinced. So they sent her to a friend of the family who was a statistician. 'Tell me,' she said suspiciously, 'what are the chances that someone will have a bomb on a plane?' The boffin fiddled about with his calculator and said, 'A very small chance. Maybe one in five hundred thousand.' She nodded, then thought for a moment. 'So what are the odds of two people having a bomb on the same plane?' Again he went through his calculations. 'Extremely remote,' he said. 'About one in a billion.' The old lady nodded and left his office. And from that day on, every time she flew, she took a bomb with her.

✳ A school teacher was arrested today at Gatwick Airport as he attempted to board a flight while in possession of a ruler, a protractor, a set square, a slide rule, and a calculator.

At a morning press conference, the Home Secretary said he believes the man is a member of the notorious Al-gebra movement. He did not identify the man, who has been charged by the Police with carrying weapons of maths instruction. 'Al-gebra is a problem for us,' the Home Secretary said. 'They desire solutions by means and extremes, and sometimes go off on tangents in a search of absolute values. They use secret code names like "x" and "y" and refer to themselves as "unknowns", but we have determined they belong to a common denominator of the axis of medieval with co-ordinates in every country. As the Greek philanderer Isosceles used to say, 'There are three sides to every triangle.' When asked to comment on the arrest, the prime minister, speaking from his holiday resort before the planes stopped flying, said, 'If God had wanted us to have better Weapons of Maths Instruction, He would have given us more fingers and toes.'

✳ Working on an airline, you receive free or reduced-priced flights. Such was the case when Roger Gay took the opportunity of a free flight from London to Manchester. He boarded the flight some minutes before it was due to leave the terminal. The flight was filling up. Roger's allocated seat was already taken, so he sat in another, vacant seat. A few minutes later a woman in airline uniform (not a stewardess) holding a clipboard marched up to the man in Roger's originally allocated seat and in her official capacity asked, 'Are you Gay?' The man sank down in his seat, blushed and sheepishly uttered, 'Yes.' The woman said, 'Then you have to get off.' Roger, realising that the airline had over-booked and he had to give up his perk seat, put his hand up and said, 'I'm Gay,' and started to get up. Immediately another passenger stands up and militantly calls out, 'I'm gay! They can't chuck us all off!'

✳ A flight attendant is on the red-eye when a water leak develops in the galley, which eventually soaks the carpet throughout the aft cabin of the 747. A very sleepy woman who becomes aware of the dampness tugs at the attendant's skirt as she passes by. 'Has it been raining?' she asks the flight attendant. Keeping a straight face, the attendant replies, 'Yes, but we put the top up.' With a sigh of relief, the woman then goes back to sleep.

✳ Bill, Hillary, and Al Gore were in an airplane that crashed. They're up in Heaven, and God's sitting on the great white throne. God addresses Al first. 'Al, what do you believe in?' Al replies, 'Well, I believe that the combustion engine is evil and that we need to save the world from CFCs and that if any more freon is used, the whole earth will become a greenhouse and we'll all die.' God thinks for a second and says, 'OK, I can live with that. Come and sit at my left.' God then addresses Bill, 'Bill, what do you believe in?' Bill replies, 'Well, I believe in power to the people. I think people should be able to make their own choices about things and that no one should ever be able to tell someone else what to do. I also believe in feeling people's pain.' God thinks for a second and

says, 'OK, that sounds good. Come and sit at my right.' God then address Hillary. 'Hillary, what do you believe in?'
'I believe you're in my chair.'

* If God had really intended men to fly, He'd make it easier to get to the airport. *George Winters*

* During class the skydiving instructor would take time to answer any first-timer questions. One guy asked: 'If our chute doesn't open and the reserve doesn't open, how long do we have till we hit the ground?' The jump master looked at him and in perfect deadpan answered: 'The rest of your life.'

* What do you call a pregnant flight attendant? Pilot error.

* Sorry, folks, for the hard landing. It wasn't the pilot's fault, and it wasn't the plane's fault. It was the asphault.

* If you're ever faced with a forced landing at night, turn on the landing lights to see the landing area. If you don't like what you see, turn 'em back off.

* Flying is hours of boredom, punctuated by moments of stark terror.

* Airspeed, altitude, or brains; you always need at least two.

* The passenger aircraft was fully loaded and in the air after take-off when the announcement came over the loudspeaker: 'Ladies and gentlemen, we've been working on a fully automatic piloting system for years that

doesn't need a flight crew and we are proud to announce that it has been perfected. You are the first passengers to fly controlled by software only with nobody in the cockpit. We are proud that during all our testing there has never been a mistake, mistake, mistake, mistake, mistake … '

Airline dictionary:

* AIR TRAFFIC CONTROL – A game played by airline pilots and air-traffic controllers. The game has no rules, and neither side knows how it is played, but the goal is to prevent flights from arriving in time for passengers to make connecting flights.
* CARRY-ON BAG – An item, usually of large dimensions, which somehow managed to fit under the passenger's seat on the inbound flight. Regardless of what the passenger says the following are not acceptable as carry-on items: bicycles, refrigerators, truck tyres, or widescreen projection TVs.
* FLIGHT SCHEDULE – An entertaining work of paperback fiction.
* FOG – A natural weather phenomenon, which usually occurs around an airport while the surrounding areas are clear. Fog is created and controlled by the airlines and is used to delay flights.
* NO RECORD – Any passenger booked through a travel agency.
* ON TIME – An obscure term, meaning unknown.
* PASSENGER – A herding creature of widely varying intellect usually found in pairs or small groups. Often will become vicious and violent in simple and easily rectified situations. When frightened or confused these creatures collect into a group called a 'line'. This 'line' has no set pattern and is usually formed in inconvenient places. Passengers are of four known species: Paxus iratus, Paxus latus, Paxus inebriates and Paxus ignoramus.

✳ Boarded a Ryanair flight yesterday. They charged me a pound for the headphones, two quid for the pillow. And ten pounds for the goggles and armbands.

✳ When you are lost … Climb, Conserve and Confess.

✳ A young and foolish hotshot pilot wanted to sound cool and show who was boss on the aviation radio frequencies. This was his first time approaching an airfield during the night. Instead of making an official landing request to the tower, he said: 'Guess who?' The tower controller switched the field lights off and replied: 'Guess where!'

✳ There are more planes in the ocean than submarines in the sky.

✳ When one engine fails on a twin-engine airplane you always have enough power left to get you to the scene of the crash.

✳ Progress in airline flying: now a flight attendant can get a pilot pregnant.

✳ A smooth landing is mostly luck; two in a row is all luck; three in a row is prevarication.

✳ Mankind has a perfect record in aviation; we never left one up there!

✳ If something hasn't broken on your helicopter, it's about to.

ALIENS

✳ What do you call a UFO with faulty air conditioning? A frying saucer!

✳ What do aliens wear to posh functions? Space suits.

✳ Did you hear about the man who was abducted in a spaceship full of kittens? It was a close encounter of the furred kind!

✳ If Martians live on Mars and Venusians live on Venus, who lives on Pluto? Fleas.

✳ What do you call an overweight ET? An extra cholesterol!

✳ What did the alien say when it crashed on a stud farm? Take me to your breeder!

✳ What do you call a spaceship that drips water? A crying saucer.

✳ Two aliens landed in the remote countryside and went walking from the flying saucer along a narrow lane. The first thing they saw was a red pillar box. 'Take us to your leader,' said the first alien. 'Don't waste time talking to him. Can't you see he's only a child?' said the second alien.

ARCHITECTS AND ARCHITECTURE

✳ What do architectural historians drink at bedtime? Rococoa!

✳ What do architectural historians listen to? Baroque and roll.

✳ How do you catch a door? You wait at a door stop.

✳ What do interior decorators shout at a hold-up? Frieze!

✳ What do architects eat with Chinese meals? Spatial fried rice.

✳ In which *Star Trek* film did the crew of the *Enterprise* get the builders in for a new floor? The Vinyl Frontier!

✳ Which Elvis song tells of the disastrous early stage of a project? Return to Tender.

✳ What happened to the man who had a leak under his floor? He soon had a spring in his step.

✳ Waterbeds: the vinyl resting place.

✳ A man's home is his castle. In a manor of speaking.

✳ What do you do if you want to put in wooden walls? Have a panel discussion!

✳ Old architects never die. They just put things in perspective.

☺ARMY

✳ A US army platoon was marching north of Fallujah when they came
upon an Iraqi insurgent, badly injured and unconscious. On the
opposite side of the road was a British soldier in a similar but less
serious state. The soldier was conscious and alert and as first aid was
given to both men, the platoon leader asked the injured soldier what
had happened.

The soldier reported, 'I was moving north along the highway here, and
coming south was a heavily armed insurgent. We saw each other and
both took cover in the ditches along the road. I yelled to him that
Saddam Hussein was a miserable, lowlife scum bag who'd got what he
deserved, and he yelled back that Gordon Brown is a fat, useless, lying
one-eyed Jock, and Tony Blair was just Bush's lapdog.

So I said that Osama Bin Laden dresses and ponces about like a
hatchet-faced woman.

He retaliated by yelling, "Oh yeah? Well, so does Harriet Harman!"
And, there we were, in the middle of the road, shaking hands, when a
bus hit us.'

✳ The history teacher one day said to his class at the beginning of the
lesson, 'Right, we are going to have a snap quiz today to see if you
have learnt anything about military history.' A groan went round the
room but a couple of students perked up and seemed quite keen. 'I'm
going to say some quotes, you're going to tell me who said them,
where and when,' the teacher explained.

'First one. Veni, vidi, vici,' he called out.

'Sah! Sah!' cried out a little Japanese boy in the front row on the left-hand side.

'Yes, Kawachi,' said the teacher.

'Sah, that was Julius Caesar, invasion of Britain, 55 BC,' said the little fellow.

'Absolutely spot-on, Kawachi, well done.' The little Japanese boy positively beamed with pride. 'Right, next one – I can't see.'

'Sah! Sah!' cried out a little Japanese boy in the back row on the right-hand side.

'Yes, Sokomoto' said the teacher.

'Sah, that was Admiral Lord Nelson, Battle of Cophenhagen, 1801.'

'Way to go, Sokomoto, that's absolutely correct,' said the teacher.

Suddenly a voice called out from the middle of the classroom, 'Rot in hell, you Japanese scum!'

'Who said that? Who said that?' called out the teacher, enraged.

Same voice from the middle of the class, 'Sir, that was President Roosevelt, invasion of Pearl Harbor, 1941.'

* Did you hear about the soldier who survived mustard gas and pepper spray attacks? He's now a seasoned veteran!

* Landmines cost an arm and a leg.

* Did you hear about the cabin boy who was obsessed with his belly button? He was promoted to navel officer!

* When planning a military campaign, trench warfare should always be a last-ditch effort.

Army recruitment guidelines:

- Take the prospective employees you are trying to place and put them in a room with only a table and two chairs. Leave them alone for two hours, without any instruction. At the end of that time, go back and see what they are doing.
- If they have taken the table apart in that time, put them in the Royal Engineers.
- If they are screaming and waving their arms, send them off to the PT Corps.
- If they are talking to the chairs, send them to the Royal Corps of Signals.
- If they are sleeping, they are officer material.
- If they are writing up the experience, send them to the SAS.
- If they don't even look up when you enter the room, assign them to MOD Police.
- If they try to tell you it's not as bad as it looks, send them to the Intelligence Corps.
- And if they try to leave early, tell them where the RAF office is.

✳ Why shouldn't anyone called William join the army? Have you heard what they shout? Fire at Will ...

✳ Why was the overweight fighter pilot grounded? For violating the rules of engorgement.

✳ What's a soldier's favourite date? March forth!

✳ Why did the soldier stuff himself with pudding? He was a desserter.

✳ What happened to the paratroopers who refused to obey orders? They eventually fell in line.

✳ Did you hear about the woman who loved twenty soldiers? It was platonic.

✳ When in the army, what orders should you obey? General ones!

✳ Why do arrows make you scared? They come with a quiver.

✳ Why did the junior NCO have sore wrists? He had corporal tunnel syndrome!

✳ Why did the soldier refuse to carry two flags? He said it would be a double standard.

✳ Why did they villagers throw stones at the soldiers? They were rotten to the corps.

✳ The Pentagon announced today the formation of a new 500-man elite fighting unit called the United States Redneck Special Forces (USRSF). These boys will be dropped off in Afghanistan and have been given only the following facts about terrorists:

1. The season opened today.
2. There is no limit.
3. They taste just like chicken.
4. They don't like beer, pick-ups, country music or Jesus.

5. They are directly responsible for the death of Dale Earnhardt.

6. They think Daisy Duke is a slut.

* A group of army sergeants and a group of Royal Air Force Officers take a train to a conference. Each officer holds a ticket. But the entire group of sergeants has bought only one ticket for a single passenger. The officers are just shaking their heads and are secretly pleased that the army sergeants will get what they deserve.

Suddenly one of the sergeants calls out: 'The conductor is coming!' At once, all the sergeants jump up and squeeze into one of the toilets. The conductor checks the tickets of the officers. When he notices that the toilet is occupied he knocks on the door and says: 'Ticket, please!' One of the sergeants slides the single ticket under the door and the conductor continues merrily on his round.

For the return trip the officers decide to use the same trick. They buy only one ticket for the entire group but they are baffled as they realise that the sergeants didn't buy any tickets at all. After a while one of the sergeants announces again: 'The conductor is coming!' Immediately all the officers race to a toilet and lock themselves in.

All the sergeants walk leisurely to the other toilet. Before the last sergeant enters the toilet, he knocks on the toilet occupied by the officers and says: 'Ticket, please!'

* A fleeing Taliban, desperate for water, was plodding through the Afghanistan desert when he saw something far off in the distance. Hoping to find water, he hurried towards the object, only to find a little old man at a small stand selling ties.

The Taliban asked, 'Do you have water?'

The man replied, 'I have no water. Would you like to buy a tie?

They are only $5.'

The Taliban shouted, 'Idiot! I do not need an over-priced tie. I need water! I should kill you, but I must find water first!'

'OK,' said the old man, 'it does not matter that you do not want to buy a tie and that you hate me. I will show you that I am bigger than that. If you continue over that hill to the east for about two miles, you will find a lovely restaurant. It has all the ice-cold water you need. Peace be upon you.'

Muttering, the Taliban staggered away over the hill. Several hours later he staggered back, almost dead.

'Your brother won't let me in without a tie.'

✳ When the man was shot with a BB gun the case ended up in a pellet court.

Army ranks explained:

* GENERAL: Leaps tall buildings, is more powerful than a locomotive, is faster than a speeding bullet, walks on water amid hurricanes, gives policy to God.
* COLONEL: Leaps short buildings with a single bound, is more powerful than a jeep, is just as fast as a speeding bullet, walks on water if the sea is calm, talks to God.
* LT. COLONEL: Leaps short buildings with a running start and a favourable wind, is almost as powerful as a jeep, is faster than a speeding pellet, walks on water in indoor swimming pool, talks to God if a request form is approved.
* MAJOR: Barely clears a Nissan hut, loses tug of war with a jeep, can fire a speeding bullet, swims well, is occasionally addressed by God.

- CAPTAIN: Makes high marks by trying to leap buildings, gets run over by locomotive, can sometimes handle a gun without shooting himself, dog paddles, talks to animals.
- 1ST LIEUTENANT: Runs into buildings, recognises locomotives two out of three times, is not issued with live ammunition, can stay afloat in a Mae-West if properly instructed, talks to walls.
- 2ND LIEUTENANT: Falls over the doorstep when entering buildings, says, 'Look at the choo-choo, wets himself, plays in mud puddles, mumbles to himself.
- SERGEANT MAJOR: Lifts tall buildings and walks under them, kicks locomotives off the track, catches speeding bullets in his teeth and eats them, freezes water with one stare …
- HE IS GOD.

International Alert states

The British are feeling the pinch in relation to recent terrorist threats in Islamabad and have raised their security level from 'Miffed' to 'Peeved'. Soon, though, security levels may be raised yet again to 'Irritated' or even 'A Bit Cross'. Brits have not been 'A Bit Cross' since the blitz in 1940 when tea supplies all but ran out. Terrorists have been re-categorised from 'Tiresome' to a 'Bloody Nuisance'. The last time the British issued a 'Bloody Nuisance' warning level was during the great fire of 1666.

The French government announced yesterday that it has raised its terror alert level from 'Run' to 'Hide'. The only two higher levels in France are 'Collaborate' and 'Surrender'. The rise was precipitated by a recent fire that destroyed France's white flag factory, effectively paralysing the country's military capability.

It's not only the French who are on a heightened level of alert:

* Italy has increased the alert level from 'Shout loudly and excitedly' to 'Elaborate Military Posturing'. Two more levels remain: 'Ineffective Combat Operations' and 'Change Sides'.
* The Germans also increased their alert state from 'Disdainful Arrogance' to 'Dress in Uniform and Sing Marching Songs'. They also have two higher levels: 'Invade a Neighbour' and 'Lose'.
* Belgians, on the other hand, are all on holiday as usual and the only threat they are worried about is NATO pulling out of Brussels.
* The Spanish are all excited to see their new submarines ready to deploy. These beautifully designed subs have glass bottoms so the new Spanish navy can get a really good look at the old Spanish navy.
* Americans meanwhile are carrying out pre-emptive strikes on all of their allies, just in case.

And on the other side of the globe ...

* New Zealand has also raised its security levels from 'baaa' to 'BAAAA!' Due to continuing defence cutbacks, the air force being down to a squadron of spotty teenagers flying paper aeroplanes and the navy just a few toy boats in the Prime Minister's bath, New Zealand only has one more level of escalation, which is 'Hell, I hope Australia will come and rescue us'.
* Australia, meanwhile, has raised its security level from 'No worries' to 'She'll be right, mate'. Four more escalation levels remain: 'Crikey!' 'We've run out of snags for the barbie,' 'I think we'll need to cancel the barbie this weekend' and 'The barbie's cancelled!' There has not been a situation yet that has warranted the use of this final escalation level.

✳ Did you hear about the high-ranking military father who cloned himself? The result was a Major Faux Pa!

✳ Three squaddies were captured by Iraqi terrorists. They were buried up to their necks in sand, just within reach of a lovely stretch of water. The most senior said to the others: 'They want us to suffer from thirst, while baking in the sun close to water. Don't give them the satisfaction ... don't give in.'
After hours of this, the terrorists sitting in the shade, watching, noticed that the squaddies' heads were moving in time, from side to side.
One of the terrorists said, 'Hakim, go and see what they are doing.'
Hakim returned looking bewildered and said, 'Malik, they are singing.'
Malik, stunned, said, 'Singing? What are they singing?'
'They are singing ... '
"Ohhhhh liiiiii dooo like to be beside the seaside!"'

✳ A young corporal dislocated his arm during a battle but kept going. You could say he was shouldering on.

✳ The Queen is inspecting three armed forces personnel, one from each of her fighting forces.
She asks each one what they would do if they woke up and found a redback spider in their tent on operations?
The squaddie says, 'I'd reach over, grab my bayonet and stab it to death!'
The navy man says, 'I'd reach over, grab my boot and batter it to death!'
The airman says, 'I'd reach over, pick up my phone, call reception and ask "Who the hell has put a tent up in my hotel room?"'

✳ Why don't Al-Qaida have clarinets? Because then the terrorists woodwind!

✳ A Russian general and an American general meet in a Brussels restaurant and rapidly get engaged in a spot of one-upmanship.
'The American GI is the best-trained soldier in the world. Every GI gets twelve months of rigorous basic training.'
'Huh, that is nothing. The Russian squaddie is made of iron and does two years of training … in the permafrost.'
'Well, the American fighting man is the best equipped in the world. Every GI carries over $3,000 worth of equipment on his person.'
'Hah. Only $3,000? Every Russian soldier has over $5,000 worth of equipment when he goes into battle.'
'All right. The American soldier is the best-fed soldier in the world. Every day each GI eats over 8,000 calories.'
'Now you lie, sir. No one can eat that many potatoes!'

✳ Was depressed last night, rang lifeline. Got a call centre in Afghanistan, told them I was suicidal. They got all excited and asked if I could drive a truck.

✳ Late one afternoon, the US air force folks out at Area 51 were very surprised to see a Cessna landing at their 'secret' base. They immediately impounded the aircraft and hauled the pilot into an interrogation room.
The pilot's story was that he took off from Vegas, got lost, and spotted the base just as he was about to run out of fuel. The air force started a full FBI background check on the pilot and held him overnight during the investigation.

By the next day, they were finally convinced that the pilot really was lost and wasn't a spy. They fuelled up his airplane, gave him a terrifying 'you-did-not-see-a-base' briefing, complete with threats of spending the rest of his life in prison, told him Vegas was that-a-way on such-and-such a heading, and sent him on his way.

The day after that though, to their total disbelief, the same Cessna showed up again. Once again, the military police surrounded the plane … only this time there were two people in the plane.

The same pilot jumped out and said, 'Do anything you want to me, but my wife is in the plane and you have to tell her where I was last night!'

✳ A Taliban commander is patrolling when he hears a shout from behind a sand dune.'One SAS soldier is better than ten Taliban fighters!'

The Taliban commander is enraged at this cheek so quickly sends his ten best soldiers over the dune.

A few shots can be heard. When all is quiet there is no sign of the ten fighters. Another shout rings out.

'One SAS soldier is better than a hundred Taliban fighters!'

The enraged commander rustles up a hundred fighters and sends them over the dune. A firefight erupts. When all is quiet there is no sign of the Taliban fighters. Another shot rings out.

'One SAS soldier is better than a thousand Taliban fighters!'

The commander, now livid, sends a thousand fighters over the dune.

A firefight lasting one hour ensures. When all is quiet, one dying fighter crawls back over the dune and into the arms of his commander.

'Don't send any more fighters. It's a trap. There's two of them!'

✳ Why is it hard to count anything in Afghanistan?
Because of the tally-ban!

✳ A file arrives on a general's desk. On the front in red letters it says: 'TOP SECRET: JAM.' The general opens the file to see what it could be. Inside is a single piece of paper. Printed on it is: 'I can't tell you more in case you spread it about.'

✳ Tom was in his early fifties, retired and started on a second career. However, he just couldn't seem to get to work on time. Every day, five, ten, fifteen minutes late. But he was a good worker, real sharp, so the boss was in a quandary about how to deal with it. Finally, one day he called him into the office for a talk.
'Tom, I have to tell you, I like your work ethic, you do a bang-up job, but you're being late so often is quite bothersome.'
'Yes, I know boss, and I am working on it.'
'Well good, you are a team player. That's what I like to hear. It's odd though, you're coming in late. I know you're retired from the army. What did they say if you came in late there?'
'They said, "Good morning, General."'

✳ Fifty-one years ago, Herman James, a Norfolk man, was drafted by the army. On his first day in basic training, the army issued him a comb. That afternoon the army barber sheared off all his hair.
On his second day, the army issued Herman a toothbrush. That afternoon the army dentist yanked seven of his teeth.
On the third day, the army issued him a jock strap. The army has been looking for Herman for fifty-one years.

✳ A young fresh-faced soldier lost his head during a firefight and ran for cover some distance from the action. He had not only lost his prized beret but had also lost his backpack and weapon.

He was crouched down behind a wall when he felt a strong hand grip his shoulder and a calming voice behind him say, 'What the devil do you think you're doing here, soldier? Think of the regiment ... get back there and do what you're paid to do.'

The young soldier got himself back under control and said, 'Sorry, mate, you're right.'

The voice behind him bellowed, 'MATE! MATE! I'm the bloody general!!!'

The young soldier replied, 'Sorry, sir, I didn't realise I'd run back that far ... '

✳ What do you call 100,000 Frenchmen with their hands in the air? The Army.

✳ How many French troops does it take to defend Paris? We don't know – it hasn't been tried yet.

✳ I joined the French army yesterday. Was a bit confused though – the body armour only covers the back.

✳ Have you seen those French Army Knives? No scissors or tweezers, just six corkscrews and a white flag.

✳ What's the first thing the French army teaches at basic training? How to surrender in at least ten languages.

✳ What's the difference between Frenchmen and toast? You can make soldiers out of toast!

✳ A government scientist, a diplomat and a squaddie are captured by the Taliban and are taken to a remote desert prison.

After a week in solitary, they are brought one by one in front of the prison governor, a man bored and almost permanently drunk. To each he gives the challenge: 'Tonight I will give you 3 x 2cm steel ball bearings. Go back to your cells and prepare a trick to show me tomorrow. If yours is the best trick I will let you go free.'

The three retire to their cells with their ball bearings. The next morning the diplomat is up first.

'Have you got a trick for me?' asks the governor.

'Yes, I have developed a method of standing 3 x 2cm steel ball bearings one on top of each other so they stand in an unsupported column!!' The diplomat shows his trick and is warmly congratulated by the governor.

The next up is the government scientist.

'Have you got a trick for me?'

'Yes, I have developed a method of standing 3 x 2cm steel ball bearings one on top of each other so they stand in an unsupported column AT AN ANGLE OF 45 DEGREES!!' The scientist shows his trick and is warmly congratulated by the governor.

Last up is the squaddie.

'Have you got a trick for me?'

'No!'

'What do you mean, no?'

'No, no trick!'

'What have you done with your three ball bearings?'

'Well ... I broke two and lost one!!'

You know you've been in the army too long when:

* You can't help saying 'Roger' instead of thanks.
* You cringe and mutter 'haircut' under your breath when you see men with long hair.
* You walk at a ridiculous pace and are physically incapable of walking at the shopping pace of your girlfriend.
* You refer to personal organisation as 'admin'.
* Your girlfriend is stored in your mobile phone address book as 'Zero Alpha'.
* You use patrol hand signals in a nightclub if people can't hear you.
* You can't watch war movies without giving a running commentary.
* People in prison have more contact with women than you do.
* You don't trust your mum/wife/girlfriend/any woman to iron your clothes because deep down you think that your ironing is better ...
* You point using your whole hand in a karate-chop motion.
* The sight of rolling countryside makes you scan for hidden enemies.
* You think that eating every meal for a week with the same spoon that you licked clean and kept in the pocket of the same shirt you've worn all week is perfectly normal.
* All of your food has to be prepared by a chef because you're incapable of cooking anything that can't either be boiled in a bag or eaten cold.

❊ Did you hear about the despot who made his army go without shoes and socks? It was a toe tallying regime!

❊ Two retired colonels sat in their club reading the newspapers.
'I say, old boy,' said one to the other, 'says here they've found old Carruthers.'

'What, you mean him from the Fighting Fifth that went missing in Malaya in '45?'

'Yes, that's the chap.'

'So where's he been all these years?'

'Well, says here they found him living up a tree with a bloody monkey.'

'A WHAT? A monkey! Male or female?'

Came the reply, 'Oh well, it would be female, of course, you know old Carruthers was never like that.'

* Where do infantry chaplains get their robes? From the army surplice depot.

ART AND ARTISTS

* A wealthy man commissioned Pablo Picasso to paint a portrait of his wife. Startled by the non-representational image on the final canvas, the woman's husband complained, 'It isn't how she really looks.'
When asked by the painter how she really looked, the man produced a photograph from his wallet.
Returning the photograph, Pablo observed, 'Small, isn't she?'

* I went to the still-life exhibition. It was quite good, but not moving.

* Did you hear about the Lautrec painting that fell down in the gallery? It was Toulouse!

* The unveiling of the statue was a monumental occasion.

✳ A museum is a thing of the past.

✳ A man passes an artist standing next to a small hole in the wall yelling, 'FIVE, FIVE, FIVE, FIVE!'
Interested, the guy bends down and looks in the hole. Instantly the man is poked in the eye with the sharp end of a paint brush and runs off in pain.
The artist stops yelling 'FIVE, FIVE, FIVE,' and starts yelling 'SIX, SIX, SIX, SIX!'

✳ A woman goes to her first show at an art gallery and is looking at the paintings. One is a huge canvas that has black paint with yellow blobs splattered all over it. The next painting is a murky grey colour that has drips of purple paint streaked across it. She walks over to the artist and says, 'I don't understand your paintings.' 'I paint what I feel inside me,' explains the artist. 'Have you ever tried Immodium?' she replies.

✳ What do you get if you cross an artist with a kebab? Donner-tello.

✳ Old artists never die, they just drop out of the frame.

✳ Did you hear about the artist found dead? All the details are sketchy!

✳ What do you get if you cross a painter with a boxer? Mohammed Dali.

✳ Did you hear about the artist who couldn't draw a cube?
He had a mental block!

✳ Did you hear about the man whose photos were double exposed? He was beside himself.

✳ Did you hear about the village that wanted to sculpt a statue for their mayor? They all chipped in!

✳ Why was the art dealer in debt? He didn't have any Monet.

✳ How did the graffiti artist know he was going to be caught? The writing was on the wall.

✳ What did the artist say to the dentist? Matisse hurt.

✳ Why wouldn't the artist's car start? He forgot to put in Degas!

Backpacking

✳ What's the difference between a backpacker and a tramp?
A tramp doesn't bore you about how little his stuff weighs.
With a backpacker it's a vacation. With a tramp, it's a vocation.
A backpacker doesn't have to queue for a place in the night shelter.

✳ Two hikers are talking on the trail. One asks the other, 'How do you tell the difference between a black bear and a grizzly bear?' 'Well,' replies his friend, 'when you see the bear, climb a tree. If it climbs up the tree and kills you, it's a black bear. If it knocks the tree down and kills you, it's a grizzly bear.'

Battle of the Sexes

✳ What's Tiger Woods's wife getting for Christmas? Half of everything.

* How do you know when a woman is about to say something smart? When she starts her sentence with, 'A man once told me ... '

* Home page: when your wife makes your beeper go off.

* Why do men break wind more than women? Because women can't shut up long enough to build up the required pressure.

* Did you hear about the young couple who decided to live in a tree house? It went well until they had a falling out!

* My wife lost two stones swimming last month. I don't know how, I tied them round her neck tight enough.

* Jonboy discovered his wife in the arms of her lover. Mad with rage, he shot her dead. The southern jury brought in a verdict of justifiable homicide.
  Just as Jonboy was about to leave the courtroom a free man, the judge stopped him and asked, 'Why did you shoot your wife instead of her lover?'
  'Suh,' he replied, 'I decided it was better to shoot a woman once than a different man each week.'

* When women enter middle age, it gives men a pause.

* Paula thinks she knows a lot about government, but she doesn't. Politics me off.

✳ Why didn't the woman like being massaged?
  It rubbed her up the wrong way!

✳ Why did the man suddenly shoot his wedding photographs?
  He wanted snapshots!

✳ If your dog is barking at the back door and your wife is yelling at the front door, who do you let in first? The dog, of course. He'll shut up once you let him in.

✳ Did you hear about the man who assaulted his wife with jelly?
  He was done for using a congealed weapon.

✳ My two uncles bet who would get married first.
  Then one upped the ante.

✳ What did the women driver do when she couldn't pull out of a parking space? She used her back-up plan.

✳ Our last fight was my fault: my wife asked me, 'What's on the TV?'
  I said, 'Dust.'

✳ Married men should forget their mistakes.
  There is no need for two people to remember the same thing.

✳ Sexual harassment: a touchy business.

✳ Keith was a thoughtful husband. He wanted to give his wife something special for her birthday, which was coming up soon. As he sat on the edge of the bed, he watched his wife turning back and forth and looking at herself in the mirror. 'Rita,' he said, 'what would you like for your birthday?'

His wife continued to look at herself and said, 'I'd like to be six again.' Keith knew just what to do. On the big day, he got up early and made his wife a bowl of Frosties. Then he took her to an amusement park where they rode all the rides. Five hours later, Rita's stomach felt upside down and her head was reeling. Nevertheless, Keith took her to McDonald's and bought her a Happy Meal with extra fries and a chocolate shake. Next, it was a movie with popcorn, Coke and her favourite sweets.

As Rita wobbled into the house that evening and flopped on the bed, Keith asked her, 'Well, dear, what was it like to be six again?'

Rita looked up at him. Her expression changed. She said, 'I meant my dress size!'

✳ Did you hear about the man who bought a hard guest bed?
It led to hard feelings.

✳ If all of the women left the country there would be a stagnation.

✳ Why do you notice men who make mistakes?
They have an err about them!

Some definitions:

FLATULENCE: (flach-u-lens) n.
female: An embarrassing byproduct of digestion.
male: An endless source of entertainment, self-expression and male bonding.

WANTS AND NEEDS: (wontz and nedz) n.
female: The delicate balance of emotional, physical and psychological longing one seeks to have fulfilled in a relationship.
male: Food, sex and beer.

THINGY: (thing-ee) n.
female: Any part under a car's bonnet.
male: The strap fastener on a woman's bra.

VULNERABLE: (vul-ne-ra-bel) adj.
female: Fully opening up one's self emotionally to another.
male: Playing cricket without a box.

COMMUNICATION: (ko-myoo-ni-kay-shon) n.
female: The open sharing of thoughts and feelings with one's partner.
male: Scratching out a note before suddenly taking off for a weekend with the guys.

BUM: (bum) n.
female: The body part that every item of clothing manufactured makes 'look bigger'.
male: The organ of mooning (and farting).

COMMITMENT: (ko-mit-ment) n.
female: A desire to get married and raise a family.
male: Not trying to pick up other women while out with one's girlfriend.

ENTERTAINMENT: (en-ter-tayn-ment) n.
female: A good movie, concert, play or book.
male: Anything with one ball, two folds, or three stooges.

REMOTE CONTROL: (ri-moht kon-trohl) n.

female: A device for changing from one TV channel to another.

male: A device for scanning through seventy-five channels every two and a half minutes.

TASTE: (tayst) v.

female: Something you do frequently to whatever you're cooking, to make sure it's good.

male: Something you must do to anything you think has gone bad, prior to tossing it out.

✳ A wife woke in the middle of the night to find her husband missing from bed. She got out and checked throughout the house. She heard sobbing from the basement.
After turning on the light and descending the stairs, she found her husband in a foetal position, sobbing.
'Honey, what's wrong?' she asked, worried about what could hurt him so much.
'Remember twenty years ago I got you pregnant? Then your father threatened me to marry you or go to jail?'
'Yes, of course,' she replied.
'Well, I would have been released tonight!'

✳ What happens when a woman gets married? She gets a new name and a dress!

✳ Marriage: a matter of wife and debt.

✳ I support both of my wives very well. I think that's big o' me.

✳ Pre-arranged marriages pre-pair people for the future.

✳ When a psychic showed me the girl I'll marry, it was love at second sight.

✳ They were a fastidious couple. She was fast, he was tedious.

✳ Did you hear about the two gun enthusiasts who got married? They had BBs!

✳ In marriage, two wrongs can make a riot.

✳ Why did the bored woman take up pottery? She was kiln time.

✳ He was as steady and solid as a rock; his girlfriend wished he was a little bolder.

✳ What happened to the couple who were married by candlelight? The marriage lasted only a wick.

✳ Did you hear about the two cheerleaders who got married? They met by chants!

✳ Recently a 'Husband Shopping Centre' opened, where women could go to choose a husband from among many men. It was laid out on five floors, with the men increasing in positive attributes as you ascended. The only rule was, once you opened the door to any floor, you HAD to choose a man from that floor; if you went up a floor, you couldn't go back down except to leave the place, never to return.

A couple of girlfriends went to the shopping centre to find some husbands ...

* FIRST FLOOR: The door had a sign saying, 'These men have jobs and love kids.' The women read the sign and said, 'Well, that's better than not having a job, or not loving kids, but I wonder what's further up?' So up they went.
* SECOND FLOOR: The sign read, 'These men have high-paying jobs, love kids, and are extremely good-looking.' 'Hmmm,' said the ladies. 'But, I wonder what's further up?'
* THIRD FLOOR: This sign read, 'These men have high-paying jobs, are extremely good-looking, love kids and help with the housework.' 'Wow!' said the women. 'Very tempting, BUT, there's more further up!' And up they went.
* FOURTH FLOOR: This door had a sign saying, 'These men have high-paying jobs, love kids, are extremely good-looking, help with the housework, and have a strong romantic streak.' 'Oh, mercy me. But just think! What must be awaiting us further on!' So up to the fifth floor they went.
* FIFTH FLOOR: The sign on that door said, 'This floor is empty and exists only to prove that women are impossible to please.'

Classes for men

Upon Completion of the course diplomas will be issued to the survivors.

* Topic 1 – How to Fill up the Ice Cube Trays.
  Step by Step, with Slide Presentation.

- Topic 2 – The Toilet Paper Roll: Do they Grow on the Holders?
  Round Table Discussion.
- Topic 3 – Is it Possible to Urinate by Lifting the Seat Up and Avoid
  Spraying the Floor/Walls and Nearby Bathtub?
  Group Practice.
- Topic 4 – Fundamental Differences Between the Laundry Basket and
  the Floor.
  Pictures and Explanatory Graphics.
- Topic 5 – The After-Dinner Dishes and Cutlery: Can They Levitate and
  Fly into the Kitchen Sink?
  Examples on Video.
- Topic 6 – Loss of Identity: Losing the Remote to Your Significant Other.
  Helpline Support and Support Groups.
- Topic 7 – Learning How to Find Things, Starting with Looking
  in the Right Place Instead of Turning the House Upside Down
  While Screaming.
- Topic 8 – Health Watch: Bringing Her Flowers Is Not Harmful to Your
  Health.
  Graphics and Audio Tape.
- Topic 9 – Real Men Ask for Directions When Lost.
  Real-Life Testimonials.
- Topic 10 – Is it Genetically Impossible to Sit Quietly as She Parallel-
  Parks.
  Driving Simulation.
- Topic 11 – Learning to Live: Basic Differences Between Mother and
  Wife.
  Online Class and Role-Playing.
- Topic 12 – How to be the Ideal Shopping Companion.
  Relaxation Exercises, Meditation and Breathing Techniques.

- Topic 13 – How to Fight Cerebral Atrophy: Remembering Birthdays, Anniversaries, Other Important Dates and Calling when you're Going to be Late.
Cerebral Shock Therapy Sessions and Full Lobotomies Offered.

Men can't win

- If you put a woman on a pedestal and try to protect her from the rat race, you're a male chauvinist. If you stay home and do the housework, you're a pansy.
- If you work too hard, there is never any time for her.
- If you don't work hard enough, you're a good-for-nothing bum.
- If she has a boring repetitive job with low pay, this is gender exploitation. If you have a boring repetitive job with low pay, you should get off your rear and find something better.
- If you get a promotion ahead of her, it's favouritism. If she gets a job ahead of you, it's equal opportunity.
- If you mention how nice she looks, it's sexual harassment. If you keep quiet, it's male indifference.
- If you cry, you're a wimp. If you don't, you're an insensitive idiot.
- If you make a decision without consulting her, you're a chauvinist. If she makes a decision without consulting you, she's a liberated woman.
- If you ask her to do something she doesn't enjoy, that's domination. If she asks you, it's a favour.
- If you appreciate the female form and frilly underwear, you're a pervert. If you don't, you're gay.
- If you like a woman to shave her legs and keep in shape, you're sexist. If you don't, you're unromantic.

- If you try to keep yourself in shape, you're vain. If you don't, you're a slob.
- If you buy her flowers, you're after something. If you don't, you're not thoughtful.
- If you're proud of your achievements, you're full of yourself. If you lack pride, you're not ambitious.
- If she has a headache, she's tired. If you have a headache, you don't love her any more.
- If you want it too often, you're oversexed. If you don't, there must be someone else.

* A man approached a girl at a disco: 'Would you like to dance?' he enquired. 'Not with you,' she replied with a sneer. 'Oh, come on,' he retorted, 'lower your standards a little. I did.'

* Two women were comparing notes concerning their latest boyfriends. The first said, 'He took me to his flat in Knightsbridge and showed me all these expensive jewels. There was an emerald-cut diamond of at least five carats, a tennis bracelet of six carats, and even a wrist watch with eleven carats.' 'Impressive,' said the second girl. 'Well … yes,' the first agreed. 'But the downside was that with all those carats, he expected me to behave like a rabbit.'

* A wealthy playboy met a beautiful young girl in an exclusive lounge. He took her up to his lavish apartment where he soon discovered she was not a tramp, but was well groomed and apparently very intelligent. Hoping to impress her, he began showing her his collection of expensive paintings, first editions of famous authors and offered her a glass of wine. He asked her if she preferred port or sherry and she said, 'Oh sherry by all means. To me it is the nectar of the gods. Just looking at it in a crystal-clear decanter fills me with a glorious sense of anticipation. When the stopper is removed and the gorgeous liquid is poured into my glass, I inhale the enchanting aroma and I'm lifted on the wings of ecstasy. It seems as though I'm about to drink a magic potion and my whole being begins to glow. The sound of a thousand violins being softly played fills my ears and I am transported into another world. On the other hand, port gives me gas.'

* What's the difference between stress, tension and panic? Stress is when your wife is pregnant. Tension is when your girlfriend is pregnant, and panic is when both are pregnant.

* Girl: When we get married, I want to share all your worries and troubles and lighten your burden.
Boy: It's very kind of you, darling. But I don't have any worries or troubles.
Girl: Well, that is because we aren't married yet.

* I have had three wives, and they all ran up massive debts on the phone. Unfortunately my first wife died of poisoned fish. The second wife had enormous chatline bills. She also died of poisoned fish. My third wife had a massive phone bill phoning her friends in Australia. She died from an axe in the head. (She would not eat the fish.)

* Ask any man, and he will tell you that any woman's ultimate fantasy is to have two men at once. While this has been verified by a recent sociological study, it appears that most men do not realise that in this fantasy, one man is cooking and the other is cleaning.

Is he henpecked? Checklist

- He wears the trousers in the house – under his apron.
- He has two chances of winning an argument with her: slim and none.
- She leads a double life – hers and his.
- He comes right out and says what she tells him to think.
- She does not have to raise the roof; all she has to do is raise an eyebrow.
- He always has the last word – it's 'I'm sorry.'
- The last big decision she let him make was whether to wash or to dry.
- He put a ring on her finger and she put one through his nose.
- He was a dude before marriage – now he is subdued.
- He married her for her looks, but not the kind he's getting now.
- She lost her thumb in an accident and sued for £100,000, because it was the thumb she had him under.
- He goes to a woman dentist – it's a relief to be told to open his mouth instead of to shut it.
- Every once in a while she comes to him on her bent knees. She dares him to come out from under the bed.

✳ As a new bride, Aunt Edna moved into the small home on her husband's farm. She put a shoe box on a shelf in her closet and asked her husband NEVER to touch it.

For fifty years Uncle Jack left the box alone until Aunt Edna was old and dying. One day when he was putting their affairs in order, he found the box again and thought it might hold something important. Opening it, he found two doilies and £82,500 in cash.

He took the box to her and asked about the contents.

'My mother gave me that box the day we married,' she explained.

'She told me to make a doily to help ease my frustrations every time I got mad at you.' Uncle Jack was very touched that in fifty years she'd only been mad at him twice.

'What's the £82,500 for?' he asked.

'Oh, that's the money I made selling the rest of the doilies.'

✳ A newly retired couple enjoyed their new boat together, although it was the husband who always took the wheel of the boat. He was concerned about what might happen in an emergency. So one day out on the sea he said to his wife,

'Please take the wheel, dear. Pretend that I am having a heart attack. You must get the boat safely to shore and dock it.' So she drove the boat to shore. Later that evening, the wife walked into the living room where her husband was watching television. She sat down next to him, switched the TV channel, and said to him, 'Please go into the kitchen, dear. Pretend I'm having a heart attack and set the table, cook dinner and wash the dishes.'

✳ A young man goes into a chemist's and asks the man behind the counter: 'Are you the owner?'

The pharmacist answers 'Yes.'

The man says: 'We're about to get married. Do you sell heart medication?'

Pharmacist: 'Of course we do.'

Man: 'How about medicine for circulation?'

Pharmacist: 'All kinds.'

Man: 'Medicine for rheumatism?'

Pharmacist: 'Definitely.'

Man: 'How about Viagra?'

Pharmacist: 'Of course.'

Man: 'Medicine for memory problems, arthritis, jaundice?'

Pharmacist: 'Yes, a large variety. The works.'

Man: 'What about vitamins, sleeping pills, antidotes for Parkinson's disease?'

Pharmacist: 'Absolutely.'

Man: 'You sell wheelchairs and walkers?'

Pharmacist: 'All speeds and sizes.'

Man: 'We'd like to use this store for our wedding list!'

* A little boy was at a relative's wedding. As he was coming down the aisle he would take two steps, stop, and turn to the crowd (alternating between bride's side and groom's side). While facing the crowd, he would put his hands up like claws and roar loudly.

So it went, step, step, ROAR, step, step, ROAR all the way down the aisle. As you can imagine, the crowd was near tears from laughing so hard by the time he reached the front. The little boy, however, was getting more and more distressed from all the laughing, and was near tears himself by the time he reached the pulpit.

When asked what he was doing, the child sniffed and said, 'I was being the Ring Bear.'

* A wedding ring may not be as tight as a tourniquet, but it does an equally good job of stopping the circulation.

* A man who says marriage is a fifty-fifty proposition doesn't understand two things:
1. Women.
2. Fractions.

* When walking down the aisle, there are three words on a woman's mind: 'Aisle, Altar, Hymn!'

* A little girl was at a wedding with her parents. After the wedding, she asked her mother why the bride had changed her mind. 'What do you mean?' responded her mother. 'Well, she went down the aisle with one man and came back with another!'

* One day a man inserted an advert in the local classifieds: 'Wife wanted.' Next day he received a hundred letters. They all said the same thing: 'You can have mine.'

* Marriage – an institution in which a man loses his Bachelor's Degree and the woman gets her Masters.

* When I married Mr. Right, I didn't know his first name was always!

Birds

Did you hear about the budgie that was sacked from the pet shop?
It had its hands in the trill!

There's a new GPS for birdwatchers. It does tern-by-tern directions.

CARS AND DRIVING

* When is a car driver not a car driver? When he turns into a side road.

* What should you do if you see a spaceman? Park in it, man!

* Did you hear about the man who thought installing a fan in his car would be a breeze?

* A speeding motorist was caught by radar from a police helicopter in the sky. An officer pulled him over and began to issue a speeding ticket. 'How did you know I was speeding?' the frustrated driver asked. The police officer pointed towards the sky. 'You mean,' asked the motorist, 'that even He is against me?'

* Three blokes are driving around, drinking beers and having a laugh when the driver looks in the mirror and sees the flashing lights of a police car telling him to pull over.

The other two are really worried. 'What are we going to do with our beers? We're in trouble!'

'No,' the driver says, 'it's OK, just pull the labels off your bottles and stick them on your foreheads,' and pulls over.

The police officer then walks up and says, 'You lads were swerving all around the road back there. Have you been drinking?'

'Oh, no, officer,' says the driver, pointing to his forehead. 'We're trying to give up, so we're on the patches!'

* A policeman flagged down a motorist and said, 'I'm arresting you for going through three red lights.' 'Yeah, well, I'm colour-blind,' said the motorist. 'In addition to that, you were exceeding the speed limit,' said the policeman. 'So what?' said the motorist. 'And on top of all that you were going the wrong way down a one-way street,' added the officer. 'I always did have a lousy sense of direction,' said the motorist with a smile. At that point, his wife leaned forward from the back seat and said, 'Don't pay any attention to him, officer. He always talks like this when he's had a few drinks.'

* Vandals destroyed some road signs recently. They pulled out all the stops.

* A dilapidated and very ancient Ford pulled into the local garage. 'Could you let me have half a gallon of petrol?' asked the old fellow at the wheel. 'Why don't you fill her up, now that you're here?' said the attendant. 'Well,' said the old chap, 'she might not run that far.'

* The new Skoda has an air bag. When you sense an impending accident, start pumping fast.

✳ Two men in a Skoda were arrested last night in Manchester following a push-by shooting incident.

✳ What do you call shock absorbers in a Skoda? Passengers!

✳ An old lady was waiting to park when a young man in his brand-new car drove around her and parked in the space that she had been waiting for. She was so annoyed that she approached the young fellow and said, through gritted teeth, 'I was about to park there.' The man looked at her with disdain and replied, 'That's what you can do when you're young and bright.' This annoyed the old lady even more, so she got back in her car, backed it up and then stamped on the accelerator and rammed straight into his car. The young man ran back to his car and shouted in a stunned voice, 'What did you do that for?' She smiled at him and said, 'That's what you can do when you're old and rich.'

✳ A very dignified gentleman walks into a leading city bank and enquires about taking out a loan for two thousand pounds. 'What security can you offer?' The banker enquires. 'Well, I've parked my Rolls-Royce Phantom in one of your parking bays. I'll be away for a few weeks so here are the keys.' Four weeks later the dignified gentleman returns and pays off the loan – two thousand and twenty-four pounds including interest – and collects his keys. 'Pardon me,' the banker says, 'but why would a man of your obvious means bother with a loan of two thousand pounds? 'Very simple,' the gent replied, 'where else in the middle of the city could I get secured parking for twenty-four pounds!'

✳ A married couple are driving down the motorway, travelling at seventy mph. The husband is behind the wheel. His wife looks over at him and says, 'I know we've been married for fifteen years, but I want a divorce.' The husband says nothing but slowly increases his speed to eighty mph. She then says, 'I don't want you to try to talk me out of it, because I've been having an affair with your best friend, and he's a better lover than you.' Again the husband stays quiet and just speeds up as he clenches his hands on the wheel. She says, 'I want the house.' Again the husband speeds up, and now is doing ninety mph. She says, 'I want the kids, too.' The husband just keeps driving faster, and faster, until he's up to one hundred mph. She says, 'I want the car, the credit account, and all the credit cards too.' The husband slowly starts to veer towards a bridge, as she says, 'Is there anything you want?' The husband says, 'No, I've got everything I need right here.' She asks, 'What's that?' The husband replies just before they hit the wall, 'The airbag!'

✳ An engineer, a systems analyst, and a programmer were driving down a mountain when the brakes failed. They screamed down the mountain, gaining speed, and finally managed to grind to a halt, more by luck than anything else, just inches from a thousand-foot drop to jagged rocks. They all got out of the car. The engineer said, 'I think I can fix it.' The systems analyst said, 'No, I think we should take it into town and have a specialist look at it.' The programmer said, 'OK, but first I think we should get back in and see if it does it again.'

✳ There are five friends touring Europe in an Audi Quattro and they get to the Spanish border. 'Passports, please,' asks the guard. They hand them over. After a few minutes examining the passports the guard says, 'There are five of you in this four-person car.' 'There's allowed to be,' argues the driver. 'It's a five-person car, it says here in the manual.' 'No,' argues the guard. 'Quattro means four.' After more arguing the driver asks to see the border controller. 'Oh, he's busy at the moment,' replies the attendant, 'over there with those two guys in that Fiat Uno!'

✷ He had a two-tone car ... black and rust.

✷ A car I owned was so old and dilapidated someone had scrawled on it 'Rust In Peace'.

✷ I once owned a car designed for twelve people. One drove and the other eleven took turns pushing it.

✷ A man steps out in front of a car and is almost knocked down. Incensed, the motorist winds down his window and yells, 'What the hell are you doing? There's a zebra-crossing fifty feet up the road!' 'Is there?' replies the pedestrian. 'I hope it's having better luck than I am.'

✷ An MG Midget pulled alongside a Rolls-Royce at a traffic light. 'Do you have a car phone?' its driver asked the guy in the Rolls. 'Of course I do,' replied the haughty driver. 'Well, do you have a fax machine?' The driver in the Rolls sighed. 'I have that too.' 'Then do you have a double bed in the back?' the Midget driver wanted to know. Ashen-faced, the Rolls driver sped off. That afternoon, he had a mechanic install a double bed in his car. A week later, the Rolls driver passes the same MG Midget, which is parked on the side of the road – back windows fogged up and steam pouring out. The arrogant driver pulls over, gets out of the Rolls and bangs on the Midget's back window until the driver sticks his head out. 'I want you to know that I had a double bed installed,' brags the Rolls driver. The Midget driver is unimpressed. 'You got me out of the shower to tell me that?'

✳ A motorist, after being bogged down in a muddy road, paid a passing farmer five pounds to pull him out with his tractor. After he was back on dry ground he said to the farmer, 'At those prices, I should think you would be pulling people out of the mud night and day.' 'Can't,' replied the farmer. 'At night I haul water for the hole.'

✳ Two man sat down for a pint in the pub. 'Hey, whatever happened to Pete who used to work here?' one asked.
'He got this harebrained notion he was going to build a new kind of car,' his friend replied.
'How was he going to do it?'
'He took an engine from a Porsche, tyres from a Mercedes, seats from a TVR, and chassis from a Lotus and, well, you get the idea.'
'So what did he end up with?'
'Ten years in prison.'

✳ Two truck-driving brothers are taking a driving test, and the instructor asks one a question. 'You're driving the truck and you are at the top of a mountain and your brakes fail. You notice an accident at the bottom of the mountain, what do you do?' The trucker replies, 'The first thing I do is wake up my brother.' The instructor asks, 'What good is that going to do?' The trucker replies, 'In all of the years we've been driving he ain't never seen an accident like the one we're about to get in to.'

✳ A man was helping his new girlfriend clean out the boot of her car. Inside, he noticed a bag labelled 'Emergency Repair Kit'. Looking at it a little closer, he noticed a stick of dynamite inside. Thinking that was a bit strange, he asked her what it was for. She said, 'It's part of my emergency repair kit.' Puzzled, he said, 'I can see that, but why?' She replied, 'In case I have a flat and need to blow up one of my tyres.'

✳ A man was on his way home from work when the most remarkable thing happened. Traffic was heavy as usual, and as he sat there at a red light, out of nowhere a bird slammed into the windscreen. If that wasn't bad enough, the poor creature got its wing stuck under the wiper. Just then the light turned green and there he was with a bird stuck on his screen. Without any other options, turning on the wipers seemed the only thing to do. On the upswing, the bird flew off and slammed right onto the windscreen of the car behind, a police car. The officer walked up and told the driver he saw what had happened at the light. Trying to plead his case, the driver's protests fell on deaf ears. The policeman took out his pad and pencil: 'I'm going to have to write you a ticket for flipping me the bird.'

✳ A police officer pulls over this guy who's been weaving in and out of the lanes. He goes up to the guy's window and says, 'Sir, I need you to blow into this breathalyser tube.' The man says, 'Sorry, officer, I can't do that. I am an asthmatic. If I do that, I'll have a really bad asthma attack.' 'OK, fine. I need you to come down to the station to give a blood sample.'
'I can't do that either. I am a haemophiliac. If I do that, I'll bleed to death.'
'Well, then, we need a urine sample.'
'I'm sorry, officer, I can't do that either. I am also a diabetic. If I do that, I'll get really low blood sugar.'
'All right, then I need you to come out here and walk this white line.'
'I can't do that, officer.'
'Why not?'
'Because I'm drunk.'

✳ A lady bought a new Mercedes and proudly drove it off the showroom floor to take home. Halfway home, she attempted to change radio stations and saw that there appeared to be only one station.

She immediately turned around and headed back to the dealer. Once at the dealer, she found her salesman and began to excitedly explain that her radio was not working, and they must replace it since she only had one radio station. The salesman calmed her down and told her that her car radio was voice-activated, and that she would only need to state aloud the type of music that she wanted and the car would find it.

She got into the car and started the engine and then said the word 'country', and the radio changed to a station playing a Johnny Cash song. She was satisfied and started home. After a while she decided to try out the radio and said 'rock 'n' roll';' the radio station changed and a song by the Rolling Stones came from the speakers. Quite pleased, the woman continued driving. A few blocks from her house, another driver ran a light causing her to slam on her brakes to avoid a collision. The woman angrily exclaimed, 'Idiot!' The radio cut over to a Gordon Brown press conference.

✳ Two cab drivers met. 'Hey,' asked one, 'why did you paint one side of your cab red and the other side blue?'

'Well,' the other responded, 'when I get into an accident, you should see how all the witnesses contradict each other.'

✳ A father, who worked away from home all week, always made a special effort with his family at the weekends. Every Sunday morning he would take his daughter out for a drive in the car.

One particular Sunday however, he was so full of cold that he really didn't feel like driving at all. Luckily, his wife came to the rescue and

decided that for this week she would take their daughter out.
They returned just before lunch and the little girl ran upstairs to see her father.

'Well,' the father asked, 'did you enjoy your ride with Mummy?'

'Oh yes, Daddy,' the girl replied, 'and do you know what … we didn't see a single idiot!'

✳ The parents of two boys went on a trip for the weekend with friends. They left early Friday morning and the boys were left alone at home. That evening the younger boy made the suggestion that they take their dad's car, pick up some girls and go to the local disco. The sixteen-year-old boy could drive a bit but was too scared. After some nagging he gave in and off they went to enjoy the evening. When they got back to the car after a lot of partying, they noticed a huge dent in the rear of the car – someone must have bumped into the car and driven off. Frantically they phoned their friends to find a repairer to fix their dad's car. Finally they found one who said they must have the car at his house early next morning. The car was fixed properly and they parked it back in the garage that afternoon. Their parents returned the next day but the boys were too terrified to say anything about the accident. The father went to get something from the garage, came back very amazed and announced to the family in the lounge, 'A miracle has happened! A guy drove into the back of my car on Thursday and now it's fixed without a scratch!'

✳ An elderly couple were driving cross-country, and the woman was driving. She gets pulled over by the highway patrol. The officer says, 'Ma'am, did you know you were speeding?' The woman turns to her husband and asks, 'What did he say?' The old man yells, 'HE SAYS YOU WERE SPEEDING.'

The patrolman says, 'May I see your licence?' The woman turns to her husband and asks, 'What did he say?' The old man yells, 'HE WANTS TO SEE YOUR LICENCE.' The woman gives him her licence.

The patrolman says, 'I see you are from Coventry. I spent some time there once, had the worst night with a woman I have ever had.'

The woman turns to her husband and asks, 'What did he say?'

'HE THINKS HE KNOWS YOU,' the old man yells.

* What do you call a Skoda with twin exhausts? A wheelbarrow!

* I saw a sign at a petrol station. It said: 'Help wanted.' There was another sign below it that said: 'Self service.' So I hired myself. Then I made myself the boss. I gave myself a raise. I paid myself. Then I quit.

* What's the smallest part in a Skoda? The owner's brain.

* A man walks into a bar and demands to know: 'Who's the strongest in here?' A huge Hell's Angel stands up: 'I'm the strongest around here!' The other guy politely asks, 'Can you help me push my car to the petrol station?'

* What's the difference between a used-car salesman and a software salesmen? The used-car salesman knows when he's lying.

* What kind of cars are in the Bible?
God drove Adam and Eve out of the garden in a fury.

* What kind of motor vehicles are in the Bible?
Honda ... because the Apostles were all in one accord.

✳ A man's wife borrowed his car and parked in the supermarket car park. Just as she came out laden with shopping, she saw a young lad break into the car, hot-wire it and drive off. Naturally she reported the matter to the police. 'What did he look like?' the sergeant asked. 'I don't know,' she replied, 'but I got the licence plate.'

✳ My grandad drove so slowly that he had to have a sign on his car: 'This is not an abandoned vehicle.'

✳ A man's wife phoned him while she was out in the car to tell him she'd broken down.
'There's water in the carburettor,' she said confidently. The man, not a little impressed, asked, 'Where's the car?'
'In the river.'

✳ Know why the British car industry doesn't make computers? They couldn't figure out how to make them leak oil!

✳ Harry was at his golf club and went into the clubhouse to see whether anyone could offer him a lift home. His own car was off the road being serviced.
'Sure,' said Jim, 'I'll give you a lift. My Rolls-Royce is just outside.'
As they're driving along, Harry says, 'Jim, what's that thing on the dashboard ticking all the time?'
'That's my digital clock.'
A few minutes later, Harry asks, 'And what's that thing on the dashboard moving up and down?'
'That's my tachometer,' says Jim.
Then a few minutes after that, Harry starts to ask, 'But what's that … '

'Hold on a minute, Harry,' says Jim, 'I can see you've never been in a Rolls-Royce before.'
'Never in the front seat,' says Harry.

* What make of car do shepherds drive? Lamb drovers.

* In the pub one night Keith is telling his friends about the perils of women on the road.' 'I tell you, women drivers are a hazard to traffic. Driving to work this morning on the motorway, I looked over to my left and there was a woman in a red Ferrari doing eighty-five miles per hour with her face up next to her rear-view mirror putting on her eyeliner! I looked away for a couple seconds and when I looked back she was halfway over in my lane.' 'What happened next?' asked his friend. 'It scared me so bad,' said Keith, 'that I dropped my electric shaver in my coffee, and it spilled all over my mobile phone!'

* My wife drives her car like lightning. You mean she drives very fast? No, she hits trees.

* I had a dream the other night. I was in the old west riding in a stagecoach. Suddenly, a man riding a horse pulls up to the left side of the stagecoach, and a riderless horse pulls up on the right. The man leans down, pulls open the door, and jumps off his horse into the stagecoach. Then he opens the door on the other side and jumps onto the other horse. Just before he rode off, I yelled out, 'What was all that about?' He replied, 'Nothing. It's just a stage I'm going through.'

Driving styles

- One hand on steering wheel, one hand out of window – Sydney.
- One hand on steering wheel, one hand on horn – Japan.
- One hand on steering wheel, one hand on newspaper, foot solidly on accelerator – London.
- Both hands on steering wheel, eyes shut, both feet on brake, quivering in terror – New York.
- Both hands in air, gesturing, both feet on accelerator, head turned to talk to someone in back seat – Italy.
- One hand on horn, one hand greeting, one ear on cell phone, one ear listening to loud music, foot on accelerator, eyes on female pedestrians, conversation with someone in next car – India.

✳ A woman was getting petrol at a Shell station off the motorway. As she whistled while pumping, a UFO parked beside her car and a tall green alien came out. It too was pumping fuel. The woman, out of curiosity, asked, 'UFO stands for unidentified flying object, right?' The alien replied, 'Stupid humans. It means unleaded fuel only!'

✳ One day, a bus driver went to the bus garage, started his bus, and drove off along the route. No problems for the first few stops, a few people got on, a few got off, and things went generally well. At the next stop, however, a big hulk of a guy got on. Six feet eight, built like a wrestler, arms hanging down to the ground. He glared at the driver and said, 'Big John doesn't pay!' and sat down at the back.
The driver was five feet three, thin, and very meek. Naturally, he didn't argue with Big John, but he wasn't happy about being intimidated.
The next day the same thing happened – Big John got on again, made

a show of refusing to pay and sat down. And the next day and the one after that and so on every day. This grated on the bus driver, who started losing sleep over the way Big John was taking advantage of him. Finally he could stand it no longer. He signed up for body building courses, karate, judo, and boxing. By the end of the summer, he had become strong, and brimming with confidence.

So on the next Monday, when Big John once again got on the bus and said, 'Big John doesn't pay!' the driver stood up, glared back at the passenger, and screamed, 'And why not?'

With a surprised look on his face, Big John replied, 'Big John has a bus pass.'

✳ What does Fiat stand for? Fix it again, Toni.

✳ Why are Fiat drivers like corned beef? They both come in tin cans.

✳ What do you call a Skoda full of food? A Lada!

✳ Why do Skoda's have a rear wiper? To clean off the flies that crash into them.

✳ What do you call a Skoda driver who says he has a speeding ticket? A dreamer.

✳ What's the difference between a Skoda and a Jehovah's Witness? You can shut the door on a Jehovah's Witness.

✳ What do you call a Skoda at the top of a hill? A miracle!

CATS

✳ Did you hear about the cat who drank five bowls of water?
He set a new lap record.

✳ What is a cat's way of keeping law and order?
Claw enforcement!

✳ What is the name of the unauthorised autobiography of the cat?
Hiss and Tell.

✳ What do you call the cat that was caught by the police?
The purrpetrator.

✳ What do you call a cat that lives in an igloo?
An eskimew.

✳ What has more lives than a cat?
A frog, because it croaks every night.

✳ What do you call a septic cat?
Pus.

✳ Why do cats make awful storytellers?
They only have one tail.

✳ What would you get if you crossed a cat and a donkey?
A mewl.

✳ What song do heartbroken cats sing?

'Felines … nothing left but felines …'

✳ Why do cats never shave?

Because eight out of ten of them prefer Whiskers.

✳ What's furry, has whiskers and chases outlaws?

A posse cat.

CHILDBIRTH AND PREGNANCY

Things NOT to say in childbirth:

- Gosh, you're lucky. I wish men could experience the miracle of childbirth.
- Do you think the baby will come before Monday night football starts?
- If you think this hurts, I should tell you about the time I twisted my ankle playing football.
- That was the kids on the phone. Did you have anything planned for dinner?
- When you lay on your back, you look like a python that swallowed a wild boar.
- You don't need an epidural. Just relax and enjoy the moment.
- Oops! Which cord was I supposed to cut?
- Stop your swearing and just breathe.
- Your stomach still looks like there's another one in there.

✳ A lady from a foreign country who could not understand much English wasn't feeling well and went to see her doctor. After examining her he said, 'You are pregnant. Please understand that you have an insufficient passage and if you have a baby it will be a miracle.' The lady rushed home crying and told her husband, 'The doctor says I'm pregnant and I have a fish in the passage and if I have a baby it will be a mackerel!'

✳ A woman goes to her doctor who verifies that she is pregnant. This is her first pregnancy. The doctor asks her if she has any questions.
She replies, 'Well, I'm a little worried about the pain. How much will childbirth hurt?'
The doctor answered, 'Well, that varies from woman to woman and pregnancy to pregnancy and besides, it's difficult to describe pain.'
'I know, but can't you give me some idea?' she asks.
'Grab your upper lip and pull it out a little …'
'Like this?'
'A little more …'
'Like this?'
'No. A little more …'
'Like this?'
'Yes. Does that hurt?'
'A little bit.'
'Now stretch it over your head!'

If men could get pregnant …

- Maternity leave would last for two years … with full pay.
- There would be a cure for stretch marks.

- Natural childbirth would become obsolete.
- Morning sickness would rank as the nation's number one health problem.
- All methods of birth control would be 100% effective.
- Children would be kept in the hospital until potty-trained.
- Briefcases would be used as nappy bags.
- Paternity suits would be a fashion line of clothes.
- They'd stay in bed during the entire pregnancy.
- Restaurants would include ice cream and pickles as entreés.
- Women would rule the world.

Questions from new mothers answered

- Q: When will my baby move?
  A: With any luck, right after he finishes school.
- Q: What is the most reliable method to determine a baby's sex?
  A: Childbirth.
- Q: How long is the average woman in labour?
  A: Whatever she says, divided by two.
- Q: When is the best time to get an epidural?
  A: Right after you find out you're pregnant.
- Q: What does it mean when the baby's head is crowning?
  A: It means you feel as though not only a crown but the entire throne is trying to make its way out of you.
- Q: Where is the best place to store breast milk?
  A: In your breasts.
- Q: What does it mean when a baby is born with teeth?
  A: It means that the baby's mother may want to rethink her plans to nurse.

- Q: What is colic?
  A: A reminder for new parents to use birth control.
- Q: What are night terrors?
  A: Frightening episodes in which the new mother dreams she's pregnant again.

＊ Three men at a bar were discussing coincidences. The first man said, 'My wife was reading *A Tale of Two Cities* and she gave birth to twins!' 'That's funny,' the second man remarked, 'my wife was reading *The Three Musketeers* and she gave birth to triplets.'
The third man shouted, 'Good God, I have to rush home!'
When asked what the problem was, he exclaimed, 'When I left the house, my wife was reading *Ali Baba and the Forty Thieves*!!!'

＊ An American man is riding a train in France. His seatmate knows some English, and they end up chatting. The seatmate asks if the American has children. The American says no.
'Ah, so sad,' says the Frenchman. 'Your wife, she is impregnable?'
'Well, um, that's not exactly the word,' says the American. 'Oh!' interrupts the Frenchman. 'I mean, she is inconceivable?' 'Um, not quite –' the American begins, only to be interrupted again. 'Oh, no, that isn't right,' says the Frenchman. 'She is, what is it, she is unbearable?'
'Well, actually, that's pretty much sums it up,' says the American.

＊ Brenda, pregnant with her first child, was paying a visit to her obstetrician's office. When the exam was over, she shyly began, 'My husband wants me to ask you if it's still OK …'
'I know, I know,' the doctor said, placing a reassuring hand on her shoulder, 'I get asked that all the time. Sex is fine until late in the pregnancy.'

'No, that's not it at all,' Brenda confessed. 'He wants to know if I can still mow the lawn.'

* The room was full of pregnant women and their partners, and the class was in full swing. The instructor was teaching the women how to breathe properly, along with informing the men how to give the necessary assurances at this stage of the plan.
The teacher then announced, 'Ladies, exercise is good for you. Walking is especially beneficial. And, gentlemen, it wouldn't hurt you to take the time to go walking with your partner!'
The room really got quiet. Finally, a man in the middle of the group raised his hand.
'Yes?' replied the teacher.
'Is it all right if she carries a golf bag while we walk?'

* No matter what you colic, a baby crying for hours is a pain!

* Sometimes a pregnancy is so long it seems like a maternity.

* Having children is a heir-raising experience.

* Before a mother knows the sex of her baby it's a hidden a gender.

* Unborn twins are womb-mates.

* What do you call twin boys? Sunsets!

* Men have no control over whether their child will be a boy or girl. It's a sperm-of-the-moment decision.

* To heir is human.

CHILDREN

✳ A couple had two little boys, aged eight and ten, who were excessively mischievous. They were always getting into trouble and their parents knew that, if any mischief occurred in their town, their sons were probably involved.

The boys' mother heard that a clergyman in town had been successful in disciplining children, so she asked if he would speak with her boys. The clergyman agreed, but asked to see them individually. So the mother sent her eight-year-old first, in the morning, with the older boy to see the clergyman in the afternoon.

The clergyman, a huge man with a booming voice, sat the younger boy down and asked him sternly, 'Where is God?'

They boy's mouth dropped, but he made no response, sitting there with his mouth hanging open, wide-eyed. So the clergyman repeated the question in an even sterner tone, 'Where is God!!?' Again the boy made no attempt to answer. So the clergyman raised his voice even more and shook his finger in the boy's face and bellowed, 'WHERE IS GOD!?'

The boy screamed and bolted from the room, ran directly home and dived into his room, slamming the door behind him. When his older brother found him there, he asked, 'What happened?'

The younger brother, gasping for breath, replied, 'We are in BIG trouble this time, dude. God is missing – and they think WE did it!'

✳ What happens if you get too big for your britches?
You get exposed in the end!

✳ Most teenagers find a lecturing parent hear-resistable.

✳ What do you call a small girl in charge of a tribe? Little miss-chief.

✳ What did the child say to its mother?
It's true I don't like soap, but you don't have to rub it in my face!

✳ How do you make antifreeze? Steal her blanket.

✳ A young man agreed to baby-sit one night so a single mother could have an evening out. At bedtime he sent the youngsters upstairs to bed and settled down to watch football. One child kept creeping down the stairs, but the young man kept sending him back to bed. At nine p.m. the doorbell rang, it was the next-door neighbour, Mrs Brown, asking whether her son was there. The young man brusquely replied, 'No.' Just then a little head appeared over the banister and shouted, 'I'm here, Mum, but he won't let me go home!'

✳ When I had my PlayStation stolen, my family were there to console me.

✳ What do you call a two-year-old with a ghetto blaster? A baby boomer!

✳ When Dad came home he was astonished to see Alec sitting on a horse, writing something. 'What on earth are you doing there?' he asked. 'Well, the teacher told us to write an essay on our favourite animal. That's why I'm here and that's why Susie's sitting in the goldfish bowl!'

✳ A four-year-old boy and his father went to the beach. There was a dead seagull lying on the sand. The boy asked his father, 'Dad, what happened to the birdie?' His dad told him, 'Son, the bird died and went to Heaven.' Then the boy asked, "And God threw him back down?'

✳ Little girl to her friend: 'I'm never having kids. I hear they take nine months to download.'

✳ Teddy came thundering down the stairs, much to his father's annoyance.
'Teddy,' he called, 'how many more times have I got to tell you to come down the stairs quietly? Now, go back up and come down like a civilised human being.'
There was a silence, and Teddy reappeared in the front room.
'That's better,' said his father. 'Now will you always come downstairs like that?'
'Suits me,' said Teddy. 'I slid down the bannister.'

✳ When do children wake up? In the wee wee hours of morning.

✳ Rules of thumb suck.

✳ Sibling rivalry is all relative.

✳ One day a little girl was sitting and watching her mother do the dishes at the kitchen sink. She suddenly noticed that her mother had several strands of white hair sticking out in contrast on her brunette head. She looked at her mother and inquisitively asked, 'Why are some of your hairs white, Mum?'
Her mother replied, 'Well, every time that you do something wrong and make me cry or unhappy, one of my hairs turns white.'
The little girl thought about this revelation for a while and then said, 'Mum, how come ALL of Grandma's hairs are white?'

✳ A six-year-old boy called his mother from his friend Charlie's house and confessed he had broken a lamp when he threw a football in their living room.

'But, Mum,' he said, brightening, 'you don't have to worry about buying another one. Charlie's mother said it was irreplaceable.'

✳ If children were allowed to dig for coal, would they be minor miners?

✳ George knocked on the door of his friend's house. When his friend's mother answered he asked, 'Can Albert come out to play?'

'No,' said the mother, 'it's too cold.'

'Well, then,' said George, 'can his football come out to play?'

✳ You know what they say about unruly youths: vandalism is just a stone's throw away.

✳ Little Johnny's new baby brother was screaming at the top of his voice. He asked his mum, 'Where'd we get him?' His mother replied, 'He came from Heaven, Johnny.' Johnny says, 'WOW! I can see why they threw him out!'

✳ Big Brother: 'That planet over there is Mars.'
Little Brother: 'Then that other one must be Pa's.'

✳ Did you hear about the fight in the launderette?
The washing machine beat the crap out of a nappy.

✳ An irate woman burst into the baker's shop and said, 'I sent my son in for two pounds of biscuits this morning, but when I

weighed them there was only one pound. I suggest that you check your scales.'
The baker looked at her calmly for a moment or two and then replied, 'Ma'am, I suggest you weigh your son.'

* Little Jimmy's class went on a field trip to the fire station. The firefighter giving the presentation held up a smoke detector and asked the class: 'Does anyone know what this is?'
Little Jimmy's hand shot up and the firefighter called on him.
Little Jimmy replied: 'That's how Mummy knows supper is ready!'

* Doris had been talking on the phone for about half an hour before she hung up. Her father said, 'Wow! That was short. You usually talk for an hour. What happened?'
Doris replied, 'It was a wrong number.'

CHRISTMAS

* What beats his chest and swings from Christmas cake to Christmas cake? Tarzipan!

* Why did the little boy call Father Christmas Santa Cause?
Because there was Noel!

* Mum, can I have a dog for Christmas?
No, you can have turkey like everyone else!

✳ What did the Eskimos sing when they got their Christmas dinner?
'Whalemeat again, don't know where, don't know when!'

✳ Who is never hungry at Christmas? The turkey – he's always stuffed!

✳ What happens when you eat Christmas tree decorations?
You get tinsel-itus!

✳ Will the Christmas pudding be long? No, it'll be the traditional round!

✳ Why does Santa go down the chimney? It soots him.

✳ Who's the bane of Santa's life? The elf and safety officer!

✳ Be careful drinking at Christmas. I got so drunk last night I ended up in
a cheesy bar … or as you might call it, a delicatessen.

✳ Nurse! I want to operate. Take this patient to the theatre.
Ooh! Good! I love a nice pantomime at Christmas!

✳ Doctor, Doctor, Father Christmas gives us oranges every Christmas.
Now I think I'm turning into an orange!
Have you tried playing squash?

✳ Did Rudolph go to a regular school? No, he was elf-taught!

✳ How do you get into Donner's house? You ring the deer-bell!

✳ How does Rudolph know when Christmas is coming?
He looks at his calen-deer!

✳ Who delivers cat's Christmas presents? Santa Paws!

✳ Why does Father Christmas go down the chimney?
Because it soots him!

✳ Why are Christmas trees like bad knitters?
They both drop their needles!

✳ What's Christmas called in England? Yule Britannia!

✳ What's Scrooge's favourite Christmas game? Mean-opoly.

✳ What's the name of the reindeer with three humps on its back?
Humphrey.
And that black and blue reindeer? Bruce.

✳ How do you make an idiot laugh on Boxing Day?
Tell him a joke on Christmas Eve!

🎃 CLOWNS

✳ What is the gooey red stuff between an elephant's toes? Slow clowns.

✳ Why did the clown wear loud socks? So his feet wouldn't fall asleep!

✳ Why aren't you allowed to incinerate clowns? They burn funny.

✳ When the human cannonball retired they couldn't find a replacement of the right calibre.

✳ A clown decided to retire and hand over the business to his son. His son said, 'I don't know, Dad, those are big shoes to fill.'

✳ A clown walks into a music shop and says to the owner, 'I want to buy that red trumpet and that accordian.' 'Well,' replies the owner, 'you can buy that fire extinguisher, but I have to keep the radiator.'

✳ Learning to juggle isn't hard. You just need the balls.

Signs you may have hired the wrong clown for your kids party

Clown car must be started with breathalyser device.

Tells the kids he killed Noddy in a blood match in Hackney.

Prefaces each trick with, 'Here's a little number I learned in the joint.'

Wears a T-shirt that says, 'Drug-free since March!'

Only balloon animals he can make are a snake and a 'snake on acid'.

Business cards include the phrase 'From the mind of Stephen King ...'

* Why did the circus manager make the clowns undress in his office? He was fond of comic strips!

* What happened when the human cannonball was late for work? He got fired!

* Acrobats are always doing good turns.

* To learn rope tricks you have to be taut.

* Old tightrope walkers never die, they just get highly strung.

COMPUTERS

* FERN BRITTON VIRUS: Your 1.3gb hard drive suddenly shrinks to 80mb and then slowly expands back to 1.3gb.

* LONDON TRANSPORT VIRUS: Every three minutes it tells you what great service you are getting.

* ARNOLD SCHWARZENEGGER VIRUS: Terminates and stays resident. It'll be back …

* PANTOMIME VIRUS: Prints 'Oh no you don't' whenever you choose 'Abort'.

* METROPOLITAN POLICE VIRUS: It claims it feels threatened by the other files on your PC and erases them in 'self-defence'.

✳ TITANIC VIRUS: Makes your whole computer go down.

✳ DISNEY VIRUS: Everything in the computer goes Goofy.

✳ MIKE TYSON VIRUS: Quits after one byte.

✳ FRANK SPENCER VIRUS: Appears helpful, only to destroy your hard drive.

✳ WOODY ALLEN VIRUS: Bypasses the motherboard and turns on daughter card.

✳ OSAMA VIRUS: Won't let you into any of your programmes.

✳ RONALD REAGAN VIRUS: Saves your data, but forgets where it is stored.

✳ DR HAROLD SHIPMAN VIRUS: Deletes your old files.

✳ ADAM AND EVE VIRUS: Takes a couple of bytes out of your Apple.

✳ AIRBAG VIRUS: Can only cause harm if you are a small computer operator who sits too close to the screen.

✳ AIRLINE LUGGAGE VIRUS: You're in London, but your data is in Singapore.

✳ BILL CLINTON VIRUS v 1.0: It has a six-inch hard drive and no memory. Freezes entire system due to unresolved memory conflicts.

✳ BILL CLINTON VIRUS v 2.0: Automatically connects to every URL in your internet browser's list of bookmarks, then it tells you emphatically that your computer never made any connections ... to any URL ... because since it didn't transmit and receive simultaneously, it wasn't really connected.

✳ BILL GATES VIRUS: This dominant strain searches for desirable features in all other viruses via the internet. It then either engulfs the competing viruses or removes their access to computers until they die out.

✳ BIN LADEN (AKA AL-QAEDA) VIRUS: Displays threatening messages and spawns numerous smaller viruses that periodically destroy files. The Bin Laden virus and its spawned viruses are being seen less and less frequently and may be becoming extinct due to the spread of the George W. Bush virus.

✳ BIRTHDAY VIRUS: Keeps advancing your clock by another year.

✳ BUREAUCRAT VIRUS: Divides your hard disk into hundreds of little units, each of which does practically nothing, but all of which claim to be the most important part of your computer.

✳ CHILD VIRUS: It constantly does annoying things, but is too cute to get rid of.

✳ PARLIAMENT VIRUS v 1.0: Computer locks up, screen splits vertically with a message appearing on each half blaming the other side for the problem.

✳ PARLIAMENT VIRUS v 2.0: Classifies all your internet shopping receipts as expenses.

✳ DIET VIRUS: Allows your hard drive to lose weight by eliminating the FAT table.

✳ DOLLY PARTON VIRUS: It sounds pretty good, but you'd swear your monitor looks larger and has more knobs than it used to. DEFLATE.COM removes it.

✳ LINDSAY LOHAN VIRUS: Disks can no longer be inserted.

✳ ELVIS VIRUS: Your computer gets fat, slow and lazy and then self-destructs, only to resurface at shopping malls and service stations across rural America.

✳ FREUDIAN VIRUS: Your computer becomes obsessed with marrying its own motherboard. Becomes very jealous of the size of your friend's hard drive.

✳ FRENCH VIRUS: Garbles some files and then displays a message asking you for help. If you click OK, it just garbles more files and asks for help again. If you click Cancel, it displays the message, 'I surrender!' and shuts down your computer. If you click Ignore, it scans your computer for the German and Russian viruses. If the French, Russian, and German viruses find each other, they merge into a single virus that conflicts with the ENGLISH virus, slowing it down.

✳ POLL VIRUS: 60% of the PCs infected will lose 30% of their data 14% of the time (plus or minus a 3.5% margin of error).

✳ GEORGE MICHAEL VIRUS: Runs its course, occasionally releasing excess data build-up.

✳ GORDON BROWN VIRUS v 1.0: Doesn't do anything, but you only get one chance to delete it every five years.

✳ TONY BLAIR VIRUS: Tells you it's going to eliminate all other viruses from your computer but that it may take a long time. Then it actually does scan your computer and eliminate viruses. It also scans for Programs of Mass Destruction (PMD), which are programmes that destroy a lot of files if they are run. PMDs may be caused by a number of other viruses, such as the Saddam Hussein virus. It never seems to find any PMDs, and it keeps switching the background colour on your computer screen back and forth between yellow and orange.

✳ GOVERNMENT ECONOMIST VIRUS: Nothing works, but all your diagnostic software says everything is fine.

✳ CAR CARE VIRUS: Tests your system for a day, finds nothing wrong, and sends you a bill for £450.

✳ RUSSELL BRAND VIRUS: One of the dirtiest viruses around. It writes four-letter words to all of your files just to annoy the operating system. It also installs an X-rated GIF on your hard drive. Very popular.

✳ INLAND REVENUE VIRUS: It comes in with very little warning, digs through all your files then sells all your worldly possessions on eBay, and there's not a damn thing you can do about it. It doubles the files on your hard drive while it states it is decreasing the number of files, increases the cost of your computer, taxes its CPU to maximum capacity, and then accesses your bank accounts and depletes your balances.

✳ JEFFREY DAHMER VIRUS: Eats away at your systems resources piece by piece.

✳ JERRY SPRINGER VIRUS: Appears on your screen and says it has something to tell you and you may not like it.

✳ PRIEST VIRUS: Warns you repeatedly not to reproduce illegitimate files, but meanwhile, it's reproducing illegitimate files in the background.

✳ JIMINY CRICKET VIRUS: Changes your Zip disk into a Zip-A-Dee-Doo-Dah disk.

✳ LORD LUCAN VIRUS: Nobody can find it. Your programmes can never be found again.

✳ LINUX VIRUS: Causes the computer to hang for several days while it tracks down hardware drivers, networking how-to's, and Window managers. Then it quits, saying that if you had better programming skills, your hard drive would be wiped by now.

✳ MAFIA VIRUS: You don't want it, but you're afraid to get rid of it.

❋ LAWRENCE LLEWELYN-BOWEN VIRUS: Takes all your files, sorts them by category and folds them into little doilies to be displayed on your desktop.

❋ MICHAEL JACKSON VIRUS v 1.0: Hard to identify because it is constantly altering its appearance.

❋ MICHAEL JACKSON VIRUS v 2.0: It's BAD. Computer freaks out when you put a flame or Pepsi next to it. Some people think it's identical to the Latoya Jackson virus because they have never been seen together.

❋ MILITIA VIRUS: Wipes out your operating system claiming it has no right to control your PC.

❋ MUM VIRUS: Places a phone call to your mother every time you click on an adult website.

❋ FEMINIST VIRUS: Forces your PC to recognise its male connections as female connections.

❋ NEW WORLD ORDER VIRUS: Probably harmless, but is feared by conspiracy theorists.

❋ NIKE VIRUS: Just does it.

❋ O.J. SIMPSON VIRUS: It claims that it did not, could not, and would not delete two of your files and vows to find the virus that did it.

* NICK GRIFFIN VIRUS v 1.0: Shifts all your output to the extreme right of your screen.

* NICK GRIFFIN VIRUS v 2.0: Your system works fine, but it complains loudly about foreign software.

* POLITICALLY CORRECT VIRUS v 1.0: Never calls itself a 'virus', but instead refers to itself as an 'electronic micro-organism'.

* POLITICALLY CORRECT VIRUS v 2.0: Rephrases the 'Abort, Retry, Fail' prompt as 'Choice, Retry, Success-Impaired'.

* POPE JOHN PAUL VIRUS: Deletes all your dirty files and blesses the rest.

* PROZAC VIRUS: Messes up your RAM, but your processor doesn't care.

* PUBLIC TRANSPORT VIRUS: Makes your browser stop at every website.

* QUANTUM LEAP VIRUS: One day your PC is a laptop, the next day it's a Mac, then a Nintendo.

* CONSERVATIVE VIRUS: Sells off your system resources to the highest bidder.

* RIGHT TO LIFE VIRUS v 1.0: Won't allow you to delete a file, regardless of how old it is. Prints, 'Oh, no, you don't!', whenever you choose Abort from the 'Abort, Retry, Fail' message.

✳ RIGHT TO LIFE VIRUS v 2.0: Before allowing you to delete any file, it first asks you if you've considered the alternatives.

✳ SADDAM HUSSEIN VIRUS v 1.0: This virus, first developed in the software labs of Western democracies, attacks its closest neighbours first and then fragments to hide its most virulent components in the hidden folders of your disk drive. As a defence mechanism, it claims that commercial virus detection software insults its national dignity.

✳ SADDAM HUSSEIN VIRUS v 2.0: Discovered to have mutated into a harmless, ugly graphic hiding in the Trash/Recycle Bin.

✳ SHARON STONE VIRUS: Makes a huge initial impact, then you forget it's there.

✳ STUDENT VIRUS: Uses 80% of your computer's resources, yet does absolutely nothing.

✳ STAR TREK VIRUS: Invades your system in places where no virus has gone before.

✳ BIG BROTHER VIRUS: Deletes your files one by one over thirteen weeks until only the most annoying one remains.

✳ TEENAGER VIRUS: Your PC stops every few seconds to ask for money.

✳ TEXAS VIRUS: Makes sure that it's bigger than any other file.

✳ TIGER WOODS VIRUS: Assumes pre-eminence over other applications, which are left to operate at consistently humiliating performance levels. Is liable to integrate with any available passing files.

✳ TOBACCO INDUSTRY VIRUS: It contends that there is no reliable scientific evidence that viruses can harm you computer.

✳ WARREN BEATTY VIRUS: Constantly tries to prove its virility by attaching itself to younger or newer files.

✳ WONDERBRA VIRUS: Results in overflow stack.

✳ BILLY GRAHAM VIRUS: When you save a file, it prints, 'I am saved!' on the screen.

✳ LORENA BOBBITT VIRUS v 1.0: It turns your hard disk into a 3.5 inch floppy ... then discards it through Windows.

✳ LORENA BOBBITT VIRUS v 2.0: Removes a vital part of your hard disk then reattaches it. Unfortunately, the area is permanently disabled.

✳ Did you hear about the man who dropped a PC on his foot? It megahertz!

✳ Trust your calculator. It's something to count on.

✳ It's tough to be in the computer business when the chips are down.

✳ Who likes being online? Tightrope walkers!

COOKiNG

* A man was crying at the bar, so the barman gave him a free drink. 'What's the trouble?' he asked. 'I got kicked out of chef school,' replied the man. 'They said I gave them the oldest excuse in the book, and all I did was tell the truth.' 'What did you say?' asked the barman. To which the chef student answered, 'I told them my dog ate my homework.'

* Wife: The two things I cook best are meatloaf and apple pie.
  Husband: Which is this?

* Why don't men cook at home?
  No one's invented a steak that will fit in the toaster.

* Did you hear about the new Chinese cookbook being sold only at pet shops? *101 Ways to Wok Your Dog.*

* Why couldn't the sesame seed leave the gambling casino?
  Because he was on a roll!

* My wife taught the dog not to beg at the table. She let him taste her cooking.

* What's an astronaut's favourite food? Launch meat!

* A lady was picking through the frozen turkeys at the supermarket, but couldn't find one big enough for her family. She asked an assistant,

'Do these turkeys get any bigger?' The assistant replied, 'No, missus, they're dead.'

✳ A young man saw an elderly couple sitting down to lunch at Burger King. He noticed that they ordered one meal, and an extra drink cup. As he watched, the gentleman carefully divided the hamburger in half, then counted out the fries. One for him, one for her, until each had half of them. Then he poured half of the soft drink into the extra cup, and set it in front of his wife. The old man began to eat, and his wife sat watching, with her hands folded in her lap.
The young man decided to ask if they would allow him to purchase another meal for them so that they didn't have to split theirs.
The old gentleman said, 'Oh, no. We've been married fifty years, and everything has always been and will always be shared, 50/50.'
The young man than asked the wife if she was going to eat, and she replied, 'Not yet. It's his turn using the teeth.'

✳ A customer in a bakery was observed carefully examining all the rich-looking pastries displayed on trays in the glass cases. The assistant approached him and asked, 'What would you like?' He answered, 'I'd like that chocolate-covered, cream-filled doughnut, that jam-filled doughnut and that cheese Danish.' Then with a sigh he added, 'But I'll take an oat-bran muffin.'

✳ Waiter, waiter! There's a spider in my salad! Yes, sir, the chef's using Webb lettuces today.

✳ What kind of lettuce did they serve on the *Titanic*? Iceberg!

✳ What is the most romantic fruit salad? A date with a peach.

✳ Two cartons of yoghurt walk into a bar. The barman looks them up and down and says 'We don't serve your kind in here.'
One of the yogurt cartons replies, 'Why not? We're cultured individuals.'

✳ The problem with fast food is that it slows down when it hits your stomach. It just parks there and lets the fat have time to get off and apply for citizenship.

✳ 'My wife has to be the worst cook. In my house, we pray after we eat.'
Rodney Dangerfield

✳ A Jewish man was eating in a Chinese restaurant and was chatting to his Chinese waiter. He commented what a wise people the Chinese were.
'Yes,' replied the waiter, 'we're wise because our culture is four thousand years old. But Jewish people are also very wise, are they not?'
'Yes, we are,' replied the Jewish man. 'Our culture is five thousand years old.' The waiter was surprised to hear this. 'That can't be true,' he replied, 'where did your people eat for the first thousand years?'

✳ Did you hear about the gambler whose wife was terrible in the kitchen? He hid his winnings in her cookbooks.

✳ Her soup was so thick that when she stirred it the room went round.

✳ An ambitious young waiter left the second best restaurant in town to join the best one. On his second night in the dining room, as he was serving soup to Lord and Lady Farquar at table fourteen, he noticed that one of her ladyship's breasts had fallen out of her gown and was, as they say, hanging loose. With perfect aplomb, he replaced it in her bodice with a soup spoon and returned to his station, where he was met by a glowering maitre d'. 'That may be how they do things at your old job, Higgins,' he snapped furiously, 'but here we would always use a warm spoon.'

* Checking the menu, a restaurant customer ordered a bowl of vegetable soup. After a couple of spoonfuls, he saw a circle of wetness right under the bowl on the tablecloth. He called the waitress over and said, 'It's all wet down here. The bowl must be cracked.' The waitress said, 'You ordered the vegetable soup, didn't you?' 'Yes,' he replied. 'Well, maybe it has a leek in it.'

* Newlywed: Do you want dinner?
  Spouse: Sure, what are my choices?
  Newlywed: Yes and no.

COWBOYS

* Visitor: Wow, you have a lot of flies buzzing round your horses and cows. Do you ever shoo them?
  Cowboy: No, we just let them go barefoot.

* The cowboy didn't want to volunteer for the rodeo but he got roped into it.

✳ What do zombie cowboys fight? Deadskins!

✳ A city lady was on holiday in the West. She wanted to take a horseback ride and asked the local cowboy if he could get her a nice gentle pony. 'Sure,' said the cowboy. 'What kinda saddle you want, English or Western?' 'What's the difference?' asked the lady. 'The Western saddle has a horn on it,' said the cowboy. The lady considered this and then replied, 'If the traffic is so bad here in the mountains that I need a horn on my saddle, I don't believe I want to ride after all.'

✳ An old cowhand was tending cattle late one evening out on the prairie when he noticed a dark cloud of dust from the north headed towards him. When the dust settled he saw a big, rough-looking cowboy riding a grizzly bear and whipping him with a rattlesnake. The big cowboy hopped off his bear and asked the cowhand if he had anything to eat and drink. The cowhand informed the big cowboy that he had a pot of boiling beans and a pot of boiling coffee on the fire and when it cooled off that he was welcome to all he wanted. The big cowboy told the cowhand that he didn't have time for the beans or the coffee to cool off. The big cowboy grabbed that cast iron bean pot and just chugged them down and then grabbed the boiling coffee pot and washed the beans down with the coffee. The big cowboy then darted out towards a cactus bush and squatted down behind it to relieve himself, wiping himself with cactus leaf. The old cowhand didn't know what to think about this fellow. The big cowboy, wiping the bean juice off his chin, apologised to the old cowhand for having to eat and run. As the big cowboy untied the rattlesnake from around the grizzly bear's neck to ride south he told the old cowhand, 'I got a bad son of a bitch chasing me!!!!'

✳ Did you hear about the cowboy who walked into a German car showroom and went, 'Owdy!'

✳ Three cowboys are sitting around a campfire, out on a lonesome Texas prarie, each with the bravado for which cowboys are famous. A night of tall tales begins. The first one says, 'I must be the meanest, toughest cowboy there is. Why, just the other day a bull got loose in the corral and gored six men before I wrestled it to the ground by the horns with my bare hands.' The second cowboy wasn't to be outdone, 'Why that's nothing. I was walking down the trail yesterday and a fifteen-foot rattlesnake slid out from under a rock and made a move for me. I grabbed that snake with my bare hands, bit its head off and sucked the poison down in one gulp. And I'm still here today.'
The third cowboy remained silent, silently stirring the coals with his hands.

✳ One Sunday, a cowboy went to church. When he entered, he saw that he and the preacher were the only ones present. The preacher asked the cowboy if he wanted him to go ahead and preach. The cowboy said, 'I'm not too smart, but if I went to feed my cattle and only one showed up, I'd feed him.' So the minister began his sermon. One hour passed, then two hours, then two and a half hours. The preacher finally finished and came down to ask the cowboy how he had liked the sermon. The cowboy answered slowly, 'Well, I'm not very smart, but if I went to feed my cattle and only one showed up, I sure wouldn't feed him all the hay.'

✳ A devout cowboy lost his Bible while he was mending fences out on the range. Three weeks later, a cow walked up to him carrying the Bible in its mouth. The cowboy couldn't believe his eyes. He took the precious book out of the cow's mouth, raised his eyes heavenward and exclaimed, 'It's a miracle!' 'Not really,' said the cow. 'Your name is written inside the cover.'

* More than anything, Bob wanted to be a cowpoke. Taking pity on him, a rancher decided to hire the lad and give him a chance. 'This,' he said, showing him a rope, 'is a lariat. We use it to catch cows.' 'I see,' said Bob, trying to seem knowledgeable as he examined the lariat. 'And what do you use for bait?'

* When it's branding season, cowboys always have sore calves.

* Lots of cowboys only do rodeos for the bucks.

* Cowboy wisdom: don't squat with your spurs on.

* Anyone should know how to put a saddle on a horse so it won't slip and cause an injury. It's a cinch.

* More cowboy wisdom: always drink upstream from the herd.

* I think the political correctness is getting ridiculous. Today I overheard a little boy say he was going to go and play a game of Cattle Management Specialists and Native Americans.

* Cowboy Joe was telling his fellow cowboys back on the ranch about his first visit to a big-city church. 'When I got there, they had me park my old truck in the corral,' Joe began.

'You mean the parking lot,' interrupted Charlie, a worldly fellow.

'I walked up the trail to the door,' Joe continued.

'The sidewalk to the door,' Charlie corrected him.

'Inside the door, I was met by this dude,' Joe went on.

'That would be the usher,' Charlie explained.

'Well, the usher led me down the chute,' Joe said.

'You mean the aisle,' Charlie said.

'Then, he led me to a stall and told me to sit there,' Joe continued.

'Pew,' Charlie retorted.

'Yeah,' recalled Joe. 'That's what that pretty lady said when I sat down beside her.'

* A cowboy and a biker are on death row, and are to be executed on the same day. The day comes, and they are brought to the gas chamber. The warden asks the cowboy if he has a last request, to which the cowboy replies, 'Ah shore do, ward'n. Ah'd be mighty grateful ifn yood play "Achy Breaky Heart" fur me bahfore ah hafta go.' 'Sure enough, cowboy, we can do that,' says the warden. He turns to the biker, 'And you, friend, what's your last request?' 'That you kill me first.'

* A police officer saw a man dressed as a cowboy in the street, complete with huge Stetson hat, spurs, and six shooters. 'Excuse me, sir,' said the police officer, 'who are you?' 'My name's Tex, officer,' said the cowboy. 'Oh?' said the police officer. 'Are you from Texas?' 'Nope, Louisiana.' 'Louisiana? So why are you called Tex?' 'Don't want to be called Louise, do I.'

* Back in the old West three Texas cowboys were about to be hung for cattle rustling. The lynch mob brought the three men to a tree right at

the edge of the Rio Grande. The idea was that when each man had died, they'd cut the rope and he'd drop into the river and drift out of sight. They put the first cowboy in the noose, but he was so sweaty and greasy he slipped out, fell in the river and swam to freedom. They tied the noose around the second cowboy's head. He, too, oozed out of the rope, dropped into the river and got away. As they dragged the third Texan to the scaffold, he resisted, 'Please! Would you'all tighten that noose a little bit? I can't swim!'

* If a cowboy rides into town on Friday and three days later leaves on Friday, how does he do it? The horse's name is Friday!

* Rex and Red, two Texan cowboys, were resting their horses out on the range. 'What'd Miss Eadie give yew for yore birthday?' asked Rex. 'Pair of cufflinks,' said Red. 'But I ain't got no use for them. I can't even find any place to get my wrists pierced.'

CRIME

* Two robbers were robbing a hotel. The first one said, 'I hear sirens. Jump!'
The second one said, 'But we're on the thirteenth floor!'
The first one screamed back, 'This is no time to be superstitious!!'

* Did you hear about the lingerie thief who gave police the slip?

* 'Police?' came the voice on the phone. 'I want to report a burglar trapped in an old maid's bedroom!' After ascertaining the address,

the police sergeant asked who was calling. 'This,' cried the frantic voice, 'is the burglar!'

* A lawyer phones his client on death row to tell him he had been granted a stay of execution. 'Great,' replied the prisoner. 'No noose is good noose.'

* Moving along a dimly lighted street, a man was suddenly approached by a stranger who had slipped from the shadows nearby. 'Please, sir,' asked the stranger, 'would you be so kind as to help a poor unfortunate fellow who is hungry and out of work? All I have in the world is this gun.'

* A criminal's best asset is his lie ability.

* Two small-time thieves had been sent by the big boss to steal a van load of goods from a bathroom suppliers. One stayed in the van as lookout and the other went into the storeroom. Fifteen minutes went by, then half an hour, then an hour, and no sign of him. The lookout finally grew impatient and went to look for his partner. Inside the store the two came face to face. 'Where have you been?' demanded the worried lookout. 'The boss told me to take a bath, but I couldn't find the soap and a towel.'

* The detective who went to investigate a burned-down post office figured that it must be blackmail.

* Why did the earless defendant refuse to go to court? He waived his hearing!

✳ Police take a possible witness to a house where a crime has been committed to try to jog his memory. They show him the front door and ask him if he remembers anything at all. 'Well,' he replies 'I'm not sure if I've seen that door chime before, but it rings a bell.'

✳ It was Christmas and the judge was in a merry mood as he asked the prisoner, 'What are you charged with?' 'Doing my Christmas shopping early,' replied the defendant. 'That's no offence,' said the judge. 'How early were you doing this shopping?' 'Before the store opened,' countered the prisoner.

✳ A thousand pairs of underwear were stolen. Police are making a brief inquiry.

✳ Why did the policeman never wash? He was a dirty cop.

✳ A man who was just about to be executed was asked whether he would like to have a last smoke. The man answered, 'No, thank you, I don't smoke. I don't want to get lung cancer.'

✳ The criminal mastermind found one of his gang sawing the legs off his bed. 'What are you doing that for?' demanded the crook boss. 'Only doing what you ordered,' said the stupid thug. 'You told me to lie low for a bit!'

✳ 'It's a pity you've gone on hunger strike,' said the convict's girlfriend on visiting day. 'Why?' 'I've put a file in your cake.'

✳ Did you hear about the thief who was caught stealing from the blood bank? He was caught red-handed!

✳ Old burglars never die, they just steal away.

✳ Two crooks bought a hotel. They were innmates.

✳ After the transvestite escaped from prison the only thing the police could tell the press was that she was still a broad.

✳ Criminal motto: What you seize is what you get.

✳ When can police search your house? When it's warranted!

✳ Criminal: Why don't you hire these twins for the robbery, boss?
Criminal boss: I'm afraid of a double-cross.

✳ An elderly woman had just returned to her home from an evening of religious service when she was startled by an intruder. As she caught the man in the act of robbing her home of its valuables, she yelled, 'Stop! Acts 2:38!' [Turn from your sin]
The burglar stopped dead in his tracks. Then the woman calmly called the police and explained what she had done.
As the officer cuffed the man to take him in, he asked the burglar, 'Why did you just stand there? All the old lady did was yell a scripture at you.'
'Scripture?' replied the burglar. 'She said she had an axe and two 38s!'

❋ Why did the judge always pass the toughest sentence?
No one likes to be called acquitter!

❋ Good police officers never miss a beat.

❋ Old judges never die, they just slur their sentences.

❋ What do you call it when a judge recites verse from the bench?
Poetic justice!

❋ Police have said that professional card cheats will be dealt with.

❋ One beautiful autumn day, a park ranger discovered a man sitting in the
woods chewing away on a dead bald eagle. 'Hey mister, the bald eagle
is a protected species, and killing one is punishable offence,'
said the park ranger.
The man was swiftly arrested, and ushered before the judge.
In court, he pleaded innocent to the charges against him, claiming that
if he didn't eat the bald eagle he would have died from starvation.
'I was so hungry,' complained the defensive camper, 'the bald eagle
was the only food I could find!'
To everyone's amazement, the judge ruled in his favour.
In the judge's closing statement he asked the man, 'I would like you to
tell me something before I let you go. I have never eaten a bald eagle,
nor ever plan on it. But I'd like to know: what did it taste like?'
The man answered, 'Well, it tasted like a cross between an osprey and
a snowy owl.'

✳ How did the woman know a carpenter had broken into her home?
She saw dust.

✳ After a two-week criminal trial in a very high-profile bank robbery case, the judge turns to the jury foreman and asks, 'Has the jury reached a verdict in this case?'

'Yes, we have, your honour,' the foreman responded.

'Would you please pass it to me,' the judge declared, as he motioned for the clerk to retrieve the verdict slip from the foreman and deliver it to him.

After the judge reads the verdict himself, he delivers the verdict slip back to his bailiff to be returned to the foreman and instructs the foreman, 'Please read your verdict to the court.'

'We find the defendant not guilty of all four counts of bank robbery,' stated the foreman.

The family and friends of the defendant jump for joy at the verdict and hug each other as they shout expressions of gratitude.

The man's lawyer turns to his client and asks, 'So, what do you think about that?'

The defendant, with a bewildered look on his face, turns to his lawyer and asks, 'Well, does that mean I can keep the money, or do I have to give it back?'

✳ Why didn't the police arrest the man without a passport?
It was a borderline infraction.

✳ Did you hear about the criminal who was so hardened he couldn't think straight?

✳ Police had good luck with a robbery suspect who just couldn't control himself during a line-up. When detectives asked each man in the line-up to repeat the words, 'Give me all your money or I'll shoot,' the man shouted, 'That's not what I said!'

✳ Did you hear about the police case against a doughnut thief? It was full of holes!

✳ Convicts are always committed people.

✳ The phone rings at police headquarters. 'Hello?'
'Hello, is this Scotland Yard?'
'Yes. What do you want?'
'I'm calling to report my neighbour Tom. He is hiding marijuana in his firewood.'
'This will be noted.'
Next day, the police come over to Tom's house. They search the shed where the firewood is kept, break every piece of wood, find no marijuana, swear at Tom and leave.
The phone rings at Tom's house. 'Hey, Tom! Did the police come?'
'Yeah!'
'Did they chop your firewood?'
'Yeah they did.'
'OK, now it's your turn to call. I need my garden ploughed.'

✳ A streaker was found dead this morning. Police looking for clues say the body is quite revealing.

✳ What do you call an arrogant fugitive falling from a building? Condescending.

✳ A gang of robbers broke into a lawyer's club by mistake. The old solicitors gave them a fight for their life and their money.
The gang was very happy to escape. 'It's not so bad,' one crook noted. 'We got twenty-five pounds between us.'
The boss screamed: 'I warned you to stay clear of lawyers! We had a hundred pounds when we broke in!'

✳ Did you hear about the man who was caught trying to steal stamps?
He philately denied it.

✳ The dentist's alibi was full of holes, so the police performed a cavity search.

✳ Three robbers break into a bank, but when they open the safe, there's no money, only boxes. One robber opens a box and finds cups full of yogurt. 'We didn't find any money, but we got something to eat,' he tells his partners. They eat their fill and leave. The next morning's newspaper reads: 'World's Largest Sperm Bank Robbed.'

✳ Some burglars are always looking for windows of opportunity. When just one prisoner working on a gang on a country road attempted to escape there was a chain reaction.

✳ A prisoner in jail receives a letter from his wife: 'Dear Keith, I have decided to plant some lettuce in the back garden. When is the best time to plant them?'
The prisoner, knowing that the prison guards read all mail, replied in a letter: 'Dear Helen, whatever you do, do not touch the back garden. That is where I hid all the money.'

A week or so later, he received another letter from his wife: 'Dear Keith, you wouldn't believe what happened, some men came with shovels to the house, and dug up all the back garden.'

The prisoner wrote another letter back: 'Dear Helen, now is the best time to plant the lettuce.'

* A lady was called to serve for jury duty, but asked to be excused because she didn't believe in capital punishment and didn't want her personal views to prevent the trial from running its proper course. But the judge liked her thoughtfulness, and tried to convince her that she was appropriate to serve on the jury. 'Madam,' he explained, 'this is not a murder trial! It's a simple civil lawsuit. A wife is bringing this case against her husband because he gambled away the twelve thousand pounds he had promised to use to get the kitchen done.' 'Well, OK,' agreed the lady, 'I'll serve. I suppose I could be wrong about capital punishment after all.'

* Pillaging: when a chemist is robbed.

* The priest was instructing a class of third-graders at All Saints grammar school:

'There were two brothers, and one of them chose the wicked path of Satan. The brother was evil and corrupt and did great damage to many people, and wound up a convicted criminal in a tiny, dark cell.

But the other brother studied hard and became a great, rich, knowledgeable lawyer.

'Now, children, what is the difference between these two brothers, who started out in the same place, who together embarked upon life's stormy seas?'

Keith Jnr. raised his hand and said, 'Easy. One of them got caught.'

* A librarian was caught stealing books. The police booked him.

* What do you call two robbers? A pair of knickers!

* There was a shootout in Gap. There were numerous casual-tees.

* Loads of dogs were stolen yesterday. Police have no leads.

CRUISE SHIPS

* An old lady was standing at the railing of the cruise ship holding her hat on tight so that it would not blow off in the wind. A gentleman approached her and said: 'Pardon me, madam. I do not intend to be forward, but did you know that your dress is blowing up in this high wind?' 'Yes, I know,' said the lady, 'I need both hands to hold onto this hat.' 'But, madam, you must know that your privates are exposed!' said the gentleman in earnest. The woman looked down, then back up at the man and replied, 'Sir, anything you see down there is eighty-five years old. I just bought this hat yesterday!'

* A musician who joined an orchestra on a cruise ship was having difficulty keeping time with the rest of the band. Finally, the captain said, 'Either you learn to keep time or I'll throw you overboard … It's up to you, sync or swim.'

* A panhandler was caught trying to sneak aboard a Princess liner about to embark on a three-day trip to the Bahamas. He was caught by the purser who threw him off the ship, telling him, 'Beggars can't be cruisers.'

✳ An elderly couple was on a cruise. The weather was really rough. They were standing at the stern of the boat watching the moon when a wave came up and washed the old woman overboard. The crew searched for days and couldn't find her, so the captain sent the old man back to shore with the promise that he would notify him as soon as they found something. Three weeks went by and finally the old man got a message from the boat. It read: 'Sir, sorry to inform you, we found your wife dead at the bottom of the ocean. We hauled her up to the deck and attached to her buttocks was an oyster; in it was a pearl worth £50,000 … please advise.' The old man messaged back: 'Send pearl, re-bait trap.'

Dear Diary

MONDAY: What a wonderful cruise this is going to be! I felt singularly honoured this evening. The captain asked me to dine at his table.

TUESDAY: I spent the entire afternoon on the bridge with the captain.

WEDNESDAY: The captain made proposals to me unbecoming an officer and a gentleman.

THURSDAY: Tonight the captain threatened to sink the ship if I do not give in to his indecent proposals!

FRIDAY: This afternoon I saved 1,600 lives.

DANCE

✸ What's a vampire's favourite dance? The Fangtango!

✸ Where can you dance in California? San Frandisco!

✸ How do they dance in Arabia? Sheikh-to-sheikh.

✸ What dance did the pilgrims do? The Plymouth Rock.

✸ What dance do hippies hate? A square dance.

✸ What kind of dance do buns do? Abundance.

✸ What do you get if you cross an insect and a dance? A cricket ball.

✸ Who is tall, dark and mysterious and great at dancing? Darth Raver!

✳ What dance do chickens avoid? The foxtrot.

✳ How many line dance instructors does it take to change a light bulb? Five! ... Six! ... Seven! ... Eight!

✳ What do ghosts dance to? Soul music.

✳ What do you call a belly dancer with a sword? A veiled threat.

✳ What kind of crowds do belly dancers hang out in? Hip circles!

✳ *A guide to the Arts of the Levant* by Belle E. Danzer

✳ Where can you go to learn how to belly dance? A navel academy!

✳ A man had just been laid off from work. He was standing on the railing of a high bridge getting ready to jump off, when he happened to look down and see a little man with no arms dancing all around on the river bank below. He thought, 'Life isn't so bad after all,' and got off the railing.
He then walked down to the river bank to thank the little man for saving his life.
'Thank you,' he said. 'I was going to jump off that bridge and kill myself, but when I saw you dancing even though you have no arms, I changed my mind.'
'Dancing? I'm not dancing!' the armless man replied bitterly. 'My bum itches, and I can't scratch it!'

✳ What's a Morris-dancing stick good for? Kindling for an accordion fire.

✳ What's a pig's favourite ballet? Swine Lake!

✳ Have you seen the new ballroom? It's got waltz to waltz carpeting!

✳ When people say ballet can be bad for the feet they've got a pointe.

✿DATING

✳ An ardent traveller named Joan spent most of her vacation sunbathing on the roof of her hotel. She wore a swimsuit the first day, but on the second, she decided that no one could see her way up there, and she slipped out of it for an overall tan. She'd hardly started when she heard someone running up the stairs; Joan was lying on her stomach, so she just pulled a towel over her rear.
'Excuse me, miss,' said the flustered hotel manager, out of breath from dashing up the stairs. 'The hotel doesn't mind you sunbathing on the roof but we would very much appreciate you wearing a bathing suit as you did yesterday.'
'What difference does it make,' Joan asked calmly. 'No one can see me up here, and besides, I'm covered with a towel.'
'Not exactly,' said the manager. 'You're lying on the dining room skylight.'

✳ She didn't want to go to the dance because she had bad skin. It was a pore excuse.

* Two strangers skated to the middle of a frozen pond and broke the ice.

* A lady aboard a cruise ship was not impressed by the jazz trio in one of the ship's restaurants. When her waiter came around, she asked, 'Will they play anything I ask?'
'Of course!' replied the waiter.
'Then tell them to go play chess!'

* The young man quit dating the telephone operator because he felt disconnected. Besides, she had too many hang-ups.

* What do you call a party for shy people? Abash.

* It's better to love a short girl than not a tall.

* Did you hear about the woman whose fiancé had a wooden leg?
She broke it off!

* Did you hear about the builder who spotted a beautiful girl from the top of his ladder? He fell for her.

* What happens if you are in a love triangle?
It soon becomes a wreck-tangle!

* Why did the couple go to the party dressed as a barcode?
They were an item.

* She was the apple of his eye and he liked to sit down be cider.

✳ What do squirrels give for Valentine's Day? Forget-me-nuts.

✳ What did the light bulb say to the switch? You turn me on!

✳ Did Adam and Eve ever have a date? No, but they had an apple.

✳ What did one snake say to the other snake?
  Give me a little hug and a hiss, honey.

✳ Knock, knock,
  Who's there?
  Olive.
  Olive who?
  Olive you!

✳ Why did the banana go out with the prune?
  Because it couldn't get a date.

✳ What is a ram's favourite song on Valentine's Day?
  I only have eyes for ewe!

✳ What travels around the world but stays in one corner? A stamp.

✳ What happens when you fall in love with a French chef?
  You get buttered up.

✳ What is a vampire's sweetheart called? His ghoul-friend.

✳ If your aunt ran off to get married, what would you call her? Antelope.

✳ Did you hear about the man who met a girl, took her on a date to the local bean restaurant, and was immediately inflatuated?

✳ It was Valentine's Day and their first date. They sat in the darkened cinema waiting for the film to start. The screen finally lit up with a trailer for a new blockbuster. They realised that there was no sound. The film began but the silence continued.
Suddenly, out of the darkness, an irritated voice in the crowd loudly shouted, 'OK, who's got the remote control?'

✳ What do farmers give their wives on Valentine's Day? Hogs and kisses!

✳ Why did the pig give his girlfriend a box of chocolates?
It was Valenswine's Day!

✳ Do skunks celebrate Valentine's Day? Of course, they're very scentimental.

✳ Two fonts meet in a bar on a blind date. 'Sorry, you're too bold,' says one. 'Never mind,' replies the other. 'You're not my type.'

✳ What did the French chef give his wife for Valentine's Day?
A hug and a quiche!

✳ What did one pickle say to the other? You mean a great dill to me.

✳ Why couldn't the day traders agree where to have lunch together?
They all wanted to keep their options open until the last minute.

Economist's Valentines

You raise my interest rate thirty basis points without a corresponding drop-off in consumer enthusiasm.

You stoke the animal spirits of my market.

Despite your decade of inflation, I still love you.

Dating vs marriage: a woman's view

- When you are dating … Farting is never an issue.
- When you are married …You make sure there's nothing flammable near your husband at all times.

- When you are dating … He takes you out to have a good time.
- When you are married … He brings home a six-pack, and says, 'What are you going to drink?'

- When you are dating … He holds your hand in public.
- When you are married … He flicks your ear in public.

- When you are dating … You are aroused at the sight of him naked.
- When you are married … You think to yourself, 'Was he ALWAYS this hairy?'

- When you are dating … You enjoyed foreplay.
- When you are married … You tell him, 'If we have sex, will you leave me alone?'

- When you are dating … You picture the two of you, growing old together.
- When you are married … You wonder who will die first.

- When you are dating … He understands if you 'aren't in the mood'.
- When you are married … He says, 'It's your job.'

- When you are dating … He likes to 'discuss' things.
- When you are married … He develops a thousand-yard stare.

- When you are dating … He calls you by name.
- When you are married … . He calls you 'Hey' and refers to you when speaking to others as 'She'.

When women decline a date, what they really mean is:

- I think of you as a brother. (You remind me of the banjo-playing weirdo in *Deliverance*.)
- There's a slight difference in our ages. (You're one Jurassic geezer.)
- I'm not attracted to you in that way. (You are the ugliest dork I have ever laid eyes upon.)
- My life is too complicated right now. (I'm waiting for a rich sugar daddy.)
- I've got a boyfriend. (I'd rather stay home alone.)
- I don't date men where I work. (Hey, I wouldn't even date you if you were in the same solar system, much less the same building.)

- It's not you, it's me. (It's not me, it's you.)
- I'm concentrating on my career. (Even something as boring as my job has got to be better than dating you.)
- I'm celibate. (One look at you and I'm ready to swear off men altogether.)
- Let's be friends. (I want you to stay around so I can tell you in excruciating detail about all the other men I meet and fall in love with.)

.....and what men really mean:

- I think of you as a sister. (You're ugly.)
- There's a slight difference in our ages. (You're ugly.)
- I'm not attracted to you in that way. (You're ugly.)
- My life is too complicated right now. (You're ugly.)
- I've got a girlfriend. (You're ugly.)
- I don't date women where I work. (You're ugly.)
- It's not you, it's me. (You're ugly.)
- I'm concentrating on my career. (You're ugly.)
- I'm celibate. (You're ugly.)
- Let's be friends. (You're ugly.)

* Two women met for a drink. 'How was your blind date?' enquired the first woman. 'Terrible! He showed up in a 1932 Rolls-Royce,' replied her friend. 'What's so terrible about that?' 'He was the original owner.'

* My boyfriend and I started to date after he backed his car into mine. We met by accident.

❋ At the bar one night, a man approached one of the ladies standing near the edge of the dance floor. 'Would you like to dance?' he asked.
The girl didn't even look at him when she replied, 'I don't like this song, and even if I did, I wouldn't dance with you.' The man immediately said, 'Oh, I'm sorry, but you must have misunderstood me. I said, "You look fat in that dress."'

❋ A young man was going out with a nice girl and finally popped the question. 'Will you marry me, darling?' he asked.
She smiled coyly and said, 'Yes, if you'll buy me a mink.'
He thought for a moment and then replied, 'OK, it's a deal, on one condition.'
'What is that?' she asked.
'You'll have to clean the cage,' he replied.

❋ A boy took a girl out on her first date. When they pulled off into a secluded area, around midnight, the girl said, 'My mother told me to say no to everything.'
'Well,' he said, 'do you mind if I put my arm around you?'
'No,' the girl replied.
'Do you mind if I put my other hand on your leg?'
'Nooo,' the girl said.
'You know,' said the boy, 'we're going to have a lot of fun if you're on the level about this, and follow your mother's advice.'

❋ Keith sets up Andy to go on a blind date with Shirley, a friend of his. But Andy is a little worried about going out with someone he has never seen before.
'What do I do if she's ugly?' says Andy. 'I'll be stuck with her all night.'

'Don't worry,' Keith says. 'Just go up to her door and meet her first. If you like what you see, then everything goes as planned. If you don't, just shout Aaauuuggghhh! and fake an asthma attack.'

So that night, Andy knocks at Shirley's door, and when she comes out he is awestruck at how beautiful and sexy she is. Andy's about to speak when the girl suddenly shouts, 'Aaauuuggghhh!'

✳ A woman confided to her girlfriend, 'My ex-husband wants to marry me again.'

The friend said, 'How flattering.'

The woman replied, 'Not really. I think he's after the money I married him for.'

✳ What did the female furniture saleswoman say to her boyfriend?

Couch me if you can, but before that you need to chaise me!

✳ Two men were talking after one had been on a blind date. 'So your blind date had measurements of 39-23-35?'

'That's right,' replied his friend. 'Sadly, they weren't in that order.'

✳ A man is taking a woman home after their first date. When they get to her door, he asks if he can come inside.

'Absolutely not,' the woman says. 'I never allow a man to come in on the first date.'

'All right then,' the man replies, 'how about on the last date?'

✳ When asked the whereabouts of her fancy fur scarf, the minx replied it was stole.

✳ A man walks into a bookstore not looking for anything in particular. On his way to the back of the store, he spots something of interest. A book with a very interesting title: *Dating for the New Millennium. What Women Want.* So he picks it up and opens it at a random page. 'Chapter 1: The First Date.' He glances the chapter over for a few minutes, and rushes out of the bookstore to call a girl he's wanted to ask out for quite a while. When he gets home, he picks up the phone and calls her.

She answers, 'Hello?'

He says, 'Hi. Listen, I was wondering if you would want to go see a movie with me tonight?'

She says, 'Sure, I don't see anything wrong with that.'

He gets excited. He thought she'd say, 'No way!' but she didn't. So, he decided to take it one step further. He asks, 'Great, well how about dinner before the movie?'

She replies, 'Sure, that would be great too!'

'Fine, I'll pick you up about nine, you should be finished eating by then.'

✳ A crab and a lobster are secretly dating. Pretty soon, the lobster tires of the lying and tells her father, who then forbids her to see the crab any more.

'It'll never work, honey.' he says to her. 'Crabs walk sideways and we walk straight.'

'Please,' she begs her father. 'Just meet him once. I know you'll like him.'

Her father finally relents and agrees to a one-time meeting, and she runs off to share the good news with her crab sweetie. The crab is so excited he decides to surprise his beloved's family.

He practises and practises until he can finally walk straight!

On the big day, he walks the entire way to the lobster's house as straight as he can. Standing on the porch, and seeing the crab walking towards him, the lobster dad yells to his daughter ...

'I knew it! Here comes that crab and he's drunk!'

✳ Keith got off the elevator on the fiftieth floor and nervously knocked on his blind date's door. She opened it and was as beautiful and charming as everyone had said.

'I'll be ready in a few minutes,' she said. 'Why don't you play with Spot, my dog, while you're waiting? He does wonderful tricks. He rolls over, shakes hands, sits up and if you make a hoop with your arms, he'll jump through.'

The dog followed Keith onto the balcony and started rolling over. Keith made a hoop with his arms and Spot jumped through – over the balcony railing. Just then Keith's date walked out.

'Isn't Spot the cutest, happiest dog you've ever seen?'

'To tell the truth,' Keith replied, 'Spot seemed a bit depressed to me!'

✳ After waiting more than an hour and a half for her date, the young lady decided she had been stood up. She changed from her dinner dress into pyjamas and slippers, fixed some popcorn and resigned herself to an evening of TV.

No sooner had she flopped down in front of the TV than her doorbell rang. There stood her date. He took one look at her and gasped, 'I'm two hours late ... and you're still not ready?'

✳ You know it's love when she's happy to make a pair of trousers for you, or at least sew its seams.

DEATH AND DYING

✳ An elderly fisherman is on his deathbed and summons his three sons to his bedside. 'Well, boys, the time is near, and when I pass I'd like to be buried at sea.' The boys agreed. A few days after his passing, the local front page read, 'Local Fishermen Shocked When Nets Brought in Patrick McRay in a Coffin, three Shovels and the Bodies of His Three Sons … Funeral arrangements haven't yet been made, but, it is believed all wished to be buried at sea.'

✳ Have you seen the 3-D exhibit depicting a modern funeral parlour at the V&A? It's a die-orama!

✳ Phoning the florist to order some flowers for her lover's funeral, a woman was caught off guard when asked what message she wanted on the card. 'Message?' she sputtered. 'Well, I suppose, "You will be missed."' Visiting the funeral home, she was pleased that her floral tribute had arrived but mortified that the card had her exact words: 'I suppose you will be missed.'

✳ What happened to the prisoner who died before his parole?
He was put in a halfway hearse!

✳ A man is calling on his best friend to pay a condolence visit the day after the friend's wife has died. When he knocks on the door, he gets no answer, so he decides to go in and see if everything is all right. Upon entering the house, the man discovers his friend in the living room kissing a woman. 'John!' says the man, 'Your wife just died yesterday.'

His friend looks up and says, 'In this grief, do you think I know what I'm doing?'

✳ A Texan is boasting away about how great things are in his state. Finally, he starts describing the tall buildings in the cities. 'There is a building so tall, it took my friend seventy-two hours to fall off it!' 'Oh, my God!' says his friend. 'Surely he must have died!' 'Of course. He was without food or water for three days!'

✳ At the inquest into her husband's death by food poisoning a woman was asked by the coroner if she could remember her husband's last words. 'Yes,' she replied. 'He said "I don't know how that shop can make a profit from selling this salmon at only five pence a tin … "'

✳ What do you call a man who's been dead for thousands of years? Pete!

✳ The man who was about to die said to the sheriff, 'Say, do I really have to die swinging from a tree?' 'Course not,' replied the sheriff. 'We just put the rope round your neck and kick the horse away. After that it's up to you.'

✳ Did you hear about the do-it-yourself funeral? They just loosen the earth and you sink down by yourself.

✳ First zombie: You don't look too well today. Second zombie: No, I'm dead on my feet.

✳ What lies one hundred feet up in the air and smells? A dead centipede.

* What is the last thing you eat before you die? You bite the dust.

* What did the little kid do with the dead battery? He buried it.

* What has four legs, a tail, whiskers and flies? A dead cat.

* An old preacher was dying. He sent a message for his accountant and his lawyer (both church members) to come to his home. When they arrived, they were ushered up to his bedroom. As they entered the room, the preacher held out his hands and motioned for them to sit on each side of the bed. The preacher grasped their hands, sighed contentedly, smiled and stared at the ceiling. For a time, no one said anything. Both the accountant and lawyer were touched and flattered that the old preacher would ask them to be with him during his final moment.
They were also puzzled because the preacher had never given any indication that he particularly liked either one of them.
Finally, the lawyer asked, 'Preacher, why did you ask the two of us to come?'
The old preacher mustered up some strength, then said weakly, 'Jesus died between two thieves, and that's how I want to go, too.'

* Richard Dawkins dies and is laid out in an open coffin for people to pay their respects. The Archbishop of Canterbury passes by, looks down into the coffin and shakes his head sadly: 'So sad. All dressed up and no place to go.'

* A man is reading the paper when he is surprised to see his own obituary. Perturbed, he phones his friend. 'Mike,' he says, 'have you

seen the paper? They say I'm dead.' 'I did,' replies Mike. 'Where are you calling from?'

* Beneath this stone lies Murphy
  They buried him today
  He lived the life of Reilly
  While Reilly was away

* Old software engineers never die. They just log out.

* A woman's husband died. He had only twenty thousand pounds to his name. After everything was done at the funeral home and cemetery, she told her closest friend that there was no money left.
  The friend says, 'How can that be? You told me he still had twenty thousand pounds a few days before he died. How could you be broke?'
  The widow says, 'Well, the funeral home cost six thousand. And of course, I made the obligatory donation to the church, so that was another two thousand. The rest went for the memorial stone.'
  The friend says, 'Twelve thousand pounds for the memorial stone? My goodness, how big is it?'
  Extending her left hand, the widow says, 'Three carats.'

* A workaholic man spends every second of the day trying to make money. He makes his wife promise to bury him with all his money when the time comes. One Monday, he dies from a stroke produced by his high levels of cholesterol, stress, and hypertension.
  During the funeral, the widow approaches and puts a small box next to the coffin. Her mother asks if she had been so silly to bury all the money and she replies:

'I'm Christian, and therefore I had to keep my promise. I took all his money and put it in my account. Then I wrote a cheque for the exact quantity, which is inside the box. If he can cash the cheque in, the money is his to spend.'

* Did you hear about the man who loved crosswords?
When he died they buried him six down and three across.

* Apparently Michael Jackson died picking his nose. Doctors said they couldn't blame it on the sunshine or the moonlight. They blamed it on the boogie.

* Why are undertakers nice? They're the last to let people down.

* Old philosophers never die, they just retire to their own premises.

* Old cotton pickers never die. They just bale out!

* Old electricians never die, they just keep plugging away.

* Why was the undertaker late home? He was buried in his work!

* Being burned at the stake is a rare experience but is seldom well done.

* Did you hear about the novice executioner? He couldn't get the hang of it.

* Hangmen always keep their customers in the loop.

✳ Those who defy death will face Grim Reaper-cussions.

✳ Why did the man avoid funerals? He wasn't a mourning person!

✳ Michael Jackson will always be with us … he's not biodegradable.

✳ When Beethoven passed away, he was buried in a churchyard.
A couple of days later, the town drunk was walking through the cemetery and heard some strange noise coming from the area where Beethoven was buried. Terrified, the drunk ran and got the priest to come and listen to it. The priest bent close to the grave and heard some faint, unrecognisable music coming from the grave.
Frightened, the priest ran and got the town magistrate.
When the magistrate arrived, he bent his ear to the grave, listened for a moment, and said, 'Ah, yes, that's Beethoven's Ninth Symphony, being played backwards.'
He listened a while longer, and said, 'There's the Eighth Symphony, and it's backwards, too. Most puzzling.' So the magistrate kept listening, 'There's the Seventh … the Sixth … the Fifth … '
Suddenly the realisation of what was happening dawned on the magistrate. He stood up and announced to the crowd that had gathered in the cemetery, 'My fellow citizens, there's nothing to worry about. It's just Beethoven decomposing.'

🎃 DENTISTS

✳ Be true to your teeth, or they will be false to you.

* I've been to the dentist several times so I know the drill.

* Be kind to your dentist because he has fillings too.

* Did you see the fight between the dentists and manicurist? It was tooth and nail!

* I went to my dentist to have my cavity done. He wasn't there but someone else filled in.

* They called him the king of the dentists because he specialised in crowns.

* Dentists have their own flossify on how to keep teeth clean.

* Did you hear about the man whose buck-toothed kid refused to go to the dentist's? He told him to brace himself.

* I always find dentists get on my nerves.

* To qualify as a dentist you have to go through a lot of boring drills.

* Why are dentists sad? Because they always look down in the mouth!

* Where do dentists like to shop? Gap.

* Why was the dentist arrested? For incisor trading!

✳ A dentist ran out of anaesthetic just before the last extraction for the day was scheduled.

He gave the nurse a very large needle, instructing her to jab it hard into the patient's behind when the signal was given, so it would take his attention away from the tooth extraction.

It all happened in an instant.

The nurse, patient, and pliers were in place. The signal was given, and the nurse bayoneted the patient with the needle just as the dentist yanked the tooth.

Afterwards, the dentist asked, 'Hurt much?'

The patient hesitated, 'Didn't hardly feel it come out. And those roots were really deep!'

Down on the Farm

✳ A farmer needs a bull to service his cows but needs to borrow the money from the bank. The banker who lent the money comes by a week later to see how his investment is doing. The farmer complains that the bull just eats grass and won't even look at the cows.

The banker suggests that a vet have a look at the bull.

The next week the banker returns to see if the vet helped. The farmer looks very pleased. 'The bull has serviced all my cows, broke through the fence, and has serviced all my neighbour's cows.'

'Wow,' says the banker, 'what did the vet do to that bull?'

'Just gave him some pills,' replied the farmer.

'What kind of pills?'

'I don't know,' says the farmer, 'but they sort of taste like peppermint.'

✳ Did you hear about the frog who traced his family history to Warsaw?
He was a tad Polish.

✳ Deep in the backwoods, a farmer's wife went into labour in the middle
of the night, and a doctor was called out to help. Since there was no
electricity, the doctor handed the father-to-be a lantern and said,
'Here, you hold this high so I can see what I'm doing.'
Soon, a baby boy was brought into the world. 'Whoa there,' said the
doctor. 'Don't be in a rush to put the lantern down. I think there's
another one coming.'
Sure enough, within minutes he had delivered a baby girl. 'No, no,
don't be in a great hurry to be putting down that lantern. It seems
there's yet another one in there!' cried the doctor.
The farmer scratched his head in bewilderment, and asked the doctor,
'Gee! Do you think it's the light that's attractin' 'em?'

✳ A man owned a small farm. The department of wages claimed he was
not paying proper wages to his staff and sent a representative out to
interview him.
'I need a list of your employees and how much you pay them,'
demanded the rep.
'Well,' replied the farmer, 'there's my farm hand who's been with me for
three years. I pay him three hundred and fifty pounds a week plus free
room and board. The cook has been here for eighteen months, and I
pay her two hundred and fifty pounds per week plus free room and
board. Then there's the half-wit. He works about eighteen hours every
day and does about 90% of all the work around here. He makes about
ten pounds per week, pays his own room and board, and I buy him a

bottle of whisky every Saturday night. He also sleeps with my
wife occasionally.'

'That's the person I want to talk to … the half-wit,' says the official.

'That would be me,' replied the farmer.

* A farmer in the country has a watermelon patch and upon inspection he
discovers that some of the local kids have been helping themselves to
a feast. The farmer thinks of ways to discourage this profit-eating
situation. So he puts up a sign that reads: 'WARNING! ONE OF THESE
WATERMELONS CONTAINS CYANIDE!' He smiled smugly as he
watched the kids run off the next night without eating any of his
melons. The farmer returns to the watermelon patch a week later to
discover that none of the watermelons have been eaten, but finds
another sign that reads: 'NOW THERE ARE TWO!'

* One day a travelling salesman stopped by the old Johnson farm.
The man knocked, and Johnson's wife, Fannie, came to the door.
'Is your husband home, ma'am?' the salesman asked.
Fannie replied, 'Sure is. He's over to the cow barn.'
'Well, I've got something to show him, ma'am. Will I have any difficulty
finding him?' asked the salesman.
The farmer's wife replied, 'Nope. You shouldn't have any difficulties.
He's the one with the beard and moustache.'

* Did you hear about the thief who stole some corn from a farmer's
garden? He was charged with stalking!

* Buttercup and Daisy were chatting as they chewed the cud.
''Ere, have you heard about this mad-cow disease?'

'Yes, sounds nasty.'

'I'm glad I'm a chicken.'

✳ Why was the farmer stuffing sheep into his computer?

It needed more RAM 110.

✳ The two brothers were sat in the solicitor's waiting room waiting for their father's will to be read. An argument started as to which of them was the favourite son and it was getting into full flow when they were invited into the office. After a few preliminaries including the disposal of a few small items to the cousins and old friends the important bit came – who would inherit the farm.

The solicitor took a deep breath, looked at the eldest brother and said, 'Well, John, the farm is yours.' John turned to his brother, 'See,' he said, 'I told you you were the favourite.'

✳ The farmer whittled the stick as the tourist approached him. 'How long to get to the nearest town, Paddy?' came the enquiry from the rich American. The farmer continued to whittle and started to whistle too.

'I said how long to get to the nearest town, Paddy?'

No reply. Just whistle and whittle.

'Gee, Paddy, I've been a walkin' all day. Couldn't you just tell me aw heck, what's the use,' and the American walked away from the farmer in disgust. He had gone about a hundred yards when the farmer called him back. Exasperated, the American returned.

'It will take you about an hour,' said the farmer.

'Gee, thanks Paddy. But why didn't you tell me that in the first place?'

'Had to see how fast you could walk first,' said the farmer.

✳ A farmer took B&B guests at his farm, as did his mother on her farm nearby. A dishonest tourist from the Swiss Alps stayed with the mother, heard from her about her son and when his holiday was over he left the old lady without paying and went to stay with her son. He arose at dawn on the last morning of his holiday in the son's farm, got his bags and headed off up the steep lane from the farm.

It so happened that the farmer was up early too and saw his guest trying to make his getaway without paying. Grabbing his shotgun he dashed out into the yard and called: 'Stop or I'll shoot. You owe me forty pounds for your holiday.' Knowing he was well out of shotgun reach the Swiss guest's yodel rang out across the valley: 'I owe the ole lady too.'

✳ The farmer chatted with the new curate who had been a schoolmate of his. The farmer told him of how he had been an acrobat in the circus for a few years before going back to the land. The priest looked at his watch and said, 'There'll hardly be any more for confession tonight, I'll just stand here and you show me some of the tricks you used do in the circus.' The farmer performed a few elaborate cartwheels, handstands and finished up balancing himself on one hand. Just at this stage two late-coming penitents arrived into the church and saw the farmer in the peculiar pose. One became most distressed and said, 'Will you look at the penances he's giving. I'll have to go back home and put on some pants.'

✳ The farmer's daughter was engaged to be married to a bright young solicitor. When she first brought her fiancé to visit her father engaged in conversation with the young man about his success with his crops. 'I have rhubarb sticks like hockey sticks,' he said.

'And how do you get them to grow so big?' asked the young man.

'Oh, loads of manure,' answered the farmer. 'And my turnips are as big as footballs.'

'And to what do you attribute your success with turnips?' asked the young solicitor.

'Oh loads of manure,' said the farmer again.

'Loads of manure,' was the secret of the success of the farmer's cabbage, parsnips and every other crop that he spoke to the young man about. When the evening was over an embarrassed daughter called her mother to the kitchen and, almost in tears, begged her to get her father to use the word 'fertiliser' when in polite company.

'If you only knew how long it took me to get him to say "manure",' her mother replied.

✳ Two neighbouring farmers' sons went on holidays together. One of the young men was drowned while bathing. The other young man could not face his deceased friend's parents to break the news to them and so he sent a note which, he hoped, would break the news gently.

The note read:

Dear Mr and Mrs Murphy,

Tom's swimming trunks got washed away today.

Best wishes,

Jim.

P.S. Tom was in them at the time.

✳ The farmer had been at the cattle market and was not too clean, nor did he smell too good when he went into the jeweller's shop to purchase a ring. The assistant could not help her automatic stepping back from the smell and, indeed, the young man could not avoid noticing her action but he still asked the young lady to let him see some signet rings.

'Eighteen carats?' asked the assistant.

'No, eatin' onions,' answered the farmer.

✳ A city slicker was driving through the country when he spotted a horse standing in a field. He was quite taken with the animal and so pulled over to ask the farmer if it was for sale.

'Afraid not,' said the farmer.

'I'll give you a thousand pounds!' said the city fellow.

'I can't sell you that horse. He don't look too good,' replied the farmer.

'I know horses, and he looks fine. I'll give you two thousand!'

'Well, all right, if you want him so bad.'

The next day, the man returned the horse, screaming that he had been gypped. 'You sold me a blind horse!'

'Well,' said the farmer, 'I told you he didn't look too good.'

✳ A small boy was looking at the red ripe tomatoes growing in the farmer's garden. 'I'll give you my two pennies for that tomato,' said the boy, pointing to a beautiful, large, ripe fruit hanging on the vine.

'No,' said the farmer, 'I get a pound for a tomato like that one.'

The small boy pointed to a smaller green one, 'Will you take two pennies for that one?'

'Yes,' replied the farmer, 'I'll give you that one for two pennies.'

'OK,' said the lad, sealing the deal by putting the coins in the farmer's hand, 'I'll pick it up in about a week.'

✳ How do rabbits like their beer? Hoppy!

✳ A salesman is talking to a farmer when he looks over and sees a rooster wearing pants, a shirt, and braces.

He says, 'What on earth is that all about?'

The farmer says, 'We had a fire in the chicken coop two months ago and all his feathers got singed off, so the wife made him some clothes to keep him warm.'

'OK, but that was two months ago. Why does he still wear them?'

The farmer replied, 'There ain't nothing funnier than watching him try to hold down a hen with one foot and get his pants down with the other.'

✳ A Government inspector stopped at a farm and summoned the old farmer: 'I need to inspect your farm.'

The old farmer said: 'OK, but you better not go in that field.'

In a supercilious tone the inspector said, 'I have the authority of the Government with me. See this card?'

He stuck a plastic-coated card in the farmer's face.

'This card says I can go wherever I want to on agricultural land.'

The old farmer shrugged and went about his farm chores. Later, he heard loud screams and saw the inspector running for the fence. Close behind was the farmer's prize bull, Geronimo, enraged and gaining on the inspector.

The farmer shouted, 'Show him your card!'

✳ The vicar had just finished an excellent chicken dinner at the home of a member of his congregation when he saw a rooster come strutting through the yard. 'That's certainly a proud-looking rooster you have there,' the vicar commented.

'Yes, sir,' replied the farmer. 'He has reason to be proud – one of his daughters has just entered the ministry!'

EDUCATION

* Did you hear about the man who studied pharmacy because he wanted to become … a farmer!

* Aspiring physicians go to college and get indoctorinated.

* What music do geology teachers like? Rock.

* At school I was teacher's pet. She couldn't afford a dog.

* Why don't schools teach astronomy? They don't have the space!

* My parents sent me to boarding school so that they wouldn't have to help me with my homework.

* Teacher: Billy, why have you not given me your homework?
  Billy: I made it into a paper aeroplane and someone hijacked it.

✳ Father: Well, son, how are your exam results?
  Son: They're all under water.
  Father: What do you mean?
  Son: They're all under C level.

✳ Old teachers never die. They just lose their class.

✳ Old professors never die. They just lose their faculties.

✳ 'You never get anything right,' complained the teacher. 'What kind of job do you think you'll get when you leave school?'
  'Well, I want to be the weather girl on TV.'

✳ A student who changes the course of history is probably taking an exam.

✳ A professor asked a student to remain for a few moments after class. Holding out the young man's assignment, the professor said, 'Did you write this poem all by yourself?'
  The student said, 'Every word of it.'
  The professor said, 'Well, then, I'm glad to meet you, Mr Poe. I thought you were long dead.'

✳ My school was so tough that when the teacher asked what comes at the end of a sentence, three boys answered, 'You appeal.'

✳ Teacher: 'If you had six apples and I asked you for three, how many would you have left?'
  Student: 'Six.'

✳ A school teacher injured his back and had to wear a plaster cast around the upper part of his body. It fitted under his shirt and was not noticeable at all.

On the first day of the term, still with the cast under his shirt, he found himself assigned to the toughest students in school.

Walking confidently into the rowdy classroom, he opened the window as wide as possible and then busied himself with desk work.

When a strong breeze made his tie flap, he took the desk stapler and stapled the tie to his chest.

He had no trouble with discipline that term.

✳ An infant teacher had a small number of children gathered around a table for a reading group. After the story was read she gave the children a work sheet to do. While they were working she heard a little girl say very softly, 'Damn!'

The teacher leaned over and said quietly, 'We don't say that in school.'

The little girl looked at the teacher, her eyes got very big and she said, 'Not even when things are all f@%$*ed up?'

ENGINEERS

✳ Two engineers agree to paint a flag pole. Of course they need to know how tall it is so they can purchase the paint. One shimmies up the pole with a tape measure and falls after reaching about halfway. While trying to figure out how they can possibly measure the pole, along comes a designer. After asking what they're doing he replies, 'That's easy.'

He then reaches around the pole and pulls it out of the ground and lays it down. 'There you go,' he says as he walked away. The two engineers look at each other and one said, 'That stupid idiot will never get anywhere, we don't need to know how wide it is, just how tall.'

✳ Why is it hard to become an electrician?
You have to pass a battery of tests!

✳ An architect, an artist and an engineer were discussing whether it was better to spend time with the wife or a mistress. The architect said he enjoyed time with his wife, building a solid foundation for an enduring relationship. The artist said he enjoyed time with his mistress, because of the passion and mystery he found there. The engineer said, 'I like both.' 'Both?' 'Yeah,' the engineer replied. 'If you have a wife and a mistress, they'll each assume you are spending time with the other woman, and you can go to the lab and get some work done.'

Some engineering terms:

- A NUMBER OF DIFFERENT APPROACHES ARE BEING TRIED – We are still pissing in the wind.
- CLOSE PROJECT COORDINATION – We know who to blame.
- MAJOR TECHNOLOGICAL BREAKTHROUGH – It sometimes works OK, but looks very hi-tech.
- CUSTOMER SATISFACTION IS DELIVERED ASSURED – We are so far behind schedule the customer is happy to get it delivered.
- PRELIMINARY OPERATIONAL TESTS WERE INCONCLUSIVE – It blew up when we threw the switch.
- TEST RESULTS WERE EXTREMELY GRATIFYING – We are so surprised that the stupid thing works.

- THE ENTIRE CONCEPT WILL HAVE TO BE ABANDONED –The only person who understood the thing has left.
- ALL NEW – Parts not interchangeable with the previous design.
- RUGGED – Too damn heavy to lift!
- LIGHTWEIGHT – Lighter than RUGGED.
- YEARS OF DEVELOPMENT – One finally worked.
- ENERGY SAVING – Achieved when the power switch is off.
- LOW MAINTENANCE – Impossible to fix if broken.

You may be an engineer if:

- You have a spreadsheet recording what you had for lunch.
- When your wife is pregnant, you're more interested in the ultrasound equipment than your unborn child.
- The only jokes you ever hear are via email.
- You introduce your spouse as 'mylady@home.wife'.
- You save the power leads from broken appliances.
- You need a checklist to turn on the TV.
- You thought the real heroes in the film *Apollo 13* were the men in mission control.
- You never danced with a girl at the school disco; you were too busy looking after the sound system.

✳ A physicist, an engineer and a mathematician were all in a hotel sleeping when fire broke out in their respective rooms. The physicist woke up, saw the fire, ran over to his desk, pulled out his calculator, and began working out all sorts of fluid dynamics equations. After a couple of minutes, he threw down his pencil, got a graduated cylinder out of his suitcase, and measured out a precise amount of water.

He threw it on the fire, extinguishing it, with not a drop wasted, and went back to sleep. The engineer woke up, saw the fire, ran into the bathroom, turned on the taps full-blast, flooding out the entire room and putting out the fire, and went back to sleep. The mathematician woke up, saw the fire, ran over to his desk, began working through theorems, hypotheses, equations and after a few minutes put down his pencil triumphantly and exclaimed, 'I have proof that I can put the fire out!' and went back to sleep.

✳ I've tried numerous times to apply myself, but nothing seems to stick.

✳ When considering the behaviour of artillery: a mathematician will be able to calculate where the shell will land. A physicist will be able to explain how the shell gets there. An engineer will stand there and try to catch it.

✳ Did you hear about the electrician's new van? It was a voltswagon!

✍ESTATE AGENTS

Some common estate-agent speak decoded:

✳ SPACIOUS: average.

✳ CHARMING: small.

✳ COMFORTABLE: very small.

✳ COSY: very, very small

✳ LOW MAINTENANCE: no garden, only one window.

✳ WALK TO SHOPS: your car will be stolen within hours of moving in.

✳ TOWNHOUSE: flat in tower block.

✳ CONTEMPORARY: at least fifteen years old.

✳ NATURAL, SECLUDED SETTING: ever seen *Deliverance*?

✳ NEAR HOUSES OF WORSHIP: fanatical cult next door.

✳ PARK-LIKE SETTING: a tree is growing only two streets away.

✳ UNAFFECTED CHARM: needs painting.

✳ ON THE WATER: flood in cellar.

✳ HURRY! WON'T LAST: about to collapse.

🐛Fairy Tales

✳ As a child, the wicked magician always wanted to saw people in half.
Was he an only child?
No, he had lots of half-brothers and sisters!

✳ Humpty Dumpty had a great fall – and a pretty good spring and
summer, too!

✳ Long fairy tales have a tendency to dragon.

✳ Do you know what's inside Aladdin's lamp? It would take a genie-us to
find out!

✳ 'Open Sesame' opened the doors to the robbers' cave. Which piece of
jewellery closed it?
A locket!

✳ Why couldn't Cinders use horses to pull the pumpkin coach?
Because they were too busy playing stable tennis!

✳ Why did Hansel eat all the liquorice off the witch's house?
It takes all sorts!

✳ Jack stole a golden harp from the giant. Why couldn't he play it?
Because it took a lot of pluck!

✳ Knock, knock.
Who's there?
Fifi.
Fifi who?
Fifi fiefie fofo fum I smell the blood of an Englishman!

✳ Knock, knock.
Who's there?
Sarah.
Sarah who?
Sarah giant living here?

✳ What goes: MUF OF EIF IF? A giant walking backwards!

✳ What's purple and screams from the top of a tower?
A damson in distress!

✳ How did Robin Hood tie his shoelaces? With a long bow!

✳ I keep reading *The Lord of the Rings* over and over. I guess it's just force of hobbit!

✳ What has two holes for the eyes and a slit for the beak? A Robin Hood!

✳ What is Robin Hood's favourite radio programme? *The Archers*!

✳ Why couldn't Robin Hood hit the target? Because his arrows were all in a quiver!

✳ A prince came to a small pool where the most beautiful girl in the world was bathing. On her head was a large, green frog. What was her name?
Lily!

✳ What did Sinbad eat when he was washed up on a desert island?
He ate all the sand which is there.

✳ What made Goldilocks shiver? Quaker Oats!

✳ Why did the ugly duckling stop preening himself?
He felt a little down in the mouth!

FASHION AND CLOThING

✳ Why did the man dress up as a knife? He wanted to look sharp!

✳ A young man came to the underwear department of a men's store with a complaint. He was attended to by a young woman.

'I want to return these underpants please.'

'Certainly, sir. What's wrong with them?'

'They're … not suitable.'

'In what way, sir?'

'Well, I'll put it this way. Do you know St Paul's Cathedral?'

'Yes, of course.'

'And do you know the ballroom underneath?'

'Wait a minute. There's no ballroom underneath.'

'Right. And that's just what's wrong with these underpants.'

✳ A man decides to get a bespoke suit made to impress a girl. He goes to Savile Row to get measured, and a few weeks later the tailor calls him up to tell him that his suit is finished. When he arrives he is keen to try it on, but the first thing he notices is that the arms are too long.

'No problem,' says the tailor. 'Just bend them at the elbow and hold them out in front of you. See, now it's fine.'

'But the collar is up around my ears!'

'It's nothing. Just hunch your back up a little … no, a little more … that's it.'

'But I'm stepping on my trousers!' the man shouts.

'Just bend your knees a little to take up the slack. There you go. Look in the mirror – the suit fits perfectly.'

Twisted and hunched, the man lurches out onto the street. Two office girls see him stagger past.

'Oh, look,' says one, 'that poor man!'

'Yes,' says the other, 'but what a beautiful suit!'

* The designers of jeans are always looking at the bottom line.

* 'If I didn't wear a halter top and tight jeans,' asked the girl, 'would you still find me appealing?' 'Let's find out,' the man replied gamely.

* Ron was passing a shop where the sign said: 'Suits £5.00 each, Shirts £2.00 each, Trousers £2.50 per pair.' Quickly doing some calculations he works out that he could buy a whole lot of clothes at those prices and make a fortune selling them on. He goes in and says, 'I'll take fifty suits at £5.00 each, a hundred shirts at £2.00 each, and fifty pairs of trousers at £2.50 each. I'll back up my car and …' The owner of the shop interrupts, 'You're from Ireland, aren't you?' 'Well … yes,' says a surprised Keith. 'How come you know that?' The owner says, 'This is a dry cleaner's!'

* Dating the first southern girl he'd ever known, the Yankee was surprised when she greeted him at the door in the lowest-cut gown he'd ever seen. 'Th-that's a lovely dress,' he stuttered, his eyes on her ample bosom. 'Sho' nough,' she replied. To which he answered, 'I'll say!'

* People who make necklaces often get beady eyes.

* A dry cleaner was indicted with charges pressed for money laundering. A deal is being ironed out.

* Is someone who steals shoes an arch criminal?

* As the bus approached the stop, the young woman realised she was going to have a difficult time getting on. Her dress was too tight for her

to step up, her hands were full of packages, and the line of people behind her did not seem to be in a charitable mood.

She realised that the best thing to do was to try to loosen her dress so, with great effort, she stretched her hand behind her and pulled the zipper down halfway. When that didn't seem to help, she pulled it down the rest of the way.

Just then the bus pulled up and, still unable to ascend, she was both shocked and offended when a man standing behind her picked her up and put her on the bus.

Turning, she growled, 'What right did you have to touch me?'

The man climbed on and said, 'Well, after you pulled my fly down I kind of figured we were good friends.'

＊ A rather liberal young lady came home from the store and showed her husband the new dress she'd bought, which was made of plastic and totally transparent.

'But honey,' the young man gasped, 'people will see right through it!'

'No they won't, dummy,' she replied. 'I'll be inside of it!'

＊ What do pirates keep on their foot? Booty.

＊ Did you hear about the support group for stocking-wearers?

＊ Why did the man put lipstick on his head? To make up his mind.

＊ A man took a stained sweater down to Wong's Laundry and dropped it off. Mr Wong said he'd probably be able to have it cleaned by Thursday. So on Thursday afternoon after work he stopped by Wong's again.

Mr Wong looked quite distressed when he saw the man. He brought out the sweater and, apologising profusely, explained that somehow this stain was beyond even his power to expunge.

And sure enough, though fainter than before, there was still a distinct red stain on the sweater. In an attempt to make up for his failure, Mr Wong offered to send the sweater to his brother across town, who had been in the laundry business for an even longer time, and who might have a clue as to the method of removal of this extraordinarily persistent stain.

The elder Wong brother would rush it through at no extra charge, and should have it looking as white and clean as new by Friday. So on Friday the man went back to Wong's to pick up his sweater, but when he arrived, Mr Wong regretfully informed me that his brother, too, had failed to remove the red blotch. 'No charge,' said Wong, 'but you must take sweater elsewhere to clean.'

The moral: two Wongs cannot make a white.'

Fighting and arguing

How can you tell if an Irishman is present at a cock fight?
He enters a duck.

How can you tell if a Pole is present?
He bets money on the duck.

How can you tell if an Italian is present?
The duck wins.

Why did the two jewellers remain enemies?
Neither would brooch an agreement.

Why was the hand arguing? Three fingers were willing to cooperate but the thumb and forefinger were opposed.

My friend is very paranoid. He says people are either foe him or against him.

🍏 FiLMS

✳ A man finds his seat in the cinema, but it's too far from the stage. He whispers to the usher, 'This is a mystery and I have to watch a mystery close up. Get me a better seat, and I'll give you a handsome tip.' The usher moves him to the second row, and the man hands the usher a five-pence piece. The usher looks at the coin and then leans over and whispers, 'The wife did it.'

✳ The new Sylvester Stallone Film Festival has got off to a rocky start.

✳ What do you call a film about a baby hen? A chick flick!

✳ Wanted: actor for role of hostage. A captivating part.

✳ Who's the best film star to take the lid off a jar of pickles?
Kris Twistofferson.

❋ Have you heard about the remake of the old *Dracula* film? It's a revamp!

❋ Why did the cow go to Hollywood? It wanted to be scene, not herded!

❋ Did you hear about the man who brought salt and pepper to the box office because he wanted a season ticket?

Things that films have taught us:

- It is always possible to park directly outside any building you are visiting.
- If you decide to start dancing in the street, everyone you bump into will know all the steps.
- Most laptop computers are powerful enough to override the communication systems of any invading alien civilisation.
- When a person is knocked unconscious by a blow to the head, they will never suffer a concussion or brain damage.
- No one involved in a car chase, hijacking, explosion, volcanic eruption or alien invasion will ever go into shock.
- Police departments give their officers personality tests to make sure they are deliberately assigned a partner who is their total opposite.
- When they are alone, all foreigners prefer to speak English to each other.
- You can always find a chainsaw when you need one.
- Any lock can be picked by a credit card or a paper clip in seconds, unless it's the door to a burning building with a child trapped inside.
- An electric fence, powerful enough to kill a dinosaur, will cause no lasting damage to an eight-year-old child.

- Television news bulletins usually contain a story that affects you personally at the precise moment you turn the television on.
- You're very likely to survive any battle in any war unless you make the mistake of showing someone a picture of your sweetheart back home.
- Should you wish to pass yourself off as a German officer, it will not be necessary to speak the language. Even a bad German accent will do.

✳ For the first time in many years, an old man travelled from his rural town to the city to attend a movie. After buying his ticket, he stopped at the concession stand to purchase some popcorn. Handing the attendant a five-pound note, he couldn't help but comment, 'The last time I came to the movies, popcorn was only a shilling.'
'Well, sir,' the attendant replied with a grin, 'You're really going to enjoy yourself. We have sound now.'

✳ When James Bond slept through the earthquake, he was shaken but not stirred.

✳ What do you get if you film a haircut? A short clip!

Lost in translation – some actual Chinese subtitles

- Same old rules: no eyes, no groin.
- Gun wounds again?
- Fatty, you with your thick face have hurt my instep.
- A normal person wouldn't steal pituitaries.
- The bullets inside are very hot. Why do I feel so cold? Take my advice, or I'll spank you without pants.
- Who gave you the nerve to get killed here?

- I'll fire aimlessly if you don't come out!
- You always use violence. I should've ordered glutinous rice chicken.
- Beat him out of recognisable shape!
- I got knife scars more than the number of your leg's hair!
- Beware! Your bones are going to be disconnected.
- How can you use my intestines as a gift?

* I went to see *The Hustler* last night. It started right on cue.

* Did you hear about the dad who took his kids to see the new 007 film because he wanted to bond with them?

FIRE

* The other day my house caught fire. The insurance agent said, 'Shouldn't be a problem. What kind of coverage do you have?'
I said, 'Fire and theft.'
The insurance agent frowned. 'Uh oh. Wrong kind. Should be fire OR theft.'
Apparently, the only way I can make a claim with this coverage is if the house is robbed while it's burning down.

* A lady was filling her tank at a petrol station, smoking a cigarette, even though all the signs said not to. The fumes that came out of the tank ignited, severely burning her hands. But it also lit up her arm, too! Instead of rolling on the ground to put it out, she panicked. She took off running down the street. A policeman was at the intersection where it happened and he tried to stop her, to put out her arm, but she just kept running and screaming. All the officer could think of doing was to shoot her. This took everyone by surprise. The officer ran over to her and put the fire out, then called for an ambulance. When questioned about his course of action to stop her, the officer said, 'My only thought was to stop her. After all, she was waving a fire-arm.'

* How can you tell when a fireman is dead?
  The remote control slips from his hand.

* What do you call a fire with one piece of wood? A monologue.

* How many firemen does it take to change a light bulb?
  Four. One to change the bulb and three to chop a hole in the roof.

* There was a fire at the circus. The heat was in tents.

* A fireman had two sons. What did he name them? Hosea and Hoseb.

* A fireman rescued a man who was badly injured in a car accident. The entire left half of his body was torn off. He was taken to the hospital and examined. The doctors said he was all right. The nurses said there wasn't much left.

* You won't find me sitting on top of a bonfire on 5th November. I'm not that type of guy.

* I once dragged a man out of a flaming building. Unfortunately that man was a fireman.

✳ What did the fireman say when the church caught on fire?
'Holy smoke!'

✳ Ever since the ban on flammable liquids, fewer arsonists have benzene around town.

🍎 FISHING

✳ Why did the fish miss the call?
Because he was stuck on the other line.

✳ Why did the fisherman take pills? He had a persistent haddock!

✳ Have you seen the new play about fishing?
It's got quite a cast.

✳ When fishermen get paid do they get net wages?

✳ Did you hear about the compulsive fisherman?
He was really hooked on it.

✳ Did you hear about the fisherman whose worm fell off his hook?
He carried on fishing unabated!

✳ Women who go fishing have allure.

☺FOOD

Foreign

Why was the dumpling arrested? For won ton disregard of the law!

Chinese cooks come from all woks of life.

Meat

✳ A man in a state of excessive inebriation rolled up at a fairground rifle range booth and threw down the necessary money. The booth operator at first refused to let him have a turn, considering that his inebriated state would endanger the public.

But the drunk insisted and was given a gun. He aimed unsteadily in the general direction of the target and after tying to focus pulled the trigger three times.

The booth owner, on inspecting the target, was astonished to see that he had scored three bullseyes. The star prize for the evening was a large set of glassware, but the showman was certain that the drunk wasn't aware of what he had done, and gave him instead a consolation prize, a small, live turtle.

The drunk wandered off into the crowd. An hour or so later he came back, even more drunk than before. Once again the showman demurred, but once again the drunk insisted, and once more scored three bullseyes and was given another turtle.

Eventually the drunk rolled up again and insisted on a third attempt.

Once more he picked up the rifle, waved it around in the general direction of the target, and pulled the trigger three times. Once more he had scored three bullseyes. But this time there was an onlooker with good eyesight.

'That's fantastic,' the man said. 'Hasn't he scored three bulls?'

The showman, cursing his luck, made a show of going over to the target and inspecting it closely. 'Yes, sir!' he announced to the crowd. 'This is fantastic! Congratulations, sir, you have won the star prize, this magnificent sixty-eight-piece set of glassware!'

'I don't want any bloody glasses,' the drunk replied. 'Give me another one of those little crusty meat pies!'

* How many vegans does it take to change a light bulb?
  Two, one to change it and one to check for animal ingredients.

* A ham walked out of the hospital and said, 'I'm cured.'

* Why did the vegetarian cross the road?
  Because she was protesting for the chicken, man.

* How many vegetarians does it take to eat a cow?
  One, if nobody's looking.

* Bulls wish they could live for heifer and heifer.

* A man was adding milk to my coffee when a vegan colleague said,
  'Do you know that milk belongs to a calf?'
  The man turned to his colleague and replied, 'Relax, I already ate the veal for lunch.'

✳ Did you hear about the man arrested in the butcher's?
He was choplifting!

✳ A man walks into a butcher's and asks, 'Have you got pig's feet?'
'Yes, sir,' comes the reply.
'Well, trot over and get me a couple of steaks!'

✳ There was this rabbi in a small town, and he was really curious about why so many people ate pork. He wanted to try some, but there was nowhere in town he could go and not be seen.
One weekend, he made an excuse and travelled to a distant town, went into a restaurant and ordered the first pork item on the menu. While he's waiting for his order of pork, the president of his congregation walks in. He sees the rabbi and asks if he could join him for dinner, and the rabbi has no choice but to agree.
Some time later, the waiter returns with the rabbi's meal. He takes the cover off the large platter, and there is a whole roast pig, with an apple in its mouth. The congregation president is more than a little shocked.
'What a fancy place!' exclaims the rabbi quickly. 'Just look at how they serve the apple I ordered.'

✳ A man walks into a pub with a pork pie on his head and asks the barman for a pint of lager.
BARMAN: Do you know you've got a pork pie on your head?
MAN: Yes, I always wear a pork pie on my head on Wednesday.
BARMAN: But it's Tuesday today.
MAN: Oh my God! I must look a real idiot.

＊ One day, Tim and Bill went to a restaurant for dinner. As soon as the waiter took out two steaks, Bill quickly picked out the bigger steak for himself.
Tim wasn't happy about that: 'When are you going to learn to be polite?'
'If you had the chance to pick first, which one would you pick?'
'The smaller piece, of course.'
'What are you whining about, then. You got the piece you wanted.'

＊ Why is melted butter no good? It's rendered useless

Vegetables

＊ Where did the vegetables go to have a few drinks? The Salad Bar.

＊ Have you heard about the woman who decided that becoming a vegetarian was a missed steak!

＊ What do you call a melon that's not allowed to get married?
Can't elope.

＊ Why do potatoes make good detectives?
Because they keep their eyes peeled.

＊ What do you call a stolen yam? A hot potato.

＊ What's the funniest fruit? A pun-net of strawberries!

＊ Who is king of all sauces? Mayor Naise!

* What vegetable can tie your stomach in knots? String beans.

* I've just realised that tofu is overrated. It's just a curd to me.

* What did the carrot say to the wheat? Lettuce rest, I'm feeling beet.

* We were driving and almost got creamed by a milk truck. I was udderly terrified.

* Botanists have developed a vegetable that eliminates the need to brush your teeth – bristle sprouts.

* Have you heard of the garlic diet? You don't lose much weight, but from a distance your friends think you look thinner.

* What can you make from baked beans and onions? Tear gas!

* What kind of tree has hands? A palm tree.

* What's green and likes camping? Brussels sprouts.

* What do you call a pun sandwich? A punini.

* I was a vegetarian until I started leaning towards sunlight. *Rita Rudner*

* What is small, red and whispers? A hoarse radish.

* What kind of eggs are stolen? Poached eggs!

FOREIGN TONGUES

* On a visit to the United States, Charles de Gaulle was honoured at a banquet in the White House. Seated beside his wife was an official who spoke no French, but who tried to engage her in conversation by asking, 'Madame de Gaulle, what do you think the most important thing in life is?'

'A penis,' she replied.

Overhearing, her husband said gently, 'I believe, my dear, that in English it is pronounced 'appiness.'

* Did you hear about the Frenchman who liked to stay current with the electrifying adventures of Sherlock ohms?

* An African chieftain flew to the United States to visit the president. When he arrived at the airport, a host of newsmen and television cameramen met him. One of the reporters asked the chief if he had a comfortable flight. The chief made a series of weird noises ... 'screech, scratch, honk, buzz, whistle, z-z-z-z-' ... and then added in perfect English, 'Yes, I had a very nice flight.'

Another reporter asked, 'Chief, do you plan to visit the Washington Monument while you're in the area? The chief made the same noises ... 'screech, scratch, honk, buzz, whistle, z-z-z-z' ... and then said, 'Yes, and I also plan to visit the White House and the Capitol Building.'

'Where did you learn to speak such flawless English?' asked the next reporter.

The chief replied, 'Screech, scratch, honk, buzz, whistle, z-z-z-z ... from the short-wave radio.'

✳ Two translators on a ship are talking.

'Can you swim?' asks one.

'No,' says the other, 'but I can shout for help in nine languages.'

✳ A Mexican bandit made a speciality of crossing the Rio Grande from time to time and robbing banks in Texas. Finally, a reward was offered for his capture, and an enterprising Texas Ranger decided to track him down. After a lengthy search, he traced the bandit to his favourite cantina, sneaked up behind him, put his trusty six-shooter to the bandit's head, and said,

'You're under arrest. Tell me where you hid the loot or I'll blow your brains out.' But the bandit didn't speak English, and the Ranger didn't speak Spanish.

As luck would have it, a bilingual lawyer was in the saloon and translated the Ranger's message. The terrified bandit blurted out, in Spanish, that the loot was buried under the oak tree in the back of the cantina.

'What did he say?' asked the Ranger.

The lawyer answered, 'He said, "Get lost, Gringo. You wouldn't dare shoot me."'

✳ The following were among the winners in a New York magazine contest in which contestants were to take a well-known expression in a foreign language, change a single letter, and provide a definition for the new expression.

HARLEZ-VOUS FRANCAIS?   Can you drive a French motorcycle?

IDIOS AMIGOS   We're wild and crazy guys!

VENI, VIPI, VICI	I came, I'm a very important person, I conquered.
COGITO EGGO SUM	I think; therefore I am a waffle.
RIGOR MORRIS	The cat is dead.
RESPONDEZ S'IL VOUS PLAID	Honk if you're Scottish.
LE ROI EST MORT. JIVE LE ROI	The king is dead. No kidding.
POSH MORTEM	Death styles of the rich and famous.
PRO BOZO PUBLICO	Support your local clown.
MONAGE A TROIS	I am three years old.
MAZEL TON	Tons of luck.
APRES MOE LE DELUGE	Larry and Curly got wet.
ICH LIEBE RICH	I'm really crazy about having dough.
FUI GENERIS	What's mine is mine.
CA VA SANS DIRT	And that's not gossip.

✳ Translators do it bilingually.

Interpreters do it simultaneously.

Linguists do it with their tongues.

Southern USA – English translator

BARD – verb. Past tense of the infinitive 'to borrow'.

Usage: 'My brother bard my pick-up truck.'

JAWJUH – noun. A highly flammable state just north of Florida.

Usage: 'My brother from Jawjah bard my pick-up truck.'

MUNTS – noun. A calendar division.

Usage: 'My brother from Jawjuh bard my pick-up truck, and I aint herd from himvin munts.'

IGNERT – adjective. Not smart.
Usage: 'Them boys sure are ignert!'

RANCH – noun. A tool.
Usage: 'I think I left my ranch in the back of that pick-up truck my brother from Jawjuh bard a few munts ago.'

ALL – noun. A petroleum-based lubricant.
Usage: 'I sure hope my brother from Jawjuh puts all in my pick-up truck.'

FAR – noun. A conflagration.
Usage: 'If my brother from Jawjuh doesn't change the all in my pick-up truck, that things gonna catch far.'

TARRED – adjective. Exhausted.
Usage: 'I just ran round the block, and boy my legs are tarred.'

RATS – noun. Entitled power or privilege.
Usage: 'We Southerners are willing to fight for our rats.'

FARN – adjective. Not local.
Usage: 'I cudnt unnerstand a wurd he sed … must be from some farn country.'

EAR – noun. A colourless, odourless gas.
Usage: 'He can't breathe … give 'em some ear!'

FROGS

* Why are frogs so happy? They eat whatever bugs them!

* What kind of shoes do frogs wear? Open toad!

* What do frogs do with paper? Rip-it!

* What do you get when you mix a frog with a bath flannel? A rubbit!

* How does a frog feel when he has a broken leg? Unhoppy.

* Why did the frog read Sherlock Holmes?
He liked a good croak and dagger.

* What is a frog's favourite game? Croaket.

* What does a Romulan frog use for camouflage? A croaking device!

* Why did the frog go to the bank with a gun? He wanted to robbit.

* What's a frog's favourite car? A beetle!

* What do you call a young punk frog? A radpole.

* Why couldn't the snake talk? He had a frog in his throat.

✳ A man went into a pet shop and said, 'I'd like a new frog, please.'
The assistant recognised him at once. 'But you bought one only
yesterday. What happened?' she asked. 'It Kermit-ted suicide!'

✳ What do you call the English Toad prize-giving ceremony?
The Brit Awarts!

GAMBLiNG

✳ Last night I got thrown out of the casino. I completely misunderstood what the crap table was for.

✳ What's the motto for the Eskimo lottery?
You've got to be Inuit to win it!

✳ The wife of a doctor rang the casino to get her husband paged. They refused. The house didn't make doctor calls.

✳ I know a guy at the casino who won't gamble. He just watches the games and makes mental bets. Last week, he lost his mind.

✳ Why don't English country gents play cribbage?
You can't put a squire peg in a round hole!

* At the casino I lost so badly I had to sell the car in the car park. The people at Hertz are going to be really angry.

* The Royale Casino in London is very swish. They've got special areas, like the Oak Room and the Mahogany Room. Blackpool Casino, on the other hand, is a little more basic. They've got the Chipboard Room and the Corrugated Iron Room.

* Some casinos will let you bet on anything. One will even let you bet on whether you'll win or lose.

* Ipswich must have the quietest casino in the world. I played poker. It was what I had to do to wake up the dealer.

* A man going into a casino passed some Siamese twins coming out.
'Did you win?' he asked.
'Yes and no.'

* I had nothing to do, so just for a laugh I went to the casino. In three hours I'd laughed away my car.

* The dealers at some casinos really hate you winning. I won £100 at roulette and the croupier said, 'I'll toss you, double or nothing.'

* Did you hear about the Irishman who walked around the casino with all his chips in his pocket? He couldn't get the smell of vinegar out of his trousers for weeks.

✳ Gambling is a tax that was invented for people who are bad at maths.

✳ Gambling is a good way to get nothing for something.

✳ The casino in Dublin is a bit backward. They don't even have blackjack. Instead, they've got a girl who comes up to your table and says, 'OK, I'm thinking of a number between one and ten … '

✳ 'What'll you have, Normie?'
'Well, I'm in a gambling mood, Sammy. I'll take a glass of whatever comes out of that tap.'
'Looks like beer, Norm.'
'Call me Mister Lucky.' From *Cheers*

✳ 'My husband's going to a casino in central Asia,' says one elderly bingo player to another.
'Tibet?'
'Of course,' the old woman says, quite annoyed. 'Why else would he go to a casino?'

✳ Anagram of SLOT MACHINES = CASH LOST IN 'EM.

✳ Have you heard the touching story of the young man who said to his girlfriend, 'I bet you wouldn't marry me?' The story goes that she not only called his bet, but raised him five!

✳ At an upscale Las Vegas casino, a blackjack dealer and a player begin to discuss the etiquette of tipping and if it is necessary to tip a dealer. The player contends, 'It's not the fault of the dealer when I receive bad cards, just like the dealer isn't responsible for my good cards. If both are sheer luck, why should I tip him?'

The dealer responds, 'Do you tip the waiter when dining at a restaurant?'

'Yes,' the gambler replies.

'So by this logic I am right,' says the dealer.

Confused, the player asks why.

'Well, a waiter serves you dinner, but because he doesn't make it, the quality is irrelevant as to whether or not he gets tipped. I serve you cards in the same way, so you should tip me.'

'I guess you are right,' concedes the player, 'but a waiter gives me what I order, so I'll take a queen.'

* A guy wins a big jackpot on a slot machine in Vegas. As it is paying out of the machine, but before the pit boss reaches the lucky winner, a haggard man approaches him and says, 'I don't mean to disturb you during your big moment, but my wife is sick and needs an operation. Could you see your way clear to giving me five thousand dollars of your winnings?'

The guy says, 'Well, it's all well and good for you to say that, and if it's true I sympathise, but how do I know you're not going to turn around and just gamble it away?'

The haggard man responds, 'Oh, I got gambling money.'

Poker 'Don'ts':

Don't ask the dealer about the odds on strip poker.

Don't use a Jamaican accent while playing Caribbean poker.

✳ For plumbers, a flush beats a full house.

✳ A man tried to get a job at a casino but they didn't have a slot for him. He wasn't that bothered as it was a bit of a gamble anyway.

✳ Did you hear about the man who wanted to gamble?
His wife said no dice!

✳ Some people don't have the Vegas idea of how to quit gambling.

✳ When a gambler gets up in the morning he has to pick the right suit before he shuffles off to deal with his day.

✳ He dreamt of winning the lottery when he was in the shower. He was wishy-washy.

✳ When poker players have to fold they feel a bit discarded.

GHOSTS AND GHOULS

✳ What did the mother ghost tell the baby ghost when he ate too fast?
Stop goblin your food.

✳ Vampires are always looking for their necks victim.

✳ When a vampire decided to become a poet, everyone said he went from bat to verse.

✳ Why were the two vampires fighting?
There was bad blood between them.

✳ Old mediums never die – they just give up the ghost.

✳ Fortune tellers have to work on their prophetability.

✳ How did one witch speak to the other? She cauldron the phone!

HAiR AND BALDNESS

* What's Amy Winehouse's favourite tube station? High Barnet!

* People who get complimented on their hair usually let it go to their head.

* How much does a cockney spend on shampoo? Pantene.

* Why do barbers make good criminals?
Because they're good at cutting locks.

* A boy had thin fly-away hair, so his mother often wet it to comb it into place. One morning as she applied water and slicked his hair back, she announced it was time for him to get another haircut. 'Oh no, Mum,' he moaned, 'if you'd stop watering it so much, it wouldn't grow so fast!'

✳ A mother came into the bathroom to find her expensive new shampoo bottle empty. 'Why did you use it all up?' she angrily asked her daughter, who was drying her hair in front of the mirror. 'Well, Mum,' replied the girl, 'first I washed my hair. Then I read the bottle and it said full body so I used the rest of it up having a wash!'

✳ If you don't like your haircut, don't worry! It'll grow on you.

✳ Prevent baldness. Knot your hair from the inside.

✳ Did you hear about the astronomer who left his job to become a barber? Eclipse hair now.

✳ My grandad went bald in the war. He lost it all in a hair raid.

✳ A vicar went into a barber's in Westminster. After his haircut he asked how much he owed. 'It's all right, Reverend,' replied the barber, 'there's no charge – I consider it a service to the Lord.' The vicar thanked him and went on his way. The next morning, when the barber came to open his shop, he found a new Bible on the step with a thank-you note from the vicar. Later that day a policeman came in for a haircut. Again, the barber wouldn't accept payment: 'I consider it a service to the community,' he told the grateful copper. The next morning he found a thank-you note from the policeman along with a box of doughnuts on the step. Just then an MP arrived wanting a haircut. The barber finished, but again didn't take any charge: 'I consider it a service to my country,' he told the grateful MP. The next morning he arrived at work to find a dozen MPs sitting on his step.

* A woman decided to leave her husband, a barber, after twenty years of marriage. 'Do you have any parting words?' she cried dramatically. 'Comb and brush?'

* A woman walks into a vet's waiting room dragging a wet rabbit on a lead. The rabbit does NOT want to be there. 'Sit, Bunnikins,' she says. Bunnikins glares at her, and sopping wet, jumps up on another customer's lap, getting water all over him. 'I said SIT, now there's a good Bunnikins,' says the woman, slightly embarrassed. Bunnikins, wet already, squats in the middle of the room and pees on the floor. The woman, terribly embarrassed, shouts, 'Hell, Bunnikins, will you be good?!' Bunnikins wanders over to a Dobermann and bites its nose, then chases it out of the waiting room. As the woman leaves to go after it, she turns to the rest of the flabbergasted customers and says: 'I'm so sorry, I've just washed my hare, and can't do a thing with it!'

* Where do you find a website about hair? On a mane frame.

* Why did the bald man leave nothing in his will?
He had no hair apparent!

* I'm not saying my dad was bald, but you could see what was on his mind.

* Did you hear about the man who was so bald that he got brainwashed in the shower?

* A bald man is invited to a fancy dress party. Keen to make an impression, and perhaps even meet a lady, he goes to the costume

shop to choose a suitable get-up for the do. He asks the shopkeeper to find him a costume that will hide his bald head and wooden leg.

The shopkeeper thinks for a bit, goes out the back and rummages around, and returns with a pirate costume. 'How about this?' says the shopkeeper. 'The bandana will cover your head and with your peg leg you'll look the part.'

'No, no,' says the man, 'I want something that hides my bald head and my leg. This will just draw attention to it.'

The shopkeeper disappears out the back again and re-emerges carrying a monk's habit: 'This will hide your leg, and your bald head will be perfect for a monk.'

The man is irate: 'Look, I told you I want to hide my baldness and my wooden leg. Have you got anything else?'

The shopkeeper reaches under the counter and pulls out a big jar of treacle. He plonks it down in front of the man.

'What am I supposed to do with this?' asks the angry customer.

'Pour it over your head,' replies the shopkeeper, 'and stick your wooden leg up your bum. You can go as a toffee apple.'

✳ A man can wear his hair three ways – parted, unparted, and, for bald men, departed.

✳ His hair was blonde and his head was angular: he was fair and square.

✳ Five thousand hares have escaped from the zoo. The police are combing the area.

✳ If a man is bald at the front, he is a thinker. If he is bald at the back, he is sexy. If he's bald from front to back – he thinks he's sexy.

✳ Are you bald, or is your neck blowing a bubble?

✳ The barber got out of the wet-shave business – it was too cut-throat.

✳ A girl was anxious to show her new haircut to her boyfriend.
  'So, what do you think?' she asked.
  'It reminds me of a classic Italian,' he replied.
  'What, Sophia Loren?'
  'No, spaghetti.'

✳ Two men are in a pub, and one is moaning about going bald.
  'Don't worry,' says his mate, 'just get some rabbits tattooed on
  your head.'
  'Why would I do that?' asks the balding man.
  'Well,' replies his friend, 'from a distance they'll look like hares!'

✳ What do you get if you cross a hairdresser with a werewolf?
  A monster with an all-over perm.

✳ Why was the model's hair angry? She was always teasing it.

✳ What do you call a pen with no hair? A bald point!

✳ A woman was cutting her husband's thinning hair, when their teenage
  son arrived home looking for a snack. She offered a kiwi fruit and tried
  to tempt him with its nutritious qualities. 'It has more vitamin C than an
  orange,' she pronounced.
  'And more hair than Dad,' added their son.

* America's oldest lady was 115 years old today, and she hasn't got a grey hair on her head. How come? She's completely bald.

* What do you call a proton with big hair? A froton.

* What do you call a policeman with blond hair? A fair cop!

* Why do bald men never use keys? Because they've lost their locks.

* A receptionist was at her desk in a hospital when a very angry woman stormed up to her desk. 'Someone stole my wig while I was having surgery yesterday,' she complained.
A doctor came out and tried to calm her down: 'I assure you that no one on my staff would have done such a thing,' he said. 'Why do you think your wig was taken here?'
'After the operation, I noticed the wig I was wearing was cheap-looking and ugly. It surely was not the one I came in wearing!'
'I think,' explained the surgeon gently, 'that means your cataract operation was a success.'

* What kind of wig can hear? An earwig!

HEALTH

* A man phones his doctor,'I think I've got this swine flu.'
Doctor: 'Can you describe the symptoms?'
Confused man: 'Yeah, Marge has big blue hair and Homer is a fat baldy!'

✳ With hindsight, I wouldn't have sat on that drawing pin.

✳ What's the funniest bone? The humerus!

✳ Using deodorant is no sweat.

🍎HEAVEN AND HELL

✳ Bill Gates died in a car accident. He found himself in Purgatory being sized up by God.

'Well, Bill, I'm really confused on this call. I'm not sure whether to send you to Heaven or Hell. After all, you enormously helped society by putting a computer in almost every home in the world and yet you created that ghastly Windows 95. I'm going to do something I've never done before. In your case, I'm going to let you decide where you want to go!'

Bill replied: 'Well, thanks, God. What's the difference between the two?'

God said: 'I'm willing to let you visit both places briefly if it will help you make a decision.'

'Fine, but where should I go first?' asked Bill.

God said: 'I'm going to leave it up to you.'

Bill said: 'OK, then, let's try Hell first.'

So Bill went to Hell ...

It was a beautiful, clean, sandy beach with clear waters. There were thousands of beautiful women running around, playing in the water, laughing and frolicking about. The sun was shining and the temperature was perfect. Bill was very pleased.

'This is great!' he told God. 'If this is Hell, I REALLY want to see Heaven!'

'Fine,' said God and off they went.

Heaven was a high place in the clouds, with angels drifting about playing harps and singing. It was nice, but not as enticing as Hell. Bill thought for a quick minute and rendered his decision.

'Hmm, I think I prefer Hell,' he told God.

'Fine,' retorted God, 'as you desire.'

So Bill Gates went to Hell.

Two weeks later, God decided to check up on the late billionaire to see how he was doing in Hell. When God arrived in Hell, he found Bill shackled to a wall, screaming among the hot flames in a dark cave. He was being burned and tortured by demons.

'How's everything going, Bill?' God asked.

Bill responded, his voice full of anguish and disappointment:

'This is awful, this is not what I expected. I can't believe this happened. What happened to that other place with the beaches and the beautiful women playing in the water?'

God says: 'That was the screensaver.'

* After a long illness, a woman died and arrived at the gates of Heaven. While she was waiting for Saint Peter to greet her, she peeked through the gates. She saw a beautiful banquet table. Sitting all around were her parents and all the other people she had loved and who had died before her.

They saw her and began calling greetings to her – 'Hello!' 'How are you?' 'We've been waiting for you!' 'Good to see you.'

When Saint Peter came by, the woman said to him, 'This is such a wonderful place! How do I get in?'

'You have to spell a word,' Saint Peter told her.

'Which word?' the woman asked.

'Love.'

The woman correctly spelled 'Love' and Saint Peter welcomed her into Heaven.

About six months later, Saint Peter came to the woman and asked her to watch the gates of Heaven for him that day. While the woman was guarding the gates of Heaven, her husband arrived.

'I'm surprised to see you,' the woman said. 'How have you been?'

'Oh, I've been doing pretty well since you died,' her husband told her. 'I married the beautiful young nurse who took care of you while you were ill. And then I won the lottery. I sold the little house you and I lived in and brought a big mansion. And my wife and I travelled all around the world. We were on vacation and I went water skiing today. I fell, the ski hit my head, and here I am. How do I get in?'

'You have to spell a word,' the woman told him.

'Which word?' her husband asked.

'Czechoslovakia.'

✳ A woman was worried whether or not her dead husband made it to Heaven, so she prays earnestly for God to allow him to speak to her.

'Hello, Margaret, this is Fred.'

'Fred!' she exclaimed. 'I just have to know if you're happy there in the afterlife. What's it like there?'

'Ooooooh, it's much more beautiful here than I ever imagined,' Fred answered. 'The sky is bluer, the air is cleaner, and the pastures are much more lush and green than I ever expected. I lack for nothing; the only things we do, all day long, are eat and sleep, eat and sleep, over and over.'

'Thank God, you made it to Heaven,' his wife cried.

'Heaven?' he answered. 'I'm a cow in Devon.'

✳ Keith was a good and pious man, and when he passed away, the Lord himself greeted him at the pearly gates of Heaven.

'Hungry, Keith?' the Lord asked.

'I could eat,' said Keith.

The Lord opened a can of tuna, and they shared it.

While eating this humble meal, Keith looked down into Hell and noticed the inhabitants devouring enormous steaks, pheasant, pastries and vodka.

The next day, the Lord again asked Keith if he were hungry, and Keith again said, 'I could eat.'

Once again, a can of tuna was opened and shared, while down below Keith noticed a feast of caviar, champagne, lamb, truffles, brandy and chocolates.

The following day, mealtime arrived and another can of tuna was opened.

Meekly, Keith said, 'Lord, I am very happy to be in Heaven as a reward for the good life I lived. But, this is Heaven, and all I get to eat is tuna. But in the Other Place, they eat like kings. I just don't understand.'

'To be honest, Keith,' the Lord said, 'for just two people, is it worth cooking?'

✳ A little girl was talking to her teacher about whales.

The teacher said it was physically impossible for a whale to swallow a human because even though they were very large mammals their throat was very small.

The little girl stated that Jonah was swallowed by a whale.

The teacher reiterated that a whale could not swallow a human; it was impossible.

The little girl said, 'When I get to Heaven I will ask Jonah.'

The teacher asked, 'What if Jonah went to Hell?'
The little girl replied, 'Then you ask him.'

﹡ There's a sin dividing line between Heaven and Hell.

HOLIDAYS

﹡ There are always fortune tellers at the seaside. Two of them met on the front at Frinton one sunny summer day.
'Lovely weather,' said the first fortune teller.
'Yes,' said the second. 'It reminds me of the summer of 2010.'

﹡ My only skill is knowing driving directions, but they tell me that's not going to get me anywhere in life.

﹡ I went on safari last year and there was a cannibal there who had a wife and ate kids.

﹡ What happens if you take a book to the beach on a hot day?
You can become well red.

﹡ The sign on the nudist camp said, 'Clothed 'til May.'

﹡ I was bitten on holiday by a snake. It had me rattled.

﹡ A holidaymaker was complaining to his landlady about his room.
'Look. This wall's so thin you can almost see through it.'
'That's not a wall,' she replied, 'it's the window.'

✳ I wanted to join my local rambling club, but the man I spoke to on the phone just went on and on.

✳ A man was desperate to see some llamas, and told his wife. She said, 'Alpaca suitcase.'

✳ A man arrived at his holiday guest-house and met the landlady.
'Can you sing?' she snapped.
'No,' he replied.
'Well, you'd better learn quickly. There's no lock on the bathroom door.'

✳ After the egg hunt on Easter Sunday, the young farm boy decided to play a prank. He went to the chicken coop and replaced every single egg with a brightly coloured one.
A few minutes later the rooster walked in, saw all the coloured eggs, then stormed outside and killed the peacock.

✳ Over breakfast one morning, a woman said to her husband, 'I bet you don't know what day this is.'
'Of course I do,' he indignantly answered, going out the door to the office.
At 10 am, the doorbell rang, and when the woman opened the door, she was handed a box containing a dozen long-stemmed red roses.
At 1 pm, a wrapped box of her favourite chocolates arrived. Later, a boutique delivered a designer dress. The woman couldn't wait for her husband to come home.
'First the flowers, then the chocolates, and then the dress!' she exclaimed. 'I've never had a more wonderful Shrove Tuesday in my life!'

IN DAYS OF OLD

* Where do knights go to grab a bite to eat? To an all-knight diner!

* Why did every castle have a bank with an automatic teller?
  For making knight deposits.

* What did King Arthur listen to every evening at six? The knightly news.

* When the knight logged onto his computer there was a message:
  'You've got mail.' It was a chain letter.

* What do you call it when all the knights trade places at the round table?
  The knight shift!

* What did the dragon say when he saw St George?
  Oh no! Not more tinned food!

✳ A knight was found resting in the forest by a passing lady. As he lay slumped against a tree, she demanded, 'Sir Knight, why do you not stand in the presence of a Lady? It is most unchivalrous.'
'Sorry,' replied the weary knight. 'I've been fighting a dragon, and to be honest, it's more easily slayed than done.'

✳ How do you send a message in the forest? By moss code.

✳ What do you call a mosquito in a tin suit? A bite in shining armour.

✳ There are many castles in the world, but who is strong enough to move one? Any chess player.

✳ What king of medieval England was famous because he spent so many nights at his round table writing books? King Author!

✳ How do you find a princess? You follow the foot prince.

✳ Why did the knight run about shouting for a tin opener?
He had a bee in his suit of armour!

✳ There were three men alone in the forest. A dragon appeared, breathing fire.
The dragon flapped its wings and raised itself to its full height:
'I am going to devour you all,' it roared.
The first man, quaking, said, 'No, let's make a deal.'
The dragon, intrigued by this gambit, decided to play along and said, 'OK. What kind of deal?'

The second man said, 'If we each tell you something that we think you can't do, and you can do all of it, you may eat us.'

The dragon agreed to the deal.

So the first man said, 'Eat sixteen trees of the forest.'

The dragon did it.

The second man said, 'Drink half of the pond water over there.'

The dragon succeeded in doing this, also.

The third man burped, and said, 'Catch it and paint it green.'

The three men lived happily ever after!

＊ There were three medieval kingdoms on the shores of a lake. There was an island in the middle of the lake, which the kingdoms had been fighting over for years. Finally, the three kings decided that they would send their knights out to do battle, and the winner would take the island.

The night before the battle, the knights and their squires pitched camp and readied themselves for the fight. The first kingdom had twelve knights, and each knight had five squires, all of whom were busily polishing armour, brushing horses, and cooking food. The second kingdom had twenty knights, and each knight had ten squires. Everyone at that camp was also busy preparing for battle. At the camp of the third kingdom, there was only one knight, with his squire. This squire took a large pot and hung it from a looped rope in a tall tree. He busied himself preparing the meal, while the knight polished his own armour.

When the hour of the battle came, the three kingdoms sent their squires out to fight (this was too trivial a matter for the knights to join in). The battle raged, and when the dust cleared, the only person left was the lone squire from the third kingdom, having defeated the squires from the other two kingdoms.

Which proves that the squire of the high pot and noose is equal to the sum of the squires of the other two sides.

✳ In medieval England, it was the custom for the heir to the throne to wear a fancy ruffled collar known as a ruff. One particular prince wore an exceptionally fancy ruff known as a dandy ruff, which blocked his vision so that he kept tripping and falling.
This proves that dandy ruffs cause falling heirs.

✳ A king was preparing to ride off on a quest. Before he leaves, he locks up the queen with a chastity belt and calls in his most trusted knight and hands him the key. 'Sir Percival, here is the key to my queen's honour. Should I fall in battle, it is up to you to release her from her belt so she might marry again.' He then leaves on his journey. At the top of a hill, he turns back for one last look at his castle and is surprised to see Sir Percival riding breakneck in pursuit. 'My lord, my lord … wait! You have given me the wrong key!'

✳ A medieval astrologer prophesied to a king that his favourite mistress would soon die. Sure enough, the woman died a short time later.
The king was outraged at the astrologer, certain that his prophecy had brought about the woman's death.
He summoned the astrologer and commanded him: 'Prophesy, tell me when you will die!'
The astrologer realised that the king was planning to kill him immediately, no matter what answer he gave.
'I do not know when I will die,' he answered finally. 'I only know that whenever I die, the king will die three days later.'

✳ A Spanish knight travelling at dusk alighted at a poor inn.
The innkeeper came to the door and asked him his name.
He answered, 'Don Pedro Gonzales Gayetan de Guevara.'
'Sorry, sir,' replied the innkeeper, 'we have not food enough for
so many.'

Medieval pick-up lines

- 'Hey, Princess, you wouldn't happen to know where a lonely knight
  could scabbard his sword, would you?'
- 'Been there, slain that.'
- 'What's a nice maiden like you doing in a dungeon like this?'
- 'They don't call me Lance-A-Lot for nothing, you know.'
- 'When the Inquisition put me on the rack, my limbs weren't the only
  thing they stretched.'
- 'Thou hast hit on me harder than the black plague!'
- 'Your hovel or mine?'
- 'You should be glad I'm not a Viking. You would have been ravaged
  and plundered by now.'
- 'My! But you are a beautiful damsel in distress! Allow me to help you
  out of it.'

✳ Teacher: How was the Roman Empire cut in half?
Pupil: With a pair of Caesars!

✳ Teacher: What did Caesar say to Cleopatra?
Pupil: Toga-ether we can rule the world!

✳ Why did the fool shrug? He was the court gesture!

✳ What did the group of cavemen do? Formed clubs.

✳ What does a knight wear when courting? Armour.

✳ Can Napoleon return to his place of birth? Corsican.

✳ When do knights practice fighting? Joust at night.

✳ Why was Soviet Russia slow to develop? It kept Stalin.

✳ Ancient orators tended to Babylon.

✳ What happened when Ceasar entered the forum? All hail broke loose!

🐛 IN THE NAVY

✳ Having passed the enlistment physical, the new recruit was asked by
the doctor, 'Why do you want to join the navy, son?'
'My father said it'd be a good idea, sir.'
'Oh? And what does your father do?'
'He's in the army, sir.'

✳ An old naval officer finally retired and got the chicken farm he always
wanted. He took with him his life-long pet parrot. The first morning,
at 0430, the parrot squawked loudly and said, 'Reveille, Reveille.
Up all hands. Heave out and trice up. Make shipshape, all hands on
deck.' The officer told the parrot, 'We're no longer in the navy. Go
back to sleep.'

The next morning, the parrot did the same thing. The officer shouted at the parrot, 'If you keep this up, I'll put you out in the chicken pen.' Again the parrot did it, and true to his word, the naval man put the parrot in the chicken pen.

About 0630 the next morning, he was awakened by a riot in the chicken pen. He went out to see what was the matter. The parrot had about forty white chickens at attention in formation, and on the ground lay three bruised and beaten brown chickens. The parrot was saying, 'By God, when I say fall out in dress whites, I don't mean khakis!'

✳ Just before their first long deployment, two navy recruits were talking about the stress of leaving their families. A senior officer, a veteran of many deployments, overheard the conversation and stopped to offer advice: 'It is imperative that you are sensitive to your wives' emotional needs,' he said. 'Never, ever, whistle while you pack!'

✳ A tradition in the navy is that all of the officers dance with the captain's wife at the ship's ball. At the first ball of the year a new cadet walked over and asked the formidable wife of the captain if she would like to dance. 'I don't dance with a child,' she replied haughtily.
The cadet smiled, bowed, and replied, 'Oh! I'm sorry. If I'd known about your condition, I wouldn't have asked.'

✳ A navy officer was cutting through the crew's quarters of his ship one day and happened upon a sailor reading a magazine with his feet up on the small table in front of him. 'Sailor! Do you put your feet up on the furniture at home?' the officer demanded.
'No, sir, but we don't land planes on the roof either.'

* The grizzled old sea captain was quizzing a young naval student.
'What steps would you take if a sudden storm came up on
the starboard?'
'I'd throw out an anchor, sir.'
'What would you do if another storm sprang up aft?'
'I'd throw out another anchor, sir.'
'But what if a third storm sprang up forward?'
'I'd throw out another anchor, sir.'
'Just a minute, son. Where in the world are you getting all these
anchors?'
'From the same place you're getting all your storms, sir.'

* 'Well,' snarled the tough old admiral to the hapless able seaman.
'I suppose after you get discharged from the navy, you'll just be
waiting for me to die so you can come and pee on my grave.'
'Not me, sir!' the seaman replied. 'Once I get out of the navy,
I'm never going to stand in line again!'

* An old engineer and an old gunner were sitting at the bar arguing
about who'd had the tougher career. 'I did thirty years,' the gunner
declared proudly, 'and fought in three wars. Fresh out of boot camp
I hit the beach at Dunkirk, clawed my way up the blood-soaked sand,
and eventually took out an entire enemy machine-gun nest with a
single grenade.
'As a sergeant, I fought in Korea. We pushed back the enemy inch by
bloody inch all the way up to the Chinese border, always under a
barrage of artillery and small-arms fire.
'Finally, I did three consecutive combat tours in Vietnam. We humped
through the mud and razor grass for fourteen hours a day, plagued by

rain and mosquitoes, ducking under sniper fire all day and mortar fire all night. In a firefight, we'd fire until our arms ached and our guns were empty, then we'd charge the enemy with bayonets!'

'Ah,' said the engineer with a dismissive wave of his hand, 'all shore duty, huh?'

* A sailor dies in combat and wakes up to find he is in Hell. He's really depressed as he stands in the processing line waiting to talk to an admittance devil. He thinks to himself, 'I know I've led a wild life but, hey, I'm a sailor. We're expected to live wild lives. I wasn't that bad. I never thought it would come to this.'

Looking up he sees that it is his turn to be processed into Hell.

With fear and heavy heart, he walks up.

Devil: What's the problem? You look depressed.

Sailor: Well, what do you think? I'm in Hell.

Devil: Hell's not so bad, we actually have a lot of fun. Do you like to drink?

Sailor: Of course I do. I'm a sailor.

Devil: Well then, you are going to love Mondays. On Mondays we drink up a storm. You can have whisky, rum, tequila, beer, whatever you want and as much as you want. We party all night long. You'll love Mondays. Do you smoke?

Sailor: Yes, as a matter of fact, I do. Capstan high tar.

Devil: You are going to love Tuesdays. Tuesday is smoke day. You get to smoke the finest cigars and best cigarettes available anywhere. And you smoke to your heart's desire without worrying about cancer because you are already dead! Is that great or what? You are going to love Tuesdays. Do you like to fight?

Sailor: Of course I do. I'm a sailor!

Devil: You are going to love Wednesdays. That's fighting day. We challenge each other to fights to see who's the toughest in Hell. You don't have to worry about getting hurt or killed, because you're already dead. You are going to love Wednesdays. Do you gamble?

Sailor: Show me a sailor who doesn't!

Devil: You are going to love Thursdays, because we gamble all day and night. Blackjack, craps, poker, slots, horse races, everything! You are going to love Thursdays. Are you gay?

Sailor: Of course, not! I'm a sailor!

Devil: Oh (grimaces), you're going to hate Fridays.

＊ A navy man walks into a bar, gives the bartender a conspiratorial wink and says, 'Quick, pour me a drink, before the trouble starts.' The bartender pours a drink and watches as the sailor downs it in one gulp. The sailor slams the glass down on the bar and says, 'Quick, give me another one before the trouble starts.' The bartender pours another glass and the sailor drinks it as quickly as he had the first. The sailor pauses, lets out a belch and demands a third drink 'before the trouble starts'.

After several rounds of this, the bartender says, 'Look sailor, you've been talking about trouble for ten minutes. Just when is this "trouble" going to start?'

The sailor looks at the bartender and grins. 'The trouble starts just as soon as you figure out that I don't have any money.'

＊ A young wife, her boorish husband and a young good-looking sailor were shipwrecked on an island. One morning, the sailor climbed a tall coconut tree and yelled, 'Stop making love down there!'

'What's the matter with you?' the husband said when the sailor climbed down. 'We weren't making love.'

'Sorry,' said the sailor, 'from up there it looked like you were.'

Every morning thereafter, the sailor scaled the same tree and yelled the same thing. Finally the husband decided to climb the tree and see for himself. With great difficulty, he made his way to the top.

The husband says to himself, 'By golly, he's right! It DOES look like they're making love down there!'

* A defence contractor finally succeeded in building a computer capable of solving the most complex naval warfare problems. The top navy brass assembled around the new machine and were instructed to feed a difficult tactical problem into it. They described a complex hypothetical battle situation to the computer and then asked the pivotal question, 'Should our forces attack or retreat?'

The computer hummed and beeped for about an hour, and finally printed out an answer, 'Yes.'

The admirals stared at each other, mystified by the response.

Finally, one of them submitted a second request to the computer, 'Yes what?'

The computer responded instantly, 'Yes, sir!'

* A new ensign was assigned to submarines, where he'd dreamed of working since a young boy. He was trying to impress the master engineer with his expertise learned in submarine school.

The older man cut him off quickly and said, 'Listen, "sir", it's really simple. Add the number of times we dive to the number of times we surface. Divide that number by two. If the result doesn't come out even, don't open the hatch.'

✳ The captain went out to find that none of his sailors were there.
One finally ran up, panting heavily. 'Sorry, sir! I can explain. You see
I had a date and it ran a little late. I ran to the bus but missed it, I hailed
a cab but it broke down, found a farm, bought a horse but it dropped
dead, ran ten miles, and now I'm here.'
The captain was very sceptical about this explanation but at least the
sailor was here so he let him go. Moments later, eight more sailors came
up to the captain, panting, and he asked them why they were late.
'Sorry, sir! I had a date and it ran a little late, I ran to the bus but missed
it, I hailed a cab but it broke down, found a farm, bought a horse but it
dropped dead, ran ten miles, and now I'm here.'
The captain eyed them, feeling very sceptical, but since he let the first
guy go, he let them go, too. A ninth sailor jogged up to the captain,
panting heavily.
'Sorry, sir! I had a date and it ran a little late, I ran to the bus but missed
it, I hailed a cab but …'
'Let me guess,' the captain interrupted, 'it broke down.'
'No,' said the sailor, 'there were so many dead horses in the road,
it took for ever to get around them.'

✳ A British captain had sent some of his men off to fight for their country
in the Falklands conflict.
Upon returning to England from the South American island, three sailors
that had distinguished themselves in battle were summoned to the
captain's office. 'Since we weren't officially at war,' the captain began,
'I can't give out any medals. We did, however, want to let each of you
know your efforts were appreciated.
What we've decided to do is to let each of you choose two points on
your body. You will be given two pounds sterling for each inch of

distance between those parts. We'll start on the left, boys, so what'll it be?'

Sailor 1: 'The tip of me head to me toes, sahr!'

Captain: 'Very good son, that's 70 inches which comes to 140 pounds.'

Sailor 2: 'The tip of the finger on one outstretched hand to the tip of the other, sir!'

Captain: 'Even better son, that's 72 inches which comes to 144 pounds.'

Sailor 3: 'The palm of me hand to the tip of me left pinky, sahr!'

Captain: 'That's a strange but fair request, son!

As the captain begins the measurement: 'What! Son, where is your left pinky?'

Sailor 3: 'Falkland Islands, sahr!'

✳ A young son of a navy man asked his mother: 'Mum, don't sailors ever go to Heaven?'

'Of course they do!' protested his mother. 'What makes you ask?'

'There are so many sailors with beards but I never saw any pictures of angels with beards.'

'Oh, that's because most sailors who go to Heaven get there by a close shave.'

✳ The British Navy is developing computer chips that store music in women's breast implants. This is a major breakthrough, as women are always complaining about sailors staring at their breasts and not listening to them.

How to simulate a trip to sea on land

* Sleep on the shelf in your wardrobe.
* Replace the wardrobe door with a thin curtain.
* Four hours after you go to sleep, have your mate whip open the curtain, shine a flashlight in your eyes, and mumble, 'Your watch!'
* When taking showers, shut off the water while soaping.
* If your cellar floods, go down and start bailing.
* Bring inside some type of diesel motor (lawn mower, generator, etc.), start, and leave running while trying to listen to favourite CD, or having an in-depth conversation.
* If the wind outside is howling, race around the house to make sure all windows and doors are secure (at night, everyone takes a turn on 'watch').
* Put a fluorescent light under the coffee table, and lay there to read a book.
* Every so often, throw the cat in a tub (hot tub, large sink, etc.) and shout, 'Man overboard!'
* Run into the kitchen and sweep all the pots, pans and dishes off of the counter onto the floor, then yell at the mate for not having the place 'stowed for sea'.

✳ The doctor calls a sailor. 'Well, I have good news and bad news … '
The sailor says, 'Lay it on me, Doc. What's the bad news?'
'You have Alzheimer's disease.'
'Good Heavens! What's the good news?'
'You can go back to your ship and forget about it!'

✳ Ensign Jones was assigned to the recruitment centre, where he advised new recruits about their government benefits, especially their services personnel insurance. It wasn't long before Captain Smith noticed that Jones was having a staggeringly high success rate, selling insurance to nearly a hundred per cent of the recruits he advised. Rather than ask about this, the captain stood in the back of the room and listened to Jones's sales pitch.

Jones explained the basics of the insurance to the new recruits: 'If you have insurance and go into battle and are killed, the government has to pay £200,000 to your beneficiaries. If you don't have insurance, and you go into battle and get killed, the government only has to pay a maximum of £6,000.

Now,' he concluded, 'which group do you think they are going to send into battle first?'

✳ An old sailor was dying. His wife, Becky, was maintaining a candlelit vigil by his side. She held his fragile hand, tears running down her face. Her praying roused him from his slumber; he looked up and his pale lips began to move lightly, 'Becky my darling,' he whispered.

'Hush my love,' she said. 'Rest, don't talk.'

He was insistent. 'Becky,' he said in his tired voice, 'I have something that I must confess.'

'There's nothing to confess,' replied the weeping Becky, 'everything's all right, go to sleep.'

'No, no. I must die in peace, Becky. I … I had affairs with your sister, your best friend, her best friend, and your mother!'

'I know, sweetheart,' whispered Becky, 'let the poison work.'

✳ Air Force One crashed in the middle of rural America. Panic-stricken, the Secret Service mobilised and descended on the farm in force. When they got there, the wreckage was clear. The aircraft was totally destroyed with only a burned hulk left smouldering in a treeline that bordered a farm. Secret Service agents descended upon the wreckage but could find no remains of the crew or the President's staff. To their amazement, a lone farmer was ploughing a field not too far away as if nothing at all happened. They hurried over to surround the man's tractor.

'Sir,' the senior Secret Service agent asked, panting and out of breath. 'Did you see this terrible accident happen?'

'Yep. Sure did.' the man muttered unconcernedly.

'Do you realise that is the President of the United States airplane?'

'Yep.'

'Were there any survivors?' the agent gasped.

'Nope. They's all kilt straight out.' The farmer sighed, cutting off his tractor motor. 'I done buried them all myself. Took most of the morning.'

'The President of the United States is dead?' The agent gulped in disbelief.

'Well,' the farmer sighed, obviously wanting to get back to his work. 'He kept a-saying he wasn't … but you know what a liar he is.'

✳ A captain visits the sick soldiers in sickbay, goes up to one able seaman and asks: 'What's your problem, sailor?'

'Chronic syphilis.'

'What treatment are you getting?'

'Five minutes with the wire brush each day.'

'What's your ambition?'

'To get back to fighting duty, sir.'

'Good man.' says the captain.

He goes to the next bed.

'What's your problem, sailor?'

'Chronic piles.'

'What treatment are you getting?'

'Five minutes with the wire brush each day.'

'What's your ambition?'

'To get back to fighting duty, sir.'

'Good man,' says the Captain.

He goes to the next bed.

'What's your problem, sailor?'

'Chronic gum disease.'

'What treatment are you getting?'

'Five minutes with the wire brush each day.'

'What's your ambition?'

'To get the wire brush before the other two, sir.'

* Two friends decided they would dodge the draft by having all of their teeth pulled. They knew the navy would not take them if they were toothless. Finally, the day came where they were to report to the draft board. As they lined up they had a big truck driver stood between them, who had obviously not bathed in weeks.

When the first friend stood before the sergeant for a physical examination he told the sergeant that he had no teeth. The sergeant ran his fingers around his gums and said, 'All right, you have no teeth – you're 4F.'

Next came the big, smelly truck driver. The sergeant said to him, 'What's wrong with you?'

The truck driver replied, 'I have a terrible case of piles.'

The sergeant inserted his fingers in the truck driver's pants, and felt around, and said, 'Yep, you've got piles. You're 4F.'

Next came the second friend, and the sergeant said, 'What's wrong with you?'

The recruit stared at the sergeant's fingers and replied, 'Nothing sir, nothing at all.'

✳ London, 1942. A street corner

A gentleman walks up to a soldier: 'Pardon me, sir, which side is the Admiralty on?'

'Ours, I hope.'

✳ The elderly American gentleman arrived in Paris by plane. At French customs, he fumbled for his passport.

'You have been to France before, monsieur?' the customs officer asked sarcastically.

The old gent admitted that he had been to France previously. 'Zen, you should know enough to 'ave your passport ready for inspection.'

The American said, 'The last time I was in France, I didn't have to show a passport.'

'Impossible. Americans always have to show your passports on arrival in France!'

The American senior gave the Frenchman a long, hard look. Then he quietly explained. 'Well, when I came ashore at Omaha Beach on D-day in '44, I couldn't find any Frenchmen to show it to!'

✳ Heard the one about the sailor who bought his wife a new bag and belt for Valentine's Day? Well, the Hoover now works a treat!

✳ A sailor is receiving a medal from the Admiral. 'Well, son,' says the Admiral, 'what are you getting this decoration for?' 'I saved all the crew of my ship from death,' replies the sailor.
'That's extremely commendable,' says the Admiral. 'What did you do? Destroy an enemy aircraft, blow up a submarine, that sort of thing?'
'No sir,' replies the sailor. 'I shot the cook!'

🐛 INSECTS

✳ One ant was running across an unopened box of biscuits and urging another to speed up. 'But why do we have to hurry?' said one.
'Can't you read, you idiot! It says, "Tear along the dotted line!"'

✳ Why did the woman put insecticide on her watch? To get rid of the ticks!

✳ A flea jumped over the swinging doors of a saloon, drank three whiskys and jumped out again.
He picked himself up from the dirt, dusted himself down and said, 'OK, who moved my dog?'

✳ Communism first took off in the insect kingdom when a wary wasp joined the cagey bee.

✳ What is the difference between a flea-bitten dog and a bored visitor? One's going to itch and the other is itching to go!

✳ Two mosquitoes were buzzing round when they saw a drunken man. One said to the other, 'You bite him. I'm driving.'

✳ Why didn't the two worms get on Noah's Ark in an apple? Because everyone had to go on in pairs!

✳ What did the maggot say to the second maggot? What's a nice maggot like you doing in a joint like this?!

✳ What did the worm say to the other worm when he was late home? Where in earth have you been?!

✳ What has two wheels and flies? A rubbish bin!

✳ A surveyor visits a dilapidated house. He asks the owner, 'How come the building hasn't collapsed?' 'Well,' replies the owner, 'I think all the woodworm are holding hands.'

✳ Two roaches were munching on rubbish in an alley. 'I was in that new restaurant across the street,' said one. 'It's so clean! The kitchen is spotless, the floors are gleaming white. It's so sanitary the whole place shines.' 'Please,' said the other roach, frowning. 'Not while I'm eating!'

✳ How do you hunt for bees? With a bee-bee gun!

✳ Why did the queen bee kick out all of the other bees? Because they kept droning on and on!

* Why did the bees go on strike? Because they wanted more honey and shorter working flowers!

* Why do ants dance on jam jars? Because the lid says 'twist to open'.

* What's a bee's favourite composer? Bee-thoven!

* What do wasps do when they want to go somewhere?
Wait at a buzz stop!

* What do you get if you cross an ant and a tick? All kinds of anticks.

* How does a grasshopper watch TV? With his antennae!

* Two boy silkworms pursued a luscious girl silkworm. They ended up in a tie.

* What has six legs and walks on a head? Nits.

* What did the clean dog say to the insect? Long time no flea.

* An amorous centipede was trying to mate with a female, with no success. 'No,' she said, and crossed her legs, 'and a hundred times no.'

* Where do spiders go to learn new words? WEB-ster's dictionary.

* What's the state bird of Texas? A fly.

* What do you call a grasshopper with no legs? A grasshover!

* What is the most religious insect? A mosque-ito!

* What part of a beetle likes to play noughts and crosses?
  The X O skeleton.

INSULTS

* Meeting you, I realise now why some animal eat their young.

* Are you always this stupid or are you making a special effort today?

* Your mind isn't so much twisted as badly sprained.

* He's not stupid; he's possessed by a retarded ghost.

* He's the kind of a man that you could use as a blueprint to build an idiot.

* If you were my dog, I'd shave your butt and teach you to walk backwards.

* He has a 'full 'six-pack' of brains but lacks the plastic thing to hold it all together.

* Don't you need a licence to be that ugly?

* Don't you have a terribly empty feeling – in your skull?

✳ Are your parents siblings?

✳ Do you still love nature, despite what it did to you?

✳ She has a pretty little head – for a head, it's pretty little.

✳ She's like yesterday's coffee – a little weak in the bean.

✳ He should study to be a bone specialist – he has the head for it.

✳ He has one of those mighty minds – mighty empty.

✳ His neck reminds you of a typewriter – Underwood.

✳ He's so stupid he bought a topless bathing suit for his half-sister.

✳ He's the kind of fella that girls dream about at night– it's better than seeing him in the light.

✳ His teeth are like the Ten Commandments – all broken.

✳ She has so many wrinkles, she has to screw her hat on.

✳ Yo' Mama's so fat, when she fell down the stairs I thought *EastEnders* was ending.

✳ Did you hear about the town where everyone had a low IQ?
It was densely populated.

Jokes and comedy

Do you want to hear a story about a bed? I just made it up!

Thirsty comedians can always be seen waiting in the punch line.

Magic

Illusionists do it in tricky situations.

At a job interview, I decided to lie and say I had experience as an illusionist and as a window cleaner. They saw right through me.

Did you hear the one about the tall wizard who complained he couldn't cast any spells because he was short staffed?

Did you hear about the magician who got so angry he pulled his hare out?

MATHS

* Lumberjacks make good mathematicians because of their natural logarithms.

✳ Old mathematicians never die; they just lose some of their functions.

✳ Statisticians probably do it.

✳ Algebraists do it in groups.

✳ (Logicians do it) or [not (logicians do it)].

✳ Möbius always did it on the same side.

✳ Noah's Ark lands after the flood and Noah releases all the animals, saying, 'Go forth and multiply.'
Several months pass and Noah decides to check up on the animals. All are doing fine except a pair of snakes. 'What's the problem?' asks Noah.
'Cut down some trees and let us live there,' say the snakes.
Noah follows their advice. Several more weeks pass and Noah checks up on the snakes again. He sees lots of little snakes; everybody is happy.
Noah says, 'So tell me how the trees helped.'
'Certainly,' reply the snakes. 'We're adders, and we need logs to multiply.'

✳ Why did the mathematical tree fall over? Because it had no real roots.

✳ What does the little mermaid wear? An algae-bra.

Medical - All in the Mind

✳ Neurotics build castles in the sky.
Psychotics live in them.
Psychiatrists collect the rent.

✳ Welcome to the Psychiatric Hotline.
If you are co-dependent, please ask someone to press 2.
If you are paranoid-delusional, we know who you are and what you want. Just stay on the line so we can trace the call.
If you are schizophrenic, listen carefully and a little voice will tell you which number to press.
If you are depressed, it doesn't matter which number you press. No one will answer.
If you are delusional and occasionally hallucinate, please be aware that the thing you are holding on the side of your head is alive and about to bite off your ear.

✳ A psychiatrist was conducting a group therapy session with four young mothers and their small children. 'You all have obsessions,' he observed. To the first mother he said, 'You are obsessed with eating. You even named your daughter Candy.'
He turned to the second mum. 'Your obsession is money. Again, it manifests itself in your child's name, Penny.'
He turned to the third mum. 'Your obsession is alcohol and your child's name is Brandy.'
At this point, the fourth mother got up, took her little boy by the hand and whispered, 'Come on, Dick, let's go home.'

✳ A psychologist is at a party talking with a small group of people, when a man comes up behind him and taps him on the shoulder. The psychologist turns around and the man decks him. The psychologist gets up, brushes himself off, turns to the group and declares: 'That's his problem.'

✳ What's the difference between a psychologist and a magician? A psychologist pulls habits out of rats!

✳ Did you hear about the man who would get angry when his mobile phone battery died? His psychiatrist suggested he find an outlet.

✳ A psychologist returned from a conference in Iceland in the winter. Her husband asked her, 'How did it go?' She replied, 'Fine, but I've never seen so many Freudians slip.'

✳ Why did Freud refuse dinner? There was nothing oedipal.

✳ Why don't you need psychiatrists in the desert? There are nomad people.

✳ How do you know when your fruit basket has been sent by a psychiatrist? It's shrink-wrapped!

✳ Why did the genie go the psychiatrist? His emotions were all bottled up.

✳ What's a psychiatrist's favourite takeaway? Kentucky Freud Chicken.

✳ Why couldn't the psychiatry student understand Freud?
He was too Jung.

✳ What do you call Peruvian Rorschach tests? Inca Blots.

✳ What's a mad person's favourite food? Fruit cake.

✳ The difference between a neurotic and a psychotic is that, while a psychotic thinks that $2 + 2 = 5$, a neurotic knows the answer is 4, but it worries him.

✳ A man who had been in a mental home for some years finally seemed to have improved to the point where it was thought he might be released.
The head of the institution, in a fit of commendable caution, decided, however, to interview him first.
'Tell me,' said he, 'if we release you, as we are considering doing, what do you intend to do with your life?'
The inmate said, 'It would be wonderful to get back to real life and if I do, I will certainly refrain from making my former mistake. I was a nuclear physicist, you know, and it was the stress of my work in weapons research that helped put me here. If I am released, I shall confine myself to work in pure theory, where I trust the situation will be less difficult and stressful.'
'Marvellous,' said the head of the institution.
'Or else,' ruminated the inmate, 'I might teach. There is something to be said for spending one's life in bringing up a new generation of scientists.'
'Absolutely,' said the head.

'Then again, I might write. There is considerable need for books on science for the general public. Or I might even write a novel based on my experiences in this fine institution.'

'An interesting possibility,' said the head.

'And finally, if none of these things appeals to me, I can always continue to be a tea kettle.'

* A doctor of psychology was doing his normal morning rounds when he entered a patient's room.

He found Patient 1 sitting on the floor, pretending to saw a piece of wood in half.

Patient 2 was hanging from the ceiling, by his feet.

The doctor asked Patient 1 what he was doing.

The patient replied, 'Can't you see I'm sawing this piece of wood in half?'

The doctor enquired of Patient 1 what Patient 2 was doing.

Patient 1 replied, 'Oh. He's my friend, but he's a little crazy. He thinks he's a lightbulb.'

The doctor looks up and notices Patient 2's head is going all purple.

The doctor asks Patient 1, 'If he's your friend, you should get him down from there before he hurts himself.'

Patient 1 replies, 'What? And work in the dark?'

* Q: Why did the pilot go to the psychologist?

  A: He thought he was plane crazy.

* Patient: 'I can't decide whether to slash my wrists, or blow my brains out.'

  Psychiatrist: 'You have difficulty making decisions.'

＊ A man phones a mental hospital and asks the receptionist if there is anybody in Room 27. She goes and checks, and comes back to the phone, telling him that the room is empty.

'Good,' says the man. 'That means I must have really escaped.'

Medical – alternative

Acupuncture is a jab well done.

My daughter's studying herbal medicine. I'm rooting for her.

Cod liver oil is good for you. It's official.

MEDICAL – DISEASES

＊ Did you hear about the man who felt compelled to park on double yellow lines? He had parking zones disease.

＊ Did you hear about the man who had insomnia so badly he was awake until it dawned on him?

＊ What's a hypochondriac's favourite drink? Champagne.

＊ What sort of dreams are bad for diabetics? Sweet dreams!

🍎 MEDICAL - GENERAL

✳ Doctors at a hospital went on strike. Hospital officials were keen to find out what the doctors' demands were as soon as they could get a pharmacist over there to read the picket signs!

✳ A cosmetic surgeon knows how to raise a few eyebrows.

✳ A paediatrician is a doctor who has little patients.

✳ Deciding between two physicians: a paradox.

✳ In medical school he worried about passing as a surgeon, but he made the cut.

✳ Did you hear about the two surgeons who were joking about sutures and had each other in stitches?

✳ Why are phlebotomists good spellers? Because they can spot type-o's.

✳ Did you hear about the cut-rate ophthalmologist?
He was always cutting corneas!

✳ The old art of bloodletting was abandoned when it was discovered it was all in vein.

✳ Why didn't the doctor transplant the bowels? He didn't have the guts.

* Proctologists often have a hard day at the orifice.

* I have a fear of needles. They really get under my skin.

* Overheard in med school – 'I learned about the colon through the process of elimination.'

* Did you hear about the man who was bleeding?
  They tried to save him with an IV but it was all in vein.

* What do you call two ambulance drivers? Paramedics.

* Why do dermatologists make bad flatmates?
  They really get under your skin.

* It's hard to become an optician. There's more to it than meets the eye.

* You should always cut your fingernails before they get out of hand.

* Two five-year-old boys are sitting in a hospital waiting room. One leans over to the other and says, 'What are you in here for?'
  The other says, 'Circumcision.'
  The first boy says 'Oh, man! I had that done right after I was born.
  I couldn't walk for a year!'

* After having a knee dislocated and an elbow fractured in two bar room brawls the man should have learned to stay away from those joints.

✳ When you get a transfusion in a Taiwanese hospital, you receive Taipei blood.

✳ Why should you never lie to an X-ray technician?
They can see right through you!

✳ Proctologists can rectify some problems.

✳ Did you hear about the man who was afraid of his chiropractor?
He had an appointment but he backed out.

✳ Paddy went to the opticians about his eyesight. The optician examined him and then said: 'I don't understand it, but it appears your vision is improving!'
'Really?' replied Paddy. 'Must be the luck of the iris.'

✳ Did you hear about the medical book which had no appendix?

Actual Medical Charts

- The baby was delivered, the cord clamped and cut and handed to the paediatrician, who breathed and cried immediately.
- Exam of genitalia reveals that he is circus sized.
- The skin was moist and dry.
- Rectal exam revealed a normal size thyroid.
- She stated that she had been constipated for most of her life until 1989 when she got a divorce.
- Between you and me, we ought to be able to get this lady pregnant.

- The patient was in his usual state of good health until his airplane ran out of gas and crashed.
- I saw your patient today, who is still under our car for physical therapy.
- The patient lives at home with his mother, father and pet turtle, who is presently enrolled in daycare three times a week.
- Bleeding started in the rectal area and continued all the way to Los Angeles.
- Both breasts are equal and reactive to light and accommodation.
- She is numb from her toes down.
- Exam of genitalia was completely negative except for the right foot.
- While in the emergency room, she was examined, X-rated and sent home.
- The lab test indicated abnormal lover function.
- The patient was to have a bowel resection. However, he took a job as a stockbroker instead.
- Occasional, constant, infrequent headaches.
- Coming from Detroit, this man has no children.
- Examination reveals a well-developed male lying in bed with his family in no distress.
- Patient was alert and unresponsive.
- When she fainted, her eyes rolled around the room.

✳ A woman fell for her handsome new dentist like a ton of bricks and pretty soon had lured him into a series of passionate encounters in the dental clinic after hours. But one day he said sadly, 'Darling, we have to stop seeing each other. Your husband's bound to get suspicious.' 'No way, sweetie, he's dumb as a post,' she assured him. 'Besides, we've been together for six months now and he doesn't suspect a thing.' 'True,' agreed the dentist, 'but you're down to one tooth!'

✳ It's a fact, taller people sleep longer in bed.

✳ A mechanic was removing some engine valves from a car on the lift when he spotted a famous heart surgeon standing off to the side, waiting for the service manager.
The mechanic shouted across the garage, 'Hey, Doctor. Come over here a minute.'
The famous surgeon, a bit surprised, walked over to where the mechanic was working on the car. In a loud voice that all could hear, the mechanic said argumentatively, 'So Mr Fancy Doctor, look at this work. I too, take valves out, grind 'em, put in new parts, and when I'm finished, this baby will purr like a kitten. So how come you get the big bucks, when you and me are doing basically the same work?'
The surgeon, very embarrassed, shook his head and replied in a soft voice, 'Try doing your work with the engine running.'

✳ What do you call it when a nurse isn't in surgery?
Absent without gauze!

✳ A doctor walked into a consultation room to find a nurse knocked out on the floor with a syringe in her hand, and an angry patient standing above her rubbing his fist.
'What's happened here?' asked the doctor.
'It's this nurse,' explained the exasperated patient.' She kept needling me.'

✳ Nurses often have to check their patient's impulse without missing a beat.

✳ A young boy was just being potty-trained. When he went to the bathroom though, Tommy managed to hit everything but the toilet.

So his mum had to go in and clean up after him. After two weeks, she had had enough, and took Tommy to the doctor.

After the examination, the doctor said, 'His unit is too small. An old wives' tale is to give him two slices of toast each morning, and his unit will grow so he can hold it and aim straight.'

The next morning Tommy jumped out of bed and ran downstairs to the kitchen. There on the table, were twelve slices of toast.

'Mum!' he yelled. 'The doctor said I only had to eat two slices of toast.'

'I know,' said his mother. 'The other ten are for your father.'

✳ Organ donors put their heart into it.

✳ I noticed the article about peripheral vision out of the corner of my eye.

✳ A lady went to the doctor and complained that her husband was losing interest in sex. The doctor gave her a pill, but warned her that it is still experimental. He tells her to slip it in her husband's mashed potatoes at dinner, and so she does just that.

About a week later, she returned back to the doctor's office and said, 'That pill worked great. I put it in my husband's mashed potatoes just like you said. It wasn't five minutes later, and he jumped up, raked all the food and dishes on the floor, grabbed me, ripped all my clothes off and ravished me right there on the table!'

The doctor said, 'I'm sorry, we didn't realise that the pill was that strong. The foundation will be glad to pay for any damages.'

The lady replied, 'Naah. That's OK. We aren't going back to a Harvester anyway.'

✳ The aspiring student psychiatrists from various colleges were attending their first class on emotional extremes. 'Just to establish some parameters,' said the professor, to the student from Oxford University, 'What is the opposite of joy?'
'Sadness,' replied the student.
'And the opposite of depression?' the professor asked of the young lady from Cambridge.
'Elation,' said she.
'And you sir,' he said to the young man from Devon. 'How about the opposite of woe?'
He replied, 'Sir, I believe that would be giddy-up.'

✳ Q: What advice don't you want to hear from a doctor before an operation?
A: Whatever you do, don't go into the light.

✳ Being able to fit size 14 shoes is quite a feet.

✳ Old white blood cells just lymph around the body.

✳ A man was admitted to the hospital suffering from premature ejaculation. The doctors said it was touch and go.

✳ A pessimist's blood type is always b-negative.

✳ A patient complained to his doctor, 'I've been to three other doctors and none of them agreed with your diagnosis.'
The doctor calmly replied, 'Just wait until the autopsy, then they'll see that I was right.'

✳ An attractive young girl, chaperoned by an ugly old crone, entered the doctor's office. 'We have come for an examination,' said the young girl. 'All right,' said the doctor. 'Go behind that curtain and take your clothes off.'
'No, not me,' said the girl. 'It's my old aunt here.'
'Very well … Madam, put your tongue out.'

✳ What happened when the chiropodist broke down?
He called a toe truck!

✳ Do chiropodists charge by the foot?

✳ How do heart surgeons get to hospital? They use the bypass.

✳ What do you get if you've got an infected organ? Bach-ache!

✳ What do you call it when there's not enough nurses on the delivery ward? A mid-wife crisis!

✳ A young nurse was nervous about giving vaccinations but gave it her best shot.

✳ A man who had just undergone a very complicated operation kept complaining about a bump on his head and a terrible headache. Since his operation had been an intestinal one, there was no earthly reason why he should be complaining of a headache.
Finally his nurse, fearing that the man might be suffering from some post-operation shock, spoke to the doctor about it. 'Don't worry about a thing, nurse,' the doctor assured her. 'He really does have a bump

on his head. About halfway through the operation we ran out
of anaesthetic.'

✳ A doctor made it his regular habit to stop off at a bar for a hazelnut
daiquiri on his way home. The bartender knew of his habit, and would
always have the drink waiting at precisely 5.06 p.m.
One afternoon, as the end of the work day approached, the bartender
was dismayed to find that he was out of hazelnut extract. Thinking
quickly, he threw together a daiquiri made with hickory nuts and set it
on the bar.
The doctor came in at his regular time, took one sip of the drink and
exclaimed, 'This isn't a hazelnut daiquiri!'
'No, I'm sorry,' replied the bartender. 'It's a hickory daiquiri, Doc.'

✳ I entered a contest for the most prominent veins. I didn't win, but I
came varicose.

✳ Break a bone today, and you'll hurt to marrow.

✳ On TV, the commercial says that eight out of ten people suffer from
haemorrhoids. Does this mean the other two people enjoy them?

✳ What happens when two monocles get married?
They make a spectacle of themselves!

✳ One afternoon, two doctors from India were having an animated
discussion. 'I say it's spelled 'W-H-O-O-M',' said the first Indian doctor.
'No, it is 'W-H-O-M-B',' said the other Indian doctor.
An English nurse passing by said, 'Excuse me, you are both wrong.

It is spelled "W-O-M-B".'

'Thank you, nurse,' said one of the doctors, 'but we prefer to settle this argument ourselves. Besides, we don't think you are in a position to describe the sound of an elephant passing wind under water.'

* Two kids were trying to figure out what game to play. One suggested, 'Let's play doctor.'
'Good idea,' said the other. 'You operate, and I'll sue.'

* The proctologist quit his job because it gave him tunnel vision.

* At a mental hospital the staff found some of the patients were gaining weight, so they were put on a diet of a glass of Tab and one apple for lunch.
After eating their light lunch, the group would start to sing to everyone else.
This became known as the 'Moron Tab and Apple Choir'.

* A middle-aged spinster, well known for all her charity work and support for good causes (because she was a somewhat tedious self-publicist), was complaining to the doctor of a persistent headache.
'What's it like?' asked the doctor.
'Like a tight band around my head,' replied the spinster.
Mindful that this type of headache is most often due to an unhealthy or stressed lifestyle, the doctor asked if she smoked a lot.
'Certainly not, doctor. Never have smoked, never will,' was the emphatic reply.
'Do you drink a lot of alcohol?'
'Doctor! I am strictly teetotal.'

'How often do you have sex?'

'That is an impertinent question, I am as chaste as the driven snow.'

'Perhaps you're spending too much time going to church?'

'Impossible, doctor. As I keep telling the Mothers' Union, I go twice every Sunday and every Festival Day because it is our clear duty to do so.'

'Are you working too hard at your charity activities?'

'Well,' simpered the spinster, 'I always believe that you can never do too much for your fellow man, even to the detriment of your own health.'

'Just as I thought,' said the doctor, 'It is clear that the headaches are due to your halo being too tight.'

* Yesterday I accidentally swallowed some food colouring. The doctor says I'm OK, but I feel like I've dyed a little inside.

* Did you hear about the man who swallowed a pillow?
His condition was described as comfortable.

* This guy went to the doctor and said to him, 'Doctor … I don't know what's wrong with me, but every time I fart, it sounds like the word HONDA.'

'That's interesting, never heard of anything like that before. Do you think you could fart for me?' says the doctor. The guy says, 'Sure.'
And sure enough, the doctor hears 'HONDA'.

After several attempts to figure out what's wrong with this guy, the doctor runs out of ideas. He sends him to all sorts of stomach specialists and none of them can figure out why this guy's farts say 'HONDA'. It is a completely out-of-this-world medical condition.

Finally, as a last resort, the doctors think they should send the man to a dentist. After explaining the problem to the dentist, the dentist opened up the guy's mouth and started examining it.

The dentist says, 'A-haa!!!! … I have solved the problem.'

The patient says, 'What is it? What is it? Please tell me.'

The dentist replies, 'Well, sir, you have an abscess tooth.'

The guy says, 'Yeah … so … What has that got to do with my farts?'

The dentist replies, 'Can't you see?? … Abscess Makes The Fart Go HONDA!'

✳ A handlebar moustache may look ridiculous, but symmetrical eyelashes are even cilia.

New study reveals an alarming statistic

Senior citizens are the biggest carriers of AIDS.

- Hearing AIDS
- Seeing AIDS
- Chewing AIDS
- Band AIDS
- Walking AIDS
- Government AIDS

✳ The tired doctor was awakened by a phone call in the middle of the night.

'Please, you have to come right over,' pleaded a distraught young mother. 'My child has swallowed a contraceptive.'

The physician dressed quickly; but before he could get out the door, the phone rang again.

'You don't have to come over after all,' the woman said with a sigh of relief. 'My husband just found another one.'

✷ Patient: It's been one month since my last visit and I still feel miserable.
Doctor: Did you follow the instructions on the medicine I gave you?
Patient: I sure did. The bottle said "keep tightly closed".

✷ The medical student's desire to be a dermatologist was only skin deep. He knew he was destined for osteology. He could feel it in his bones.

✷ A distraught patient phoned her doctor's office. Was it true, the woman wanted to know, that the medication the doctor had prescribed was for the rest of her life? She was told that it was.
There was a moment of silence before the woman continued, 'I'm wondering, then, just how serious my condition is. This prescription is marked "NO REFILLS".'

✷ Did you hear about the optician who wanted to open a new practice but didn't have enough contacts?

✷ Never argue with your doctor. He has inside information.

🌐MONEY - CASH-POINT PROCEDURE

Male Procedure

1. Drive up to the cash machine.
2. Wind down your car window.
3. Insert card into machine and enter PIN.
4. Enter amount of cash required and withdraw.
5. Retrieve card, cash and receipt.
6. Wind up window.
7. Drive off.

Female Procedure

1. Drive up to cash machine.
2. Reverse back the required amount to align car window to machine.
3. Restart the stalled engine.
4. Wind down the window.
5. Find handbag, remove all contents on to passenger seat to locate card.
6. Turn the radio down.
7. Attempt to insert card into machine.
8. Open car door to allow easier access to machine due to its excessive distance from the car.
9. Insert card.
10. Reinsert card the right way up.
11. Re-enter handbag to find diary with your PIN written on the inside back page.

12. Enter PIN.
13. Press cancel and re-enter correct PIN.
14. Enter amount of cash required.
15. Check make-up in rear view mirror.
16. Retrieve cash and receipt.
17. Empty handbag again to locate purse and place cash inside.
18. Place receipt in back of cheque book.
19. Recheck make-up again.
20. Drive forwards two meters.
21. Reverse back to cash machine.
22. Retrieve card.
23. Re-empty hand bag, locate card holder, and place card into the slot provided.
24. Restart stalled engine and pull off.
25. Drive for two to three miles.
26. Release handbrake.

MONEY - CREDIT CRUNCH

✳ The credit crunch is getting bad. I let my brother borrow ten pounds a couple of weeks back. It turns out I'm now Britain's third biggest lender.

✳ I talked to my bank manager the other day and he said he was going to concentrate on the big issues from now on. He sold me one outside KFC yesterday.

✳ What have Icelandic banks and an Icelandic streaker got in common? They both have frozen assets.

✳ How do you successfully freeze your financial assets? Invest in an Icelandic bank.

✳ A lobbyist on his way home from Parliament is stuck in traffic. Noticing a police officer, he winds down his window and asks: 'What's the hold-up?'
The policeman replies: 'The Prime Minister is so depressed he's stopped his motorcade and is threatening to douse himself with petrol and set himself on fire. He says no one believes he can get us through the credit crunch. So we're taking up a collection for him.'
The lobbyist asks: 'How much have you got so far?'
The officer replies: 'About 40 gallons, but a lot of people are still siphoning.'

You know it's a credit crunch when

The cash point asks if you can spare any change.

There's a 'buy one, get one free' offer – on banks.

The Inland Revenue is offering a 25 per cent discount for cash payers.

Prime minister Gordon Brown has stopped chewing his nails and started sucking his thumb.

Your builder asks to be paid in Zimbabwean dollars rather than sterling.

✳ What's the capital of Iceland? About £3.50.

✳ The credit crunch has helped me get back on my feet. The car's been repossessed.

✳ How do you define an optimist? A bank manager who irons five shirts on Sunday night.

✳ A director decided to award a prize of fifty pounds for the best idea of saving the company money during the recession. It was won by a young executive who suggested reducing the prize money to ten pounds.

✳ Overheard in a City bar: 'This credit crunch is worse than a divorce. I've lost half my net worth and I still have a wife.'

✳ Bradford & Bingley employees are concerned they were given no notice of the takeover by Santander Bank.

✳ A Government spokesman said: 'No one expected the Spanish acquisition.'

✳ What is a banker's favourite chocolate bar? A credit crunchie!

✳ Petrol is way too expensive these days. I actually can't afford to drive.

✳ Last time I went dogging, I had to ask my mum to give me a lift.

🐷MONEY – GENERAL

✳ There is the story of a preacher who got up one Sunday and announced to his congregation: 'I have good news and bad news. The good news is, we have enough money to pay for our new building programme. The bad news is, it's still out there in your pockets.'

✳ The local pub was so sure that its landlord was the strongest man around that they offered a standing thousand-pound bet.
The landlord would squeeze a lemon until all the juice ran into a glass, and hand the lemon to a patron. Anyone who could squeeze one more drop of juice out would win the money.
Many people had tried over time, but nobody could do it.
One day this scrawny little man came in, wearing thick glasses and a polyester suit, and said in a tiny, squeaky voice, 'I'd like to try the bet.'
After the laughter had died down, the landlord said OK, grabbed a lemon, and squeezed away. Then he handed the wrinkled remains of the rind to the little man.
But the crowd's laughter turned to total silence as the man clenched his fist around the lemon and six drops fell into the glass.
As the crowd cheered, the landlord paid the thousand pounds, and asked the little man, 'What do you do for a living? Are you a lumberjack, a weightlifter, or what?'
The man replied, 'I work for the Inland Revenue.'

✳ We were so poor when I was growing up we couldn't even afford to pay attention.

* Money can't buy you friends but it can get you a better class of enemy.

* Accountants enjoy the job, figuratively speaking.

* Money won't buy happiness, but if will pay the salaries of a large research staff to study the problem.

* When the gunman walked in, he turned the bank into a flee market.

* I've got all the money I'll ever need if I die by four o' clock.

Henry Youngman

* Did you hear about the Hong Kong businessman who left £100 million when he died? It was the great will of China.

* The real measure of your wealth is how much you'd be worth if you lost all your money.

* The cost of a galvanised hull is enough to zinc a ship.

* The best way of saving money is to forget the person you borrowed it from.

* A father is explaining ethics to his son, who is about to go into business: 'Suppose a woman comes in and orders fifty pounds of goods. You wrap it up, and give it to her. She pays you with a fifty-pound note. As she goes out of the door you realise she has given you two fifty-pound notes. Now, here's where the ethics come in: should you or should you not tell your partner?'

✳ An elderly lady receives an email from the son of a deceased African general asking whether he could transfer millions of pounds into her bank account in return for a 20 per cent cut. All the son needs is the sort code and account number. Not realising she is the victim of a Nigerian email fraud, she emails back the details. A couple of minutes later she receives an email back from the general's son: 'Icesave?! What is this, some sort of scam?'

✳ Why is money called dough? Because we all knead it!

✳ Three animals were having a drink in a cafe, when the owner asked for the money.
'I'm not paying,' said the duck. 'I've only got one bill and I'm not breaking it.'
'I've spent my last buck,' said the deer.
'Then the duck'll have to pay,' said the skunk. 'Getting here cost me my last scent.'

✳ At the Dublin Chamber of Commerce meeting the treasurer reported a deficit of two hundred euros.
One of the chamber members stood up and said, 'I vote that we donate half of it to the Red Cross and then give the other fifty euros to the Salvation Army.'

✳ Johnny collected lots of money fro his birthday and took it to the sweet shop to buy some chocolate. 'You should give that money to charity,' said the shopkeeper.
'No, I'll buy the chocolate. You give the money to charity!'

* Have you heard about the new aftershave that drives women wild? It smells of fifty-pound notes!

* A businessman called his travel agent with a question about the documents he needed in order to fly to China. After a lengthy discussion about passports, the agent reminded him he needed a visa. 'Oh no I don't, I've been to China many times and never had to have one of those.' The agent double-checked, and sure enough, his stay required a visa. When he told him this the businessman said, 'Look, I've been to China four times and every time they accepted my American Express.'

* Why did the girl feed money to her cow? Because she wanted to get rich milk.

* Why did the miser purse his lips? To coin a phrase.

* Why did the schoolboy eat the cash? It was his dinner money!

Credit card application: what the terms really mean

WHAT IT SAYS: 'You have demonstrated financial responsibility … '
WHAT IT MEANS: You're breathing!

WHAT IT SAYS: 'Our membership is difficult to obtain … '
WHAT IT MEANS: Life sentence prisoners are not eligible … in most cases!

WHAT IT SAYS: 'We have shortened the application process … '
WHAT IT MEANS: We need lots of new members fast or we'll go out of business!

WHAT IT SAYS: 'You have no predetermined credit limit ... '
WHAT IT MEANS: We're not worried, we employ the Break Your Legs collection agency.

WHAT IT SAYS: 'Exceptional Customer Service ...'
WHAT IT MEANS: Except when you need it!

WHAT IT SAYS: 'Trained customer representatives await your call ... '
WHAT IT MEANS: This is the part you talk into, and this is where you listen. Any questions?

WHAT IT SAYS: 'To apply for membership, fill out this short form ... '
WHAT IT MEANS: You'll get the long form later.

WHAT IT SAYS: 'You may direct us not to share this information with anyone else ... '
WHAT IT MEANS: Catch us if you can!

WHAT IT SAYS: 'We look forward to receiving your completed application ... '
WHAT IT MEANS: We baited the hook, let's see if anyone bites!

WHAT IT SAYS: 'You've been pre-approved ... '
WHAT IT MEANS: You've been pre-approved to be rejected! or We've already prepared your letter of denial.

✳ Did you know copper wire was invented by two Scotsmen fighting over a penny?

✳ What did the cod say to the loan shark? Here's that sick squid I owe you.

✳ What do you call a rich bear? Winnie the pools!

✳ What do you call a penny that goes nee naw-nee naw? A copper.

✳ This guy is walking with his friend, who happens to be a psychologist.
He says to this friend, 'I'm a walking economy.'
The friend asks, 'How so?'
'My hairline is in recession, my stomach is a victim of inflation, and both of these together are putting me into a deep depression!'

✳ Fresh out of business school, the young man answered a wanted ad for an accountant. Now he was being interviewed by a very nervous man who ran a small business that he had started himself.
'I need someone with an accounting degree,' the man said. 'But mainly, I'm looking for someone to do my worrying for me.'
'Excuse me?' the accountant said.
'I worry about a lot of things,' the man said. 'But I don't want to have to worry about money. Your job will be to take all the money worries off my back.'
'I see,' the accountant said. 'And how much does the job pay?'
'I'll start you at eighty thousand.'
'Eighty thousand pounds!' the accountant exclaimed. 'How can such a small business afford a sum like that?'
'That,' the owner said, 'is your first worry.'

✳ October: This is one of the particularly dangerous months to invest in stocks. Other dangerous months are July, January, September,

April, November, May, March, June, December, August and February.

Mark Twain

✳ What do you get if you cross a Grotbags with a millionaire?
A very witch person.

✳ A young Scottish lad and lass were sitting on a low stone wall, holding hands, gazing out over the loch. For several minutes they sat silently, then finally the girl looked at the boy and said, 'A penny for your thoughts, Angus.'
'Well, uh, I was thinkin' … perhaps it's aboot time for a wee kiss.'
The girl blushed, then leaned over and kissed him lightly on the cheek.
Then he blushed. The two turned once again to gaze out over the loch.
Minutes passed, then the girl spoke again. 'Another penny for your thoughts, Angus.'
'Well, uh I was thinkin' … perhaps its noo aboot time for a wee cuddle.'
The girl blushed, then leaned over and cuddled him for a few seconds.
Then he blushed. Then the two turned once again to gaze out over the loch. After a while, she again said, 'Another penny for your thoughts, Angus.' The young man glanced down with a furled brow. 'Well, noo,' he said, 'my thoughts are a wee bit more serious this time.'
'Really?' said the girl in a whisper, filled with anticipation.
'Aye,' said the lad, nodding. The girl looked away in shyness, began to blush, and bit her lip in anticipation of the ultimate request.
Then he said, 'Dae ye nae think it's aboot time ye paid me the first two pennies!'

✳ Did you hear about the Scotsman who dropped a penny?
It hit him on the back of the neck.

* Money can't buy you true love. It does, however, put you in a good bargaining position.

* These days money is the stuff you use when all of your credit cards are maxed-out.

* A Scot gets to the pearly gates and asks if he can come in.
St Peter replies, 'No, actually, you've been too tight-fisted while on earth.'
'No I haven't,' replies the Scot. 'Two weeks ago I gave ten pounds to children in need, three weeks ago I gave ten pounds to help the aged and last week I gave ten pounds to Oxfam.'
St Peter looked thoughtful for a minute, then said, 'Hang on a minute' and went away.
Five minutes later he came back and said, 'Right, God agrees with me. Here's your thirty quid back, now get lost.'

* Did you hear the one about the village idiot who thought Johnny Cash was the change from a Durex machine?

* Gordon Brown was wandering around a local art gallery, muttering about the profligacy of the young. He claps eyes on a picture of baby Jesus, Mary and Joseph in the stable with the three wise men.
'Typical – that's exactly what I'm talking about,' shouts Gordon.
'Now … Joseph and Mary demonstrated prudent financial skills by having the baby in a stable … but when it comes to getting a family portrait – they blow it all and get it done by Rembrandt!'

* The collective noun for a group of bankers is a wunch.

✳ A woman enquired at her local bank about who she needed to see in order to borrow some money.

The receptionist indicated a man sitting at a desk in the corner.

She went across and sat down opposite him.

'I understand you are the man I need to see in order to borrow some money,' she said.

'Sadly no,' said the man, 'he is out at lunch at the minute. I am his assistant, Tonto. You will need to return after two in order to see the loan arranger.'

✳ A group of men are in a changing room. A mobile phone rings on the bench and one of the men answers.

'Hi darling, I'm at the shops and I have seen a lovely top for fifty pounds. Can I have it?' asks the caller.

'Sure.'

'In that case there's also a fantastic coat for three hundred pounds – can I get that too?'

'OK.'

Feeling lucky, she goes for the big one: 'The car showroom next door has just what I need for only twenty thousand pounds. Can I have that too?'

'Put it on the card.'

The man hangs up. 'Anyone know who this phone belongs to?'

✳ A man goes into a pet shop.

'Hi, I want to buy a parrot … how much are those on the bottom shelf?'

'Ten pounds each,' says the owner.

'Not bad,' says the man, 'how much are those on the middle shelf?'

'Twenty pounds each,' says the owner.

'Hmmm,' say the man, 'not bad at all, but the ones on the top shelf are the best of all, how much are they?'

'Thirty pounds,' says the owner, 'but you will have to pay for it at ten pounds a week for the next three weeks if you want one.'

'That's strange,' says the man, 'why is that?'

'Ahh,' says the owner, 'that's because those are on higher perches.'

✳ Did you hear about the bankrupt contortionist?
He can no longer make ends meet!

✳ Did you hear the Kennel Club are in financial difficulty?
They might have to call in the retrievers!

✳ Bad news from the Japanese financial sector. Following last week's news that Origami Bank had folded, we are hearing that Sumo Bank has gone belly up and Bonsai Bank's growth has been stunted and now it plans to cut back some of its branches. Karaoke Bank is up for sale and is going for a song. Meanwhile, shares in Kamikaze Bank have nose-dived and five hundred back office staff at Karate Bank got the chop. Analysts report that there is something fishy going on at Sushi Bank and staff there fear they may get a raw deal. Even Miso Bank is in the soup, and an audit of the Tofu Bank is turning up questions about its REAL assets.

✳ An alien spaceship lands in a pub car park. Out jumps your typical big green Martian and slithers into the pub. The landlord immediately says, 'Sorry mate, we don't serve extra terrestrials in here – on yer way.'
The Martian says (aided by a hi-tech translator device), 'Please Mr

Earthling pub landlord, I've just travelled thirteen light years in hyperspace and I'm gagging for a beer!'

'No,' replies the landlord.

The alien ponders for a moment and then says, 'I tell you what, I'll buy drinks for everyone in the pub all night if you'll serve me.'

So the landlord relents and the punters go wild, drinking the best champagne until the final bell rings. So as the crowd stagger off into the night, the landlord adds it all up, walks over to the Martian and presents him with a bill for £14,642.21 to cover all the night's drinks.

The Martian takes one look at it and says, 'No problem. Have you got change for a Zonk?'

✳ How does the Pope pay for stuff on eBay? Papal.

✳ Who was the world's first stockbroker?
Noah – he floated his stock while the world was in liquidation.

✳ One day a father gets out of work and on his way home he remembers that it's his daughter's birthday.

He pulls over to a toy shop and asks the salesperson, 'How much is the Barbie on the display window?'

The salesperson answers, 'Which one? We have:

Workout Barbie for £19.95

Shopping Barbie for £19.95

Beach Barbie for £19.95

Disco Barbie for £19.95

Divorced Barbie for £265.95'

The amazed father asks: 'What? Why is the Divorced Barbie £265.95 and the others only £19.95?'

'Sir, divorced Barbie comes with:

Ken's car

Ken's house

Ken's boat

Ken's furniture

Ken's computer and …

One of Ken's friends.'

* What's pink and hard in the morning? The *Financial Times* crossword.

* A blonde was filling out an application form for a job. She promptly filled the columns entitled NAME, AGE, ADDRESS, etc. Then she came to the column: SALARY EXPECTED and she entered …
'Yes.'

* When he found out he was going to inherit a fortune when his sickly father died, Pete decided he needed a woman to enjoy it with. So one evening he went to a singles bar where he spotted the most beautiful woman he had ever seen. Her natural beauty took his breath away.
'I may look like just an ordinary man,' he said as he walked up to her, 'but in just a week or two, my father will die, and I'll inherit twenty million pounds.'
The woman went home with Pete that evening, and three days later, she became his stepmother.

* A man came round the other day collecting for the local swimming pool. So I gave him a bucket of water.

＊ A tourist from India went to the bank just after he arrived in the UK. He handed over fifty thousand rupees to change to sterling. The bank clerk handed the tourist six hundred pounds back.

A week later, the same tourist went to the same bank and handed over another fifty thousand rupees to exchange. This time the bank clerk handed back five hundred and twenty-five pounds.

The tourist looked at the money and said, 'Last week I changed fifty thousand rupees and you gave me six hundred pounds. Why have you only given me five hundred and twenty-five pounds this time?'

The bank clerk said, 'Well ... fluctuations ... '

The tourist then said, 'Well f**k you English as well, but where is the rest of my money?'

＊ Prices are obviously going up since the European currency came along ... when you needed to pee, you used to be able to 'spend a penny' but now it's called 'euronating'!

＊ Two Irishmen are talking. One says to the other, 'If I was as rich as Bill Gates, I'd be even richer than him.'

'How so?' asked his friend

'I'd do a bit of window cleaning on the side.'

＊ A 4ft 11' tall bank manager from Prague goes into the British Embassy to claim political asylum. He is shown to the office of the British Ambassador, and the Ambassador says to him, 'So, what can we do for you?'

The bank manager replies, 'Can you cache a small Czech?'

✳ Why is it that a bank will happily lend billions to a third world country with little hope of getting it back, yet for us they chain down all the pens?

✳ The local children's charity office realised that it had never received a donation from the town's most successful lawyer. The volunteer in charge of contributions called him to persuade him to contribute.
'Our research shows that out of a yearly income of more than £500,000 you give not a penny to charity. Wouldn't you like to give back to the community in some way?'
The lawyer mulled this over for a moment and replied, 'First, did your research also show that my mother is dying after a long illness, and has medical bills that are several times her annual income?'
Embarrassed, the charity worker mumbled, 'Um … no.'
'Second, that my brother, a disabled veteran, is blind and confined to a wheelchair?'
The stricken charity fundraiser began to stammer out an apology but was put off.
'Third, that my sister's husband died in a traffic accident,' the lawyer says, voice rising in indignation, 'leaving her penniless with three children?'
The humiliated charity worker, completely beaten, said simply, 'I had no idea … '
On a roll, the lawyer cut him off once again, 'And I don't give any money to them, so why should I give any to you?'

✳ Who is the richest artist in the world? Monet.

✳ It was the first morning of the big sale. A long queue of bargain hunters had formed in front of the store. A small man pushed his way to the front of the line, only to be pushed back, amid loud and colourful curses. On the man's second attempt, he was punched square in the jaw and then thrown to the end of the queue again. As he got up, he said to the person at the end of the line, 'That does it! If they hit me one more time, I don't open the door!'

* Nero was talking to his financial advisers in a Roman amphitheatre. 'Why aren't we making any money from this building?' he asked them. An adviser replied, 'Because the lions are eating up all the prophets.'

* A man sees the last two pasties in a bakery shop window and goes in to ask how much the pasties are.
The lady behind the counter replies, 'They're seventy pence each or two for a pound.'
The man says, 'In that case I'll have that one there for thirty pence!'

* A man walks into a pub and sees the daily special written on the blackboard:
A pie, a pint, and a kind word, £2.
'That's a bargain,' he thinks to himself, 'I'll have some of that.'
Sitting down at the bar with his pint of beer in one hand and his meat pie in the other, he asks the barman, 'What's the kind word?'
Shaking his head the barman says, 'Wouldn't eat that pie if I was you.'

* Estate Agent – I'd put your house on the market for a hundred thousand pounds.
Seller: What's your commission?
Estate Agent: Two per cent.
Seller: Could you go any lower?
Estate Agent: Well, other than becoming a traffic warden, no.

✳ A stingy old lawyer, coming to the end of his days, finally figured out how to take at least some of his fortune with him when he died. He instructed his wife to go to the bank and withdraw enough money to fill two pillowcases. He then told her to take the bags of money to the attic and leave them directly above his bed. When he passed away, he planned to reach out and grab the bags on his way to Heaven. Several weeks after the funeral, his wife, up in the attic cleaning, came upon the two forgotten pillow cases stuffed with cash.

'Oh, that old fool!' she exclaimed. 'I knew I should have put the money in the basement.'

Stock market report

Cows steered into a bull market.

Hiking equipment was trailing.

Weights were up in heavy trading.

Light switches were off.

Shipping lines stayed at an even keel.

The market for raisins dried up.

Coca-Cola fizzled.

Caterpillar stock inched up a bit.

Sun peaked at midday.

Birds Eye Peas Split.

Stanley Tools filed for bankruptcy.

And batteries exploded in an attempt to recharge the market.

＊ Did you hear about the man who was half Scottish and half Irish? He knew how to look after his money, but he couldn't count it.

＊ What do misers do when it's cold? Sit round a candle. What do they do when it's really cold? Light it!

😮 MOTHER-IN-LAW

＊ Heard the one about the man who ran off with his mother-in-law? He's got a wife sentence.

＊ How many mothers-in-law does it take to change a light bulb? One. She just holds it up there and waits for the world to revolve around her.

＊ What's the difference between a mother-in-law and a vulture? The vulture waits until you're dead before it eats your heart out.

＊ I took my mother-in-law to Madame Tussauds chamber of horrors and one of the attendants said: 'Keep her moving, sir, we're stocktaking.'

＊ Did you hear about the man who threw his mother-in-law into the lion's den at the zoo? He's being sued by the RSPCA for cruelty to animals.

＊ Why did the mother-in-law cross the road? I don't know, but it was an ugly sight.

＊ What does a mother-in-law call her broom? Basic transportation.

✳ If butting in was an Olympic sport my mother-in-law would win the gold meddle.

✳ What are the two worst things about your mother-in-law? Her faces.

✳ How many mothers-in-law does it take to ruin a marriage?
Just one … mine!

✳ How many mothers-in-law does it take to screw in a light bulb?
None … she always gets the son-in-law to do it.

✳ Last week my wife and I went to buy a car and the salesman asked if I wanted an airbag. I said: 'No thanks. I already have a mother-in-law.'

✳ Lawyer to his client: 'Your mother-in-law passed away in her sleep. Shall we order burial, embalming or cremation?'
Son-in-law: 'Take no chances. Order all three.'

✳ 'My mother-in-law was bitten by a mad dog in the street.'
'Oh, that's awful.'
'Yes, it was terrible to watch the dog die slowly in convulsions.'

✳ An anagram of mother-in-law is woman Hitler.

✳ My mother-in-law said to me: 'I'll dance on your grave.'
I said: 'I hope you do. I'm being buried at sea.'

✳ My mother-in-law is a big woman. She got run over last week. The driver said he had enough room to get around her but he didn't have enough petrol.

✳ Last night the local peeping Tom knocked on my mother-in-law's door, and asked her to shut her blinds.

✳ I have never made a fool of my mother-in-law. I just leave her to display her natural talents herself.

✳ Marriage Anon is a club for bachelors. If any is tempted to marry, they send my mother-in-law over in curlers and dressing gown.

✳ A couple drove several miles down a country road, not saying a word. An earlier discussion had led to an argument, and neither wanted to concede their position.
As they passed a barnyard of mules and pigs, the wife sarcastically asked, 'Relatives of yours?'
'Yep,' the husband replied, 'in-laws.'

✳ What is the difference between George Washington, Richard Nixon, and your mother-in-law? Washington couldn't tell a lie, Nixon couldn't tell the truth, your mother-in-Law doesn't know the difference.

✳ I saw the mother-in-law walking down the path so I jumped from behind the garage and shouted 'BOO!'
She said, 'You nearly frightened me to death so I shouted, 'BOO! BOO! BOO!'

✳ A pharmacist explained to a disappointed customer, 'In order to buy arsenic you need a legal prescription. A picture of your mother-in-law just isn't enough.'

✳ Overheard in a restaurant:

'This wine is described as full-bodied and imposing with a nutty base, a sharp bite, and a bitter aftertaste.'

'Are you describing the wine or your mother?'

✳ 'I was sorry to hear that your mother-in-law died. What was the complaint?'

'We haven't had any yet.'

✳ Two women came before wise King Solomon, dragging between them a young man. 'This young man agreed to marry my daughter,' said one. 'No! He agreed to marry MY daughter,' said the other. And so they haggled before the king, until he called for silence.

'Bring me my biggest sword,' said Solomon, 'and I shall hew the young man in half. Each of you shall receive a half.'

'Sounds good to me,' said the first lady.

But the other woman said, 'Oh sire, do not spill innocent blood. Let the other woman's daughter marry him.'

The wise king did not hesitate a moment. 'This man must marry the first lady's daughter,' he proclaimed.

'But she was willing to hew him in two!' exclaimed the king's court.

'Indeed,' said wise King Solomon. 'That shows she is the true mother-in-law.'

✳ When Barry came home, his wife, Mary, was crying. 'Your mother insulted me,' she sobbed.

'My mother?' spluttered Barry. 'How could she do that when she is on holiday on the other side of the world?'

'I know,' Mary gulped. 'But this morning a letter addressed to you arrived. I opened it because I was curious.'

'And?'

'At the end of the letter it said: "Dear Mary, when you have finished reading this letter, don't forget to give it to my son, Barry."'

＊ My mother-in-law is banned internationally from playing poker, as she keeps all the chips on her shoulder.

＊ Did you hear the one about the cannibal who got married, and at the wedding reception toasted his mother-in-law?

＊ I'm not saying the mother-in-law's ugly, but she uses her bottom lip as a shower cap.

＊ 'Do you know, my mother-in-law has vanished, just disappeared from home. Just like that.' 'Have you given her description to the police?' 'No, they'd never believe me.'

＊ I don't know what I'd do without my mother-in-law – but it's nice dreaming about it.

＊ My mother-in-law's not ugly – it's just that when she does her make-up, the lipstick crawls back down the tube.

＊ My mother-in-law's found a new cheap way of making yoghurt and sour cream – she just buys a bottle of milk and stares at it for a couple of minutes.

＊ I wanted to do something nice so I bought my mother-in-law a chair. Now they won't let me plug it in.

✳ 'I just bought my mother-in-law a Jaguar.'

'I thought you didn't like her.'

'I know what I'm doing, it's bitten her twice already.'

✳ A couple was going out for the evening. The last thing they did was to put the cat out. The taxi arrived, and as the couple walked out of the house, the cat shoots back in. So the husband goes back inside to chase it out. The wife, not wanting it known that the house would be empty, explained to the taxi driver, 'He's just going upstairs to say goodbye to my mother.' A few minutes later, the husband got into the taxi and said, 'Sorry I took so long, the stupid thing was hiding under the bed and I had to poke her with a coat hanger to get her to come out!'

✳ My mother-in-law went to see *The Elephant Man* and the audience thought she was making a special appearance.

✳ My wife said: 'Can my mother come down for the weekend?' So I said: 'Why?' and she said: 'Well, she's been up on the roof two weeks already.'

Bob Monkhouse

🍎 MUSIC

✳ An accordion is a bagpipe with pleats.

✳ What is the difference between an Uzi and an accordion?

The Uzi stops after twenty rounds.

* Three violin manufactures have all done business for years on the same block in the small town of Cremona, Italy. After years of a peaceful co-existence, the Amati shop decided to put a sign in the window saying: 'We make the best violins in Italy.'
The Guarneri shop soon followed suit, and put a sign in their window proclaiming: 'We make the best violins in the world.'
Finally, the Stradivarius family put a sign out at their shop saying: 'We make the best violins on the block.'

* Why did Rolling Stones tickets go up in price when Mick Jagger got a knighthood? The Sir charge.

* Some orchestra conductors make their mark in the world of opera. They were in the right aria at the right time.

* What's the difference between an onion and an accordion?
No one cries when you chop up an accordion.

* What's the difference between an accordion player and a terrorist?
Terrorists have sympathisers.

* I play all the chords, bar one.

* How do you protect a valuable instrument? Hide it in an accordion case.

* What's an accordion good for? Learning how to fold a map.

* What's the difference between a chainsaw and an accordion?
A chainsaw can be tuned.

✳ Why did the Boy Scout take up the banjo?
They make good paddles.

✳ How can you tell the difference between all the banjo songs?
By their names.

✳ What is the most seldom heard comment made of banjo players?
'Say, isn't that the banjo player's Porsche?'

✳ How do you know when a drum solo's really bad?
The bass player notices.

✳ There's a five-pound note on the floor. Of a thrash guitarist, a drummer who keeps good time, and a drummer who keeps bad time, who picks it up?
The drummer who keeps bad time. The other drummer doesn't exist, and the thrash guitarist doesn't care about notes anyway.

✳ A man walks into a shop. 'You got one of them Marshall Hiwatt AC30 amplificatior thingies and a Gobson StratoBlaster gittar with a Fried Rose tremolo?'
'You're a drummer, aren't you?'
'Yeah. How'd you know?'
'This is a travel agency.'

✳ What's the definition of a minor second?
Two flutes playing a unison.

✳ Where do dirty violinists stay? In a vile inn!

✳ Flute players spend half their time tuning their instrument and the other half playing out of tune.

✳ Why do loud, obnoxious whistles exist at some factories?
To give us some sort of appreciation for flutes.

✳ What did the guitar say to the guitarist? Pick on someone your own size!

✳ What does a guitarist say when he gets to his gig?
Would you like fries with that?

✳ Why are harps like elderly parents?
Both are unforgiving and hard to get into and out of cars.

✳ Two musicians are walking down the street, and one says to the other, 'Who was that piccolo I saw you with last night?' The other replies, 'That was no piccolo, that was my fife.'

✳ What do you use to tie saplings to a piano so the saplings won't blow away? Root position cords.

✳ What do a viola and a lawsuit have in common?
Everyone is happy when the case is closed.

✳ Why was the piano invented?
So musicians would have a place to put their beer.

✳ The audience at a piano recital were appalled when a telephone rang just off stage. Without missing a note the soloist glanced towards the wings and called, 'If that's my agent, tell him I'm working!'

✳ The organ is the instrument of worship for in its sounding we sense the Majesty of God and in its ending we know the Grace of God.

✳ What is the difference between grade seven and grade eight viola? Grade eight viola requires you to assemble a music stand off by heart.

✳ How do you tell the difference between a violinist and a dog? The dog knows when to stop scratching.

✳ What's the difference between a violin and a viola? There is no difference. The violin just looks smaller because the violinist's head is so much bigger.

✳ Why do violinists put a cloth between their chin and their instrument? Violins don't have spit valves.

✳ Why should you never try to drive a roof nail with a violin? You might bend the nail.

✳ Why is a viola player like a terrorist? They both destroy bowings.

✳ What do a SCUD missile and a viola player have in common? They're both offensive and inaccurate.

✳ Why shouldn't violinists take up mountain climbing?
If they get lost, no one will look for them.

✳ What's the ideal weight for a professional viola player?
About twenty ounces – not counting the urn.

✳ Why did the Irishman only listen to his radio in the morning?
It said AM on the dial.

✳ Why are some violinists taking up the accordion? Upward mobility.

✳ How do you make a double bass sound in tune?
Chop it up and make it into a xylophone.

✳ Accordian to my music instructor and his staff, squeezing in more
rehearsal time is key to my success.

✳ A guitarist arrives at the rehearsal to find the bass player and the
drummer fighting.
'What's going on?' he asked.
The bass player replied, 'He de-tuned one of my strings!'
'That's OK,' said the guitarist. 'You can just tune it back up again.'
'I can't,' said the bass player. 'He won't tell me which one!'

✳ What did the guitarist do when his teacher told him to turn his amplifier
on? He caressed it softly and told it that he loved it.

✳ What do a vacuum cleaner and an electric guitar have in common?
Both suck when you plug them in.

✳ A man drafted a letter. 'Here on my estate on Monteverdi I attempted a Liszt of classical composers but had to go Bach because I couldn't get a Handel on it.'

✳ I'm always breaking into song – I can never find the right key!

✳ What's the difference between a banjo and a cattle grid?
You drive slowly over the cattle grid …

✳ How can you tell which kid on a playground is the child of a trombonist? He doesn't know how to use the slide, and he can't swing.

✳ What is the difference between a dead trombone player lying in the road, and a dead squirrel lying in the road? The squirrel might have been on his way to a gig.

✳ What kind of calendar does a trombonist use for his gigs?
Year-at-a-glance.

✳ Trombonists: It's difficult to trust anyone whose instrument changes shape as he plays.

✳ Why is the French horn a divine instrument?
Because a man blows in it, but only God knows what comes out of it.

✳ How do you fix a broken tuba? With tuba glue!

✳ Why are orchestra intermissions limited to twenty minutes?
So you don't have to retrain the drummers.

✳ How do you tell which car belongs to the drummer?
It's the only one with two dipsticks.

✳ What's the definition of a male quartet? Three men and a tenor.

✳ String quartet: a good violinist, a bad violinist, an ex-violinist, and someone who hates violinists, all getting together to complain about composers.

✳ What do you throw a drowning guitar player? His amp.

✳ What do you hear if you play new age music backwards?
New age music.

✳ How many guitar players does it take to cover 'House of the Rising Sun'? All of them, apparently.

✳ A trombone player and an accordion player are playing a New Year's Eve gig at a local club. The place is packed and everybody is absolutely loving the music.Shortly after midnight, the club owner comes up to the duo and says, 'You guys sound great. Everybody loves you ... I'd like to know if the two of you are free to come back here next New Year's Eve to play?'
The two musicians look at each other and then at the club owner ... and the trombone player says, 'Sure ... we'd love to ... is it OK if we leave our stuff here?'

✳ A sax player dies and goes to the pearly gates. St Peter looks in his book and says, 'Sorry: too much partying. You have to go to the other place.' The musician steps into the down elevator and pushes the button. It descends for hours, then the doors open and he finds himself looking into a huge nightclub. All the greatest musicians of all time are just leaving the stage on a break. He goes over to Charlie Parker and says, 'Hey, this can't be Hell. Look at who's in this band! Amazing.' Charlie Parker replies, 'You'd better believe it's Hell. Karen Carpenter is on drums!'

✳ What's a penguin's favourite musician? Seal.

✳ Why did the optician play jazz? So he could improve-eyes!

✳ A mind reader is at a nightclub one night and decides to give a small demonstration of her abilities.
First, she reads the mind of the lead guitarist: 'Wow, look at all the cute chicks who showed up tonight! Good crowd!'
Then the drummer: 'Lots of people showed up tonight … Great, we're going to make good money tonight.'
Then the keyboard player: 'All three of these guys have no appreciation of my talent … What a bunch of losers.'
Finally, the bass player: 'C … G … C … G … '

You're too old to be a working musician if:

- It becomes more important to find a place on stage for your fan than for your amp.
- All your fans leave by 9.30 p.m.
- All you want from groupies is a foot massage and back rub.
- You need your glasses to see the amp settings.

- You love taking the lift because you can sing along with most of your play list.
- You've thrown out your back jumping off the stage.
- You feel debauched and incoherent before the gig starts.
- You stop the set because your blood pressure pills fell behind the speakers.
- Most of your crowd just sways in their seats.
- You refuse to play without earplugs.
- You ask the club owner if you can start at 7.30 instead of 9.30.
- You check the TV schedule before booking a gig.
- Your gig stool has a back.
- You need a nap before the gig.
- During the breaks, you now go to the van to lie down.
- You prefer a music stand with a light.
- You don't recover from a Saturday night gig until Tuesday afternoon.
- You buy amps considering their weight and not their tone or cool factor.
- You can remember seven different club names for the same location …
- You think 'homey' means cosy and warm.
- You have to look over your glasses to check your PA connections.
- In consideration of your age, the audience requests some British invasion.
- You start listing your truss as a 'business expense'.
- When you get a 'Cease and Desist' letter from the Spandex co.
- When the only 'stones' you care about are in your gallbladder or kidney.
- You have to charge extra money if there are any steps to climb.
- You call out the next song only to have someone remind you played it ten minutes earlier.
- Your drugs are keeping you alive rather than killing you.

- You worry more about breaking a hip than being hip.
- The only white powder to be found among the band members is foot talc.

＊ A man walks into a pet shop wanting a parrot. The owner shows him two beautiful ones out on the floor. 'This one's five thousand pounds and the other is ten thousand,' he says.

'Wow! What does the five thousand pound one do?'

'This parrot can sing every aria Mozart ever wrote.'

'And the other?' said the customer.

'This one can sing Wagner's entire Ring cycle. There's another one in the back room for thirty thousand.'

'Holy moly! What does that one do?'

'Nothing that I can tell, but the other two parrots call him "Maestro".'

＊ A man walks into the doctor's office and says, 'Doc, I haven't had a bowel movement in a week!'

The doctor gives him a prescription for a mild laxative and tells him, 'If it doesn't work, let me know.'

A week later the guy is back: 'Doc, still no movement!'

The doctor says, 'Hmm, guess you need something stronger,' and prescribes a powerful laxative.

Still another week later the poor guy is back: 'Doc, STILL nothing!'

The doctor, worried, says, 'We'd better get some more information about you to try to figure out what's going on. What do you do for a living?'

'I'm a musician.'

The doctor looks up and says, 'Well, that's it! Here's ten pounds. Go and get something to eat!'

✳ On a music shop door: Gone Chopin: Bach soon.

✳ Did you hear about the band who were thrown out of their hotel?
  Excessive sax and violins.

The rulebook of the blues

The blues are not about limitless choice, trust funds, golden parachutes, BMWs, opera, or environmental impact statements.

Blues cars are Chevies and Cadillacs. Other acceptable blues transportation is the Greyhound bus or a southbound train. Walkin' plays a major part in the blues lifestyle. So does fixin' to die.

Teenagers can't sing the blues. Adults sing the blues. Blues adulthood means old enough to get the electric chair if you shoot a man in Memphis.

You can have the blues in New York City, but not in Paris or Vienna. Hard times in St Tropez or Jamaica are just a depression. Chicago, St Louis and Kansas City are still the best places to have the blues.

✳ The following colours do not belong in the blues:
  a. violet
  b. beige
  c. mauve
  d. taupe

✳ Good places for the blues:
  a. the highway
  b. the jailhouse
  c. an empty bed

✳ Bad places for the blues:
  a. Gallery openings
  b. Weekend in the country
  c. Harrods

✳ You can tell it's the blues if:
  a. Your first name is a southern state – like Georgia.
  b. You're blind.
  c. You shot a man in Memphis.
  d. Your woman can't be satisfied.

✳ It's not the blues if:
  a. You were once blind but now can see.
  b. You have a trust fund.
  c. You hold elected office.
  d. Your woman CAN be satisfied.

✳ Chances are if you can't find your baby, she is with your best friend.

✳ While you may share your troubles, no one will know them.

✳ The preacher man is frequently of no comfort.

✳ Your happiness is directly linked to the day of the week.

✳ A moderate case of the blues has never been recorded.

✳ What does it say on a blues player's gravestone? 'I didn't wake up this morning.'

✳ A bagpiper was asked by a funeral director to play at a graveside service for a homeless man. He had no family or friends, so the service was to be at a pauper's cemetery in the country.

As he was not familiar with the area, the bagpiper got lost; and being a typical man he didn't stop for directions. He finally arrived an hour late and saw the funeral director had evidently gone, and the hearse was nowhere in sight.

There were only the diggers and crew left and they were eating lunch. The bagpiper felt bad and apologised to the men for being late. He went to the side of the grave and looked down and the vault lid was already in place. He didn't know what else to do, so he started to play.

The workers put down their lunches and began to gather around.

He played out his heart and soul for this man with no family and friends; he played like he'd never played before for this homeless man.

And as he played 'Amazing Grace', the workers began to weep.

They wept, he wept, they all wept together. When he finished the piper packed up his bagpipes and started for his car.

As he opened the door to my car, he overheard one of the workers say, 'I never seen nothin' like that before and I've been putting in septic tanks for twenty years.'

Some musical terms

Metronome: a city-dwelling dwarf.

Allegro: leg fertiliser.

Bach chorale: the place behind the barn where you keep the horses.

Bossa nova: the car your foreman drives.

Guitars are better than women because:

- A guitar has a volume knob.
- If you break a guitar's G-string, it only costs seventy-nine pence for a new one.
- You can unplug a guitar.
- If your guitar doesn't make sounds you like, you can retune it.
- If your guitar strings are too heavy, you can just get a lighter set.
- You can have a guitar professionally adjusted to your liking.
- You can go to a guitar shop and play all the guitars you want for free.
- You can take lessons on how to play a guitar without feeling embarrassed.
- You can rent a guitar without worrying about who rented it before you.
- You can get rich playing a guitar, not broke.
- A guitar doesn't take half of everything you own when you sell it.

Some real country song titles:

* If My Nose Were Full of Nickels, I'd Blow It All On You
* Drop Kick Me, Jesus, Through the Goalposts Of Life
* Get Your Tongue Outta My Mouth 'Cause I'm Kissing You Goodbye
* Her Teeth Were Stained, But Her Heart Was Pure
* Been Roped And Thrown By Jesus In The Holy Ghost Corral
* I Don't Know Whether to Kill Myself Or Go Bowling
* I Fell In a Pile Of You And Got Love All Over Me
* I Keep Forgettin' I Forgot About You
* I Wanna Whip Your Cow
* I Would Have Wrote You A Letter, But I Couldn't Spell Yuck!
* I Wouldn't Take Her To A Dawg Fight, Cause I'm Afraid She'd Win
* If The Phone Don't Ring, Baby, You'll Know It's Me
* If You Don't Leave Me Alone, I'll Go And Find Someone Else Who Will
* Mama Get the Hammer (There's A Fly On Papa's Head)
* My Every Day Silver Is Plastic
* My Head Hurts, My Feet Stink, And I Don't Love Jesus
* My Wife Ran Off With My Best Friend, and I Sure Do Miss Him
* She Got The Gold Mine And I Got The Shaft; She Got The Ring And I Got The Finger
* She Made Toothpicks Out Of The Timber Of My Heart
* They May Put Me In Prison, But They Can't Stop My Face From Breakin' Out
* When You Leave Walk Out Backwards, So I'll Think You're Walking In
* You Can't Have Your Kate And Edith Too
* You Done Tore Out My Heart And Stomped That Sucker Flat
* You're The Reason Our Kids Are So Ugly

※ What do you call a building full of guitarists? Jail.

✳ What do you get when you cross a piccolo with a clarinet? An earache.

✳ A singer went for an audition with a pianist. After a few bars he winced and waved her to be silent. 'I'm sorry,' he said, 'you're not right for this job. I play the black notes, I play the white notes. But you, you sing in the cracks.'

✳ Why can't policeman play the drums? They are often off-beat.

✳ Did you see the radio DJ in his car? He gave a short wave.

✳ Sign on a music store window: 'Come in and pick out a drum – then beat it!'

✳ Did you hear about the woman who could only compose music in 3/4 time? She had waltz timer's disease.

✳ If you can't find anyone to sing with you have to duet yourself.

✳ I wanted to be a clarinettist but I couldn't reed music.

✳ Did you hear about the robbery at the music shop?
The thief got away with the lute!

✳ Some musicians can be sharp, which is not natural.

✳ Where would you take a faulty harpsichord?
A shop for baroque instruments.

* When a jazz musician's clothes are all worn out it's ragtime.

* Did you hear about the man who tried to play the shoehorn?
  He only got footnotes.

* What should you do if you break a guitar string? Don't fret!

* The consequence of playing drums often is re-percussions.

* Those who hate classical music have my symphony.

* What's the definition of a rock group? First, they get stoned. Then they
  get petrified.

* Have you heard the soundtrack for the killer whale film?
  It is well orcastrated.

* When a musician's toupee fell into his saxophone he blew his top.

* The novel about a musician in treble was a real clef-hanger.

* Musicians need a leader because they don't know how to conduct
  themselves.

* Old musicians never die, they are just disconcerted.

* Some soloists are so bad they should sing tenor twelve miles away.

* Violinists are often fiddling around.

* I bought a metronome for twenty quid. You can't beat that price.

* Did you hear about the drummer who broke his drum and was sacked from the band for being a dead-beat?

* Composers can use lots of note paper.

* What did the musician who refused to get out of bed write?
  Sheet music.

NATURE AND GARDENING

✳ What lives in winter, dies in summer, and grows with its root upward?
An icicle.

✳ Did you hear about the man whose new garden borders caused
a fence?

✳ The bowls club are going to relay their grass. It was a turf decision.

✳ How do you become a good gardener?
You have to know the ground rules.

✳ What kind of socks does a gardener wear? Garden hose!

✳ When I bought some fruit trees the nursery owner gave me some
insects to help with pollination. They were free bees.

✳ I saw a documentary about beavers the other night. It was the best dam programme I ever saw.

✳ Never plant a larger garden than your wife can take care of.

✳ A farmer purchased an old, run-down, abandoned farm with plans to turn it into a thriving enterprise. The fields were grown over with weeds, the farmhouse was falling apart, and the fences were broken down. During his first day of work, the town preacher stops by to bless the man's work, saying, 'May you and God work together to make this the farm of your dreams!'
A few months later, the preacher stops by again to call on the farmer. Lo and behold, it's a completely different place. The farmhouse is completely rebuilt and in excellent condition, there is plenty of cattle and other livestock happily munching on feed in well-fenced pens, and the fields are filled with crops planted in neat rows.
'Amazing!' the preacher says. 'Look what God and you have accomplished together!'
'Yes, reverend,' says the farmer, 'but remember what the farm was like when God was working it alone!'

✳ Simultaneous management of elephants and walruses requires the ability to multitusk.

✳ Have you heard of the plot by earthworms to take over the world? It's called global worming.

✳ When a snail loses its shell it looks sluggish.

* The best thing about snow is that it makes your lawn look as good as the neighbours'.

* What do you get if you cross a four-leaf clover with poison ivy? A rash of good luck.

* Beautifully manicured lawns are highly sod after.

* The chickens were distraught when the tornado destroyed their home. Hopefully they will be able to recoup.

Gardening is better than sex because:

It's absolutely acceptable to garden before you're married.

You don't have to shower and shave before gardening.

You don't have to hide your gardening magazines.

Telling gardening jokes, and inviting co-workers to garden with you, is not considered workplace harassment.

Email with gardening content is not considered offensive material.

When you become famous, you don't have to worry about pictures and videotapes of you gardening being shown on the internet.

It's perfectly respectable to enjoy gardening with a total stranger.

Every time you garden, you hope to produce fruit.

Nobody will ever tell you that you will go blind if you garden by yourself.

You can have a gardening-related calendar on your wall at the office.

No one objects if you watch the gardening channel on television.

* Why did the thieves raid the monkey house at the zoo? Because they believed in gibbon take.

* A friend told me he dug a hole in my backyard and filled it with water. I thought he meant well.

✪ OLD AGE

✳ What superhero uses public transport? Bus Lightyear!

✳ Two police officers find an old woman staggering down the street. They stop her, and can tell she has had far too much to drink. Instead of taking her to the police station they decide to just drive her home. They load her into the police car and one of the officers gets in the back with the drunk woman. As they drive through the streets they keep asking the woman where she lives. But all she will say as she strokes the officer's arm is 'You're passionate.'

They drive on and ask again, and again the same response as she strokes his arm, 'You're passionate.'

The officers by now are getting a little upset so they stop the car and say to the woman, 'Look, we've driven around for two hours and you still haven't told us where you live.'

'I keep trying to tell you,' she replies. 'You're passin' it!'

✳ By yourself you're in the right. In a group you're in the throng.

✳ My sweet old granny is so old she's started to granulate.

✳ A small-town lawyer called his first witness to the stand in a trial –
a grandmotherly, elderly woman. He approached her and asked,
'Mrs Jones, do you know me?'
She responded, 'Why, yes, I do know you, Mr Williams. I've known you
since you were a young boy. And frankly, you've been a big
disappointment to me. You lie, you cheat on your wife, you manipulate
people and talk about them behind their backs. You think you're a rising
big shot when you haven't the brains to realise you never will amount to
anything more than a two-bit paper pusher. Yes, I know you.'
The lawyer was stunned. Not knowing what else to do he pointed
across the room and asked, 'Mrs Williams, do you know the defence?'
She again replied, 'Why, yes I do. I've known Mr Bradley since he was a
youngster, too. I used to babysit him for his parents. And he, too, has
been a real disappointment to me. He's lazy, bigoted, he has a drinking
problem. The man can't build a normal relationship with anyone and his
law practice is one of the shoddiest in the entire state. Yes, I know him.'
At this point the judge rapped the courtroom to silence and called both
solicitors to the bench. In a very quiet voice, he said with menace,
'If either of you asks her if she knows me, you'll be in jail for contempt
within five minutes!'

✳ The headlines nobody likes are wrinkles.

✳ The best thing about old age senility is that you can hide your own
Easter eggs.

✳ An elderly man was moaning to a friend: 'I've got old. I've had two bypass surgeries. A hip replacement and new knees. Fought prostate cancer and diabetes. I'm half blind, can't hear anything quieter than a jet engine, take forty different medications that make me dizzy, winded, and subject to blackouts. Have bouts with dementia. Have poor circulation, hardly feel my hands and feet any more. Can't remember if I'm eighty-five or ninety-two. Have lost all my friends. But … Thank God, I still have my Eastbourne driver's licence!'

✳ Since Granny went senile all she does all day is stare through the window – maybe in this cold weather we should let her in.

✳ You know you're getting old when you can pinch an inch … on your forehead.

✳ As you get older three things happen: first, your memory goes, and I can't remember the other two.

✳ An elderly gentleman had serious hearing problems for a number of years. He went to the doctor and the doctor was able to have him fitted for a set of hearing aids that allowed the gentleman to hear one hundred per cent. The elderly gentleman went back in a month to the doctor and the doctor said, 'Your hearing is perfect. Your family must be really pleased that you can hear again.'
The gentleman replied, 'Oh, I haven't told my family yet. I just sit around and listen to the conversations. I've changed my will three times!'

✳ One day an old man approached Downing Street from across Whitehall, where he'd been sitting on a bench. He spoke to the policeman standing guard and said, 'I would like to go in and meet with Prime Minister Tony Blair.'

The policeman replied, 'Sir, Mr Blair is not Prime Minister and doesn't reside here.'

The old man said, 'OK,' and walked away.

The following day, the same man approached the gates of Downing Street and said to the same policeman, 'I would like to go in and meet with Prime Minister Tony Blair.'

The constable again told the man, 'Sir, as I said yesterday, Mr Blair is not PM and doesn't reside here.'

The man thanked him and again walked away.

The third day, the same man approached Downing Street and spoke to the very same policeman, saying, 'I would like to go in and meet with Prime Minister Tony Blair.'

The policeman, understandably agitated at this point, looked at the man and said, 'Sir, this is the third day in a row you have been here asking to speak to Mr Blair. I've told you already several times that Mr Blair is not the PM and doesn't reside here. Don't you understand?'

The old man answered, 'Oh, I understand you fine. I just love hearing your answer!'

The policeman snapped to attention, saluted, and said, 'See you tomorrow.'

✳ Artificial knees and elbows were developed during a joint project.

✳ Two old ladies, Ethel and Rose, always meet every week and always end up having a light lunch at their favourite cafe. One day over lunch, Ethel says to Rose, 'All we ever seem to do is talk about the unimportant things in life. Today, for example, we've talked about the rudeness of our local butcher, what the weather's like in Bournemouth, and our vicar's recent poor sermon. Next time we meet, why don't we have a serious discussion on world affairs?'

'A good idea,' says Rose.

So the following week, while they are waiting for their lunch to arrive, Rose says, 'So let's talk about world affairs.'

Ethel says, 'OK. What do you think about the situation with Red China?'

Rose replies, 'Not much – it won't go with your green tablecloth.'

* Two gentlemen from a retirement home were sitting on a bench under a tree when one turns to the other and says: 'Eric, I'm eighty-three years old now and I'm just full of aches and pains. I know you're about my age. How do you feel?'

Eric says, 'I feel just like a newborn baby.'

'Really!? Like a newborn baby!?'

'Yep. No hair, no teeth, and I think I just wet my pants.'

* A senior citizen said to his eighty-year-old buddy:

'So I hear you're getting married?'

'Yep!'

'Do I know her?'

'Nope!'

'This woman, is she good-looking?'

'Not really.'

'Is she a good cook?'

'Naw, she can't cook too well.'

'Does she have lots of money?'

'Nope! Poor as a church mouse.'

'Well, then, is she good in bed?'

'I don't know.'

'Why in the world do you want to marry her then?'

'Because she can still drive!'

✳ An eighty-two-year-old man went to the doctor to get a physical.

A few days later, the doctor saw the old gent walking down the street with a gorgeous young woman on his arm.

A couple of days later, the doctor spoke to him and said, 'You're really doing great, aren't you?'

The old chap replied, 'Just doing what you said, Doc: "Get a hot mamma and be cheerful."'

The doctor said, 'I didn't say that. I said, "You've got a heart murmur; be careful."'

✳ Q: As people age, do they sleep more soundly?

A: Yes, but usually in the afternoon.

Old age – if only we could live life backwards

- You start out dead and get that out of the way right off the bat.
- Then, you wake up in a nursing home feeling better every day.
- When you are kicked out of the home for being too healthy, you spend several years enjoying your retirement and collecting pension cheques.
- When you start work, you get a gold watch on your first day.
- You work forty years or so, getting younger every day until pretty soon you're too young to work.
- So then, you go to school: play sports, date, drink and party.
- As you get even younger, you become a kid again.
- You go to infants' school, play, and have no responsibilities.

- In a few years, you become a baby and everyone runs themselves ragged keeping you happy.
- You spend your last nine months floating peacefully in luxury, spa-like conditions: central heating, room service on tap.
- Until finally ... you finish off as an orgasm.

Smash hits for the ageing

The Bee Gees: How Can You Mend a Broken Hip?

Roberta Flack: The First Time Ever I Forgot Your Face

Johnny Nash: I Can't See Clearly Now

Paul Simon: Fifty Ways to Lose Your Liver

The Commodores: Once, Twice, Three Times to the Bathroom

Procol Harem: A Whiter Shade of Grey

Leo Sayer: You Make Me Feel Like Napping

The Temptations: Papa's Got a Kidney Stone

Abba: Denture Queen

Leslie Gore: It's My Heart Attack, and I'll Cry If I Want To

☀ Q: What can a man do while his wife is going through menopause?
A: Keep busy. If you're handy with tools, you can finish the extension. When you are done you will have a place to live.

* There was an old lady who was accused of stealing a brooch, but the police couldn't pin it on her.

* Old people are valuable
  They have silver in their hair,
  They have gold in their teeth.
  They have stones in their kidneys.
  They have lead in their feet.
  And they are loaded with natural gas!

The Senility Prayer

Grant me the senility to forget the people I never liked anyway,
the good fortune to run into the ones I do,
and the eyesight to tell the difference.

* Just before the funeral service, the undertaker came up to the very elderly widow and asked, 'How old was your husband?'
  'Ninety-eight.' she replied,'Two years older than I am.'
  'So you're ninety-six?' the undertaker commented.
  She responded, 'Hardly worth going home, is it?'

* The irate customer called the newspaper office, loudly demanding to know where her Sunday edition was. 'Ma'am,' said the employee, 'today is Saturday. The Sunday paper is not delivered until Sunday.' There was a long pause on the other end of the phone, followed by a ray of recognition. 'I'll bet that's why no one was in church today too.'

✳ Have you heard about the elderly keep-fit video – Pumping Rust.

✳ An elderly man was thinking about how people seem to read the Bible a whole lot more as they get older. Then, it dawned on him – they were cramming for their finals.

✳ He used to be tough and ruthless. Now he's rough and toothless.

PARENTS AND PARENTING

* The advice your son rejected is now being given by him to your grandson.

* In 1900, fathers could count on children to join the family business. Today, fathers pray their kids will soon come home from college long enough to teach them how to work the computer and set up the DVD player.

* Two ladies were discussing the planetarium show they had just seen. One said the show was fantastic. The other agreed but added, 'Most of it was over my head.'

* A boy asks his father to explain the differences between irritation, aggravation, and frustration. Dad picks up the phone and dials a number at random. When the phone is answered he asks, 'Can I speak to Alf, please?'

'No! There's no one called Alf here.' The person hangs up.

'That's irritation,' says Dad.

He picks up the phone again, dials the same number and asks for Alf a second time.

'No – there's no one here called Alf. Go away. If you call again I shall telephone the police.'

'That's aggravation.'

'Then what's frustration?' asks his son.

The father picks up the phone and dials a third time:

'Hello, this is Alf. Have I received any phone calls?'

Things only a mother would say...

- MONA LISA'S MOTHER: 'After all that money you father and I spent on braces, Mona, that's the biggest smile you can give us?'
- HUMPTY DUMPTY'S MOTHER: 'Humpty, if I've told you once, I've told you a hundred times not to sit on the wall. But would you listen to me?'
- COLUMBUS'S MOTHER: 'I don't care what you've discovered, Christopher, you could have written!'
- MICHELANGELO'S MOTHER: 'Mike, can't you paint on walls like other children? Do you have any idea how hard it is to get that stuff off the ceiling?'
- NAPOLEON'S MOTHER: 'All right, Napoleon. If you're not hiding your report card inside your jacket, then take your hand out of there and prove it!'
- MARY'S MOTHER: 'I'm not upset that your lamb followed you to school, Mary, but I would like to know how he got a better mark than you!'
- BATMAN'S MOTHER: 'It's a nice car, Bruce, but do you realise how much the insurance will be!'

- GOLDILOCK'S MOTHER: 'I've got a bill here for a broken chair from the bear family. You know anything about this, Goldie?'
- LITTLE MISS MUFFET'S MOTHER: 'Well, all I've got to say is if you don't get off your tuffet and start cleaning your room, there'll be a lot more spiders around here!'
- ALBERT EINSTEIN'S MOTHER: 'But, Albert, it's your school picture. Can't you do something about your hair? Styling gel, mousse, something … ?'
- JONAH'S MOTHER: 'That's a nice story, but now tell me where you've really been for the past three days!'
- SUPERMAN'S MOTHER: 'Clark, your father and I have discussed it, and we've decided you can have your own telephone line. Now will you stop spending so much time in all those phone booths!'
- THOMAS EDISON'S MOTHER: 'Of course I'm proud that you invented the electric light bulb, dear. Now turn off that light and get to bed!'

✳ Mary was almost driven to distraction by her three kids.
She complained to her best friend, 'They're driving me nuts.
Such pests, they give me no rest and I'm halfway to the nuthouse.'
'What you need is a playpen to separate the kids from yourself,'
her friend said. So Mary bought a playpen. A few days later, her friend called to ask how things were going.
'Superb! I can't believe it,' Mary said. 'I get in that pen with a good book and the kids don't bother me one bit!'

✳ A small boy is sent to bed by his father …
[Five minutes later]
'Da-ad … '
'What?'

'I'm thirsty. Can you bring me a drink of water?'

'No. You had your chance. Lights out.'

[Five minutes later]

'Da-aaaad … '

'WHAT?'

'I'm THIRSTY … Can I have a drink of water??'

'I told you NO! If you ask again I'll have to spank you!!'

[Five minutes later]

'Daaaa-aaaAAAAD … '

'WHAT??!!'

'When you come in to spank me, can you bring me a drink of water?'

✳ A man said to his daughter, 'I want you home by eleven o'clock.'
  She said, 'But, Dad, I'm no longer a child!'
   'I know, that's why I want you home by eleven,' he replied.

✳ A woman meant to call a record shop but dialled the wrong number
  and got a private home instead.
  'Do you have "Eyes of Blue" and "A Love Supreme"?' she asked.
  'Well, no,' answered the puzzled homeowner. 'But I have a wife and
  eleven children.'
  'Is that a record?' she enquired.
  'I don't think so,' replied the man, 'but it's as close as I want to get!'

✳ Living the dream isn't owning your own house – it's getting your kids to
  leave it.

✳ Two newlyweds were deciding whether to get a puppy or have a baby.
  They weren't sure if they wanted to ruin their lives or their carpet.

✳ The easiest way to get a child's attention is to sit down and look comfortable

Laws of nature

- A child's eagerness to assist in any project varies in inverse proportion to the ability to actually do the work involved.
- Leftovers always expand to fill all available containers plus one.
- A newly washed window gathers dirt at double the speed of an unwashed window.
- The availability of a ballpoint pen is inversely proportional to how badly it is needed.
- The same clutter that will fill a one-car garage will fill a two-car garage.
- Three children plus two biscuits equals a fight.
- The potential for disaster is in direct proportion to the number of TV remote controls divided by the number of viewers.
- The number of doors left open varies inversely with the outdoor temperature.
- The capacity of any hot water heater is equal to one and a half sibling showers.
- What goes up must come down, except for bubble gum, kites and slightly used Rice Krispies.
- Place two children in a room full of toys and they will both want to play with the same toy.

✳ A man and his wife were making their first doctor's visit, the wife being pregnant with their first child. After everything checked out, the doctor took a small stamp and stamped the wife's stomach with indelible ink. The couple was curious about what the stamp was for, so when they got home, the husband got out his magnifying glass to try to see what it was.

In very tiny letters, the stamp said, 'When you can read this, come back and see me.'

✳ A man was found passed out in a dead faint by his front door. Neighbours dialled 999. When the paramedics arrived, they helped him regain consciousness and asked if he knew what caused him to faint. 'It was enough to make anybody faint,' he said. 'My son asked me for the keys to the garage, and instead of driving the car out, he came out with the lawn mower.'

✳ A confused nine-year-old goes up to his mother and asks, 'Is God male or female?'

After thinking for a moment, his mother responds, 'Well, honey, God is both male and female.'

This confuses the little boy, so he asks, 'Is God black or white?'

'Well, God is both black and white.'

This further confuses the boy so he asks, 'Is God gay or straight?'

At this the mother is getting concerned, but answers nonetheless, 'Honey, God is both gay and straight.'

At this the boy's face lights up with understanding and he triumphantly asks, 'Mum, is God Michael Jackson?'

✳ A little girl asked her mum, 'Mum, may I take the dog for a walk around the block?' Mum says, 'No, because the dog is on heat.' 'What's that mean?' asked the child. 'Go ask your dad. I think he's in the garage'. The little girl goes to the garage and says, 'Dad, can I take Susie for a walk around the block? I asked Mum but she said the dog was on heat and that I should ask you.' Dad said, 'Bring Susie over here.' He took a rag, soaked it with petrol, and scrubbed the dog's rear with it and said, 'OK, you can go now but keep Susie on the leash and only go one time around the block.' The little girl left and returned a few minutes later with no dog on the leash. Dad said, 'Where's Susie?' The little girl said, 'Susie ran out of petrol about halfway down the street and there's another dog pushing her home.'

✳ A little boy was overheard talking to himself as he strode through his back garden, cricket cap in place and toting ball and bat.
'I'm the greatest cricket player in the world,' he said proudly.
Then he tossed the ball in the air, swung, and missed. Undaunted, he picked up the ball, threw it into the air and said to himself, 'I'm the greatest player ever!'
He swung at the ball again, and again he missed. He paused a moment to examine bat and ball carefully. Then once again he threw the ball into the air and said, 'I'm the greatest cricket player who ever lived.'
He swung the bat hard and again missed the ball.
'Wow!' he exclaimed. 'What a bowler!'

✳ A six-year-old comes crying to his mother because his little sister pulled his hair. 'Don't be angry,' the mother says, 'your little sister doesn't realise that pulling hair hurts.' A short while later, there's more crying, and the mother goes to investigate. This time the sister is bawling and her brother says, 'Now she knows.'

Preparing for parenthood

- WOMEN: To prepare for maternity, put on a dressing gown and stick a beanbag down the front. Leave it there for nine months. After nine months, remove ten per cent of the beans.
- MEN: To prepare for paternity, go the local chemist's, tip the contents of your wallet on the counter, and tell the pharmacist to help himself. Next, go to the supermarket. Arrange to have your salary paid directly to its head office. Go home. Pick up the paper and read it for the last time.

  Before you finally go ahead and have children, find a couple who are already parents and berate them about their methods of discipline, lack of patience, appallingly low tolerance levels, and how they have allowed their children to run wild. Suggest ways in which they might improve their child's sleeping habits, toilet training, table manners, and overall behaviour. Enjoy it – it's the last time in your life that you will have all the answers.

  To discover how the nights feel, walk around the living room from 5 p.m. until 10 p.m. carrying a wet bag weighing approximately 8–12 pounds. At 10 p.m. put the bag down, set the alarm for midnight, and go to sleep. Get up at midnight and walk around the living room again with the bag until 1 a.m. Put the alarm on for 3 a.m. Since you can't go back to sleep, get up at 2 a.m. and make a pot of tea. Go to bed at 2:45 a.m. Get up again at 3 a.m. when the alarm goes off, sing songs in the dark until 4 a.m. Put the alarm on for 5 a.m. Get up. Make breakfast. Keep this up for five years. Look cheerful.

  Can you stand the mess children make? To find out, smear peanut butter onto the sofa and jam onto the curtains. Hide a fish finger behind the stereo and leave it there all summer. Stick your fingers in the flowerbeds then rub them on the clean walls. Cover the stains with crayons. How does that look?

Dressing small children is not as easy as it seems: first, buy an octopus and a string bag. Attempt to put the octopus into the string bag so that none of the arms hang out. Time allowed for this – all morning. Get ready to go out. Wait outside the toilet for half an hour. Go out the front door. Come in again. Go out. Come back in. Go out again. Walk down the front path. Walk back up it again. Walk down it again. Walk very slowly down the road for five minutes. Stop to inspect minutely every cigarette butt, piece of used chewing gum, dirty tissue, and dead insect along the way. Retrace your steps. Scream that you've had as much as you can stand until all the neighbours come out and stare at you. Give up and go back in the house. You're now just about ready to try taking a small child for a walk.

Always repeat everything you say at least five times.

Go to your local supermarket. Take the nearest thing you can find to a pre-school child with you. A fully grown goat is excellent. If you intend to have more than one child, take more than one goat. Buy your week's groceries without letting the goats out of your sight. Pay for everything the goats eat or destroy. Until you can easily accomplish this DO NOT even contemplate having children.

Hollow out a melon. Make a small hole in the side. Suspend it from the ceiling and swing it from side to side. Now get a bowl of soggy Weetabix and attempt to spoon it into the hole of the swaying melon by pretending to be an aeroplane. Continue until half of the Weetabix is gone. Tip the rest into your lap, making sure that a lot of it falls on the floor. You are now ready to feed a nine-month-old child.

✳ Jimmy's mum dragged him in front of his dad during the football game on TV. 'Talk to your son,' she said. 'He refuses to obey a word I say.' The father turned to Jimmy angrily. 'Jimmy, how dare you disobey your mother? Do you think you're better than your old man?'

✳ A child went up to its father and asked, 'Daddy, what's telepathy?'
'It's when two people are thinking the same thought at the same time,' replied the dad.
'Like you and Mummy?'
'No, son, when Mummy and I are thinking the same thought, that's called coincidence.'

✳ 'Oh, no!' he gasped as he surveyed the disaster before him. Never in his forty years of life had he seen anything like it. How anyone could have survived he did not know. He could only hope that somewhere amid the overwhelming destruction he would find his sixteen-year-old son. Only the slim hope of finding him kept him from turning and fleeing the scene.
He took a deep breath and proceeded. Walking was virtually impossible with so many things strewn across his path. He moved ahead slowly. 'Son! Son!' he whispered to himself.
He tripped and almost fell several times. He heard someone, or something, move. At least he thought he did. Perhaps he was just hoping he did. He shook his head and felt his gut tighten. He couldn't understand how this could have happened. There was some light but not enough to see very much. Something cold and wet brushed against his hand. He jerked it away.
In desperation, he took another step then cried out, 'Son!'
From a nearby pile of unidentified material, he heard his son.

'Yes, Dad,' he said, in a voice so weak it could hardly be heard.
'It's time to get up and get ready for school,' the man sighed. 'And for heaven's sake, clean up this room!'

✳ One evening recently, a mother entered her daughter's bedroom to discover it empty. As she looked around, she spied a letter over the bed. With trembling hands and a terrible sense of foreboding, she read …

> *Dear Mum,*
> *Please don't be cross, but I eloped with my new boyfriend. I finally found real love and he is so nice, Mum, with all his piercings and tattoos and his big motorbike. Not only that, I'm pregnant and Osama says we're going to be really happy in his cave in the hills.*
> *He wants to have lots more children with me and you know that's one of my dreams too. Also, he taught me that marijuana doesn't hurt anyone and we're going to grow it for us and his friends, who will pay us by giving us all the cocaine and ecstasy we'll ever need and we'll pray every day for scientists to find the cure for the addiction gene so that Osama can get better. He deserves it.*
> *Don't worry, Mum, I'm fifteen years old now and I know how to take care of myself. Some day I'll visit so you can get to know your grandchildren.*
> *Your daughter, Karen*

After fainting, Mum came to and read the rest of the letter …

> *PS: Mum, it's not true. I'm next door at Chloe's house. I just wanted to show you that there are worse things in life than the report card on my desk …*

✳ A frustrated father was moaning in pub, 'When I was a youngster, I was disciplined by being sent to my room without tea. But in my son's room, he has his own TV, telephone, computer, and CD player.'
'So what did you do?' asked his friend.
'I sent him to MY room!' exclaimed the father.

✳ A country doctor went way out to the sticks to deliver a baby. It was so far out, there was no electricity. When he arrived, no one was home except for the labouring mother and her five-year-old child. The doctor instructed the child to hold a lantern high so he could see, while he helped the woman deliver the baby. The child did so, the mother pushed and after a little while the doctor lifted the newborn baby by the feet and spanked him on the bottom to get him to take his first breath. The doctor then asked the five-year-old what he thought of the baby. 'Hit him again,' the five-year-old said. 'He shouldn't have crawled up there in the first place!'

✳ A young child was practising spelling with magnetic letters on the refrigerator: cat, dog, dad, and mum had been proudly displayed for all to see.
One morning while getting ready for the day, he bounded into the room with his arms outstretched. In his hands were three magnetic letters: G-O-D.
'Look what I spelled, Mum!' he said with a proud smile on his face.
'That's wonderful!' his mum praised him. 'Now go put them on the fridge so Dad can see when he gets home tonight.'
The mum happily thought that her son's Catholic education was certainly having an impact. Just then, a little voice called from the kitchen: 'Mum? How do you spell "zilla"?'

✳ A little boy is stopped by the vicar at Sunday School: 'Your mummy is very religious, you say. She says her prayers every night, just like you should. Tell me, what does your mummy pray exactly?'
'Thank God he's in bed,' replies the little boy.

Motherhood: the evolution

YOUR CLOTHES:
First baby: You begin wearing maternity clothes as soon as your doctor confirms your pregnancy.
Second baby: You wear your regular clothes for as long as possible. .
Third baby: Your maternity clothes are your regular clothes.

THE BABY'S NAME:
First baby: You pore over baby-name books and practise pronouncing and writing combinations of all your favourites.
Second baby: Someone has to name their kid after your great-aunt Mavis, right? It might as well be you.
Third baby: You open a name book, close your eyes, and see where your finger falls. Sherlock? Perfect!

PREPARING FOR THE BIRTH:
First baby: You practise your breathing religiously.
Second baby: You don't bother practising because you remember that last time, breathing didn't do a thing.
Third baby: You ask for an epidural in your eighth month.

THE NURSERY:
First baby: You prewash your newborn's clothes, colour-coordinate them, and fold them neatly in the baby's little drawers.

Second baby: You check to make sure that the clothes are clean and discard only the ones with the darkest stains.

Third baby: Boys can wear pink, can't they?

WORRIES:

First baby: At the first sign of distress – a whimper, a frown – you pick up the baby.

Second baby: You pick the baby up when her wails threaten to wake your firstborn.

Thirs baby: You teach your three-year-old how to rewind the mechanical swing.

ACTIVITIES:

First baby: You take your infant to Baby Gymnastics, Baby Massage, and Baby Story Hour.

Second baby: You take your infant to Baby Gymnastics.

Third baby: You take your infant to the supermarket and the dry cleaner.

GOING OUT:

First baby: The first time you leave your baby with a sitter, you call home five times.

Second baby: Just before you walk out the door, you remember to leave a number where you can be reached.

Third baby: You leave instructions for the sitter to call only if she sees blood.

AT HOME:

First baby: You spend a good bit of every day just gazing at the baby.

Second baby: You spend a bit of every day watching to be sure your

older child isn't squeezing, poking, or hitting the baby.
Third baby: You spend a little bit of every day hiding from the children.

PETS AND VETS

* My pet is very agreeable. He's a seeing-eye-to-eye dog.

* The cat took up computer lessons in the hope of mastering its grip on a mouse.

* Young animal doctors are vet behind the ears.

* A man decides to go the zoo. When he arrives, all that is on display is a dog. It was a pretty Shi Tzu.

* A vicar was asked to dinner by one of his church members. He knew she was a bad housekeeper, but agreed to come. When he sat down at the table, he noticed that the dishes were the dirtiest that he had ever seen in his life. 'Were these dishes ever washed?' he asked his hostess, running his fingers over the grit and grime.
She replied, 'They're as clean as soap and water could get them.'
He felt a bit uncomfortable, but blessed the food anyway and started eating. It was really delicious and he said so, despite the dirty dishes. When dinner was over, the hostess took the dishes, went to the door and yelled, 'Here, Soap! Here, Water!'

* What's the definition of catatonic? Vitamins for a kitten.

* How can you train a dog?
  See a vet, he can make him heal!

* Why do vets make good manicurists?
  They're good at giving a pet a cure.

* How do you make a dog drink?
  Put it in a blender!

Rarely seen crossbreeds

* Pekingnese + Lhasa Apso = Peekasso, an abstract dog.

* Labrador Retriever + Curly Coated Retriever = Lab Coat Retriever,
  the choice of research scientists.

* Newfoundland + Basset Hound = Newfound Asset Hound, a dog for
  financial advisers.

* Terrier + Bulldog = Terribull, a dog prone to awful mistakes.

* Bloodhound + Labrador = Blabador, a dog that barks incessantly.

* Deerhound + Terrier = Derriere, a dog that's true to the end.

* Cocker Spaniel + Rottweiller = Cockrot, the perfect puppy for that
  philandering ex-husband.

* Bull Terrier + Shitzu = Bullshitz, a gregarious but unreliable breed.

PHONES

* Yo' momma is so stupid she tripped over a cordless phone.

* What's the difference between a man and E.T? E.T. phoned home.

* Terry and Jim phoned Bert, an acquaintance, to give their birthday greetings.
  They dialled the number and then sang 'Happy Birthday' together to him. When they had completed their terribly off-key rendition, they discovered that they had phoned the wrong number.
  'Don't let it bother you,' said the voice on the other end. 'You obviously need all the practice you can get.'

* An American phoned directory enquiries and asked for the knitwear company in Woven.
  The operator asked, 'Woven? Are you sure? There's no knitwear company that I can find.'
  'Yes,' the woman firmly responded, 'That's what it says on the label of my jersey – "Woven in Scotland."

* What did the big red phone box say to the little red phone box?
  'You're too young to be engaged.'

* Jerry was deeply in love with Myra, but couldn't pluck up enough courage to 'pop the question' face to face. So Jerry decided to ask her on the telephone.
  'Darling,' he blurted out, 'will you marry me?'

'Of course, I will, you silly boy,' Myra replied, 'but first, who's calling please?'

* If a homeless person holding a BlackBerry asks you for change, he is probably from the future.

Answer-machine messages

* A is for academics, B is for beer. One of those reasons is why we're not here. So leave a message.

* Hello, you are talking to a machine. I am capable of receiving messages. My owners do not need block-paving, windows, or a bathroom, and their carpets are clean. They give to charity through their office and do not need their picture taken. If you're still with me, leave your name and number and they may get back to you.

* You have reached the CPX-2000 Voice Blackmail System. Your voice patterns are now being digitally encoded and stored for later use. Once this is done, our computers will be able to use the sound of your voice for literally thousands of illegal and immoral purposes. There is no charge for this initial consultation. However, our staff of professional extortionists will contact you in the near future to further explain the benefits of our service, and to arrange for your schedule of payment. Remember to speak clearly at the sound of the tone. Thank you.

* Hi this is Sonya. I'm sorry I can't answer the phone right now. Please leave a message and then wait by the phone until I call you back.

✷ Hi, I'm not home right now but my answering machine is, so you can talk to it instead. Wait for the beep.

✷ Hello. I am David's answering machine. What are you?

✷ Please leave a message. However, you have the right to remain silent. Everything you say will be recorded and will be used by us.

✷ How do you keep an idiot in suspense? Leave a message and I'll get back to you.

✷ We might be in, we might be out, but leave a message and you might find out!

PHOTOGRAPHY

✷ Two photographers were talking. One said to the other, 'If you saw a man drowning and you could either save him or photograph the event ... what kind of film would you use?'

✷ Old photographers never die, they just have flashbacks.

✷ There was a haunted house on the outskirts of the town which was avoided by all the locals – the ghost which 'lived' there was feared by all.
However, an enterprising journalist decided to get the scoop of the day by photographing the fearsome phantom. When he entered the house, armed with only his camera, the ghost descended upon him, clanking

chains et al. He told the ghost, 'I mean no harm – I just want your photograph.' The ghost was quite happy at this chance to make the headlines – he posed for a number of ghostly shots.

The happy journalist rushed back to his darkroom, and began developing the photos. Unfortunately, they turned out to be black and underexposed.

So what's the moral of the story?

The spirit was willing but the flash was weak.

＊ My wife knows hundreds of photography jokes. You can't shutter up.

＠PRACTICAL ENGLISH USAGE

＊ Verbs HAS to agree with their subjects.

＊ Prepositions are not words to end sentences with.

＊ And don't start a sentence with a conjunction.

＊ It is wrong to ever split an infinitive. Avoid clichés like the plague. (They're old hat.)

＊ Also, always avoid annoying alliteration.

＊ Be more or less specific.

＊ Parenthetical remarks (however relevant) are (usually) unnecessary. Also too, never, ever use repetitive redundancies.

* No sentence fragments.

* Contractions aren't necessary and shouldn't be used.

* Foreign words and phrases are not apropos.

* Do not be redundant; do not use more words than necessary; it's highly superfluous.

* One should NEVER generalise.

* Comparisons are as bad as clichés.

* Eschew ampersands & abbreviations, etc.

* One-word sentences? Eliminate.

* Analogies in writing are like feathers on a snake.

* The passive voice is to be ignored.

* Eliminate commas, that are, not necessary. Parenthetical words however should be enclosed in commas.

* Never use a big word when a diminutive one would suffice.

* Use words correctly, irregardless of how others use them.

* Understatement is always the absolute best way to put forth earth-shaking ideas.

* Eliminate quotations. As Ralph Waldo Emerson said, 'I hate quotations. Tell me what you know.'

* If you've heard it once, you've heard it a thousand times: resist hyperbole; not one writer in a million can use it correctly.

* Puns are for children, not groan readers.

* Go around the barn at high noon to avoid colloquialisms.

* Even IF a mixed metaphor sings, it should be derailed.

* Who needs rhetorical questions?

* Exaggeration is a billion times worse than understatement.

* Proofread carefully to see if you any words out.

* The European Union commissioners have announced that agreement has been reached to adopt English as the preferred language for European communications, rather than German, which was the other possibility. As part of the negotiations, the British government conceded that English spelling had some room for improvement and has accepted a five-year phased plan for what will be known as Euro-English (Euro for short).
In the first year, 's' will be used instead of the soft 'c.'

Sertainly, sivil servants will resieve this news with joy.

Also, the hard 'c' will be replaced with 'k'. Not only will this klear up konfusion, but typewriters kan have one less letter.

There will be growing publik enthusiasm in the sekond year, when the troublesome 'ph' will be replaced by 'f'. This will make words like 'fotograf' 20 per sent shorter.

In the third year, publik akseptanse of the new spelling kan be expekted to reach the stage where more komplikated changes are possible.

Governments will enkorage the removal of double letters, which have always ben a deterent to akurate speling.

Also, al wil agre that the horible mes of silent 'e's in the languag is disgrasful, and they would go.

By the fourth year, peopl wil be reseptiv to steps such as replasing 'th' by 'z' and 'w' by 'v'.

During ze fifz year, ze unesesary 'o' kan be dropd from vords kontaining 'ou', and similar changes vud of kors be aplid to ozer kombinations of leters.

Und efter ze fifz yer, ve vil al be speking German like zey vunted in ze forst plas.

✳ The teacher asked the little girl if she was going to the school fete. 'No, I ain't going,' was the reply.

The teacher corrected the child: 'You must not say, "I ain't going," you must say, "I am not going."

And she added to impress the point: 'I am not going. He is not going. We are not going. You are not going. They are not going. Now, dear, can you say all that?'

The little girl nodded and smiled brightly. 'Sure!' she replied. 'They ain't nobody going.'

✳ A widowed Jewish lady, still in good shape, was sunbathing on a mostly deserted beach. She looked up and noticed that a man her age, also in good shape, had walked up, placed his blanket on the sand near hers and begun reading a book.

Smiling, she attempted to strike up a conversation with him. 'How are you today?'

'Fine, thank you,' he responded, and turned back to his book.

'I love the beach. Do you come here often?' she asked.

'First time since my wife passed away two years ago,' he replied and turned back to his book.

'I'm sorry to hear that. My husband passed away three years ago and it is very lonely,' she countered. 'Do you live around here?'

'Yes, I live in San Francisco,' he answered, and again he resumed reading.

Trying to find a topic of common interest, she persisted, 'Do you like pussy cats?'

With that, the man dropped his book, came over to her blanket, tore off her swimsuit and gave her the most passionate lovemaking of her life. When the cloud of sand began to settle, she gasped and asked the man, 'How did you know that was what I wanted?'

The man replied, 'How did you know my name was Katz?'

✳ A businessman arriving in Boston for a convention found that his first evening was free, and he decided to go and find a good seafood restaurant that served Scrod, a Massachussetts speciality. Getting into a taxi, he asked the cab driver, 'Do you know where I can get Scrod around here?' 'Sure,' said the cab driver. 'I know a few places ... but I can tell you it's not often I hear someone use the third-person pluperfect indicative any more!'

🍎RELiGiON

❋ The Pope was finishing his sermon. He ended it with the Latin phrase, 'Tuti homini' – Blessed be mankind. A women's rights group approached the Pope the next day. They noticed that he had blessed all of mankind, but not womankind.

So the next day, after his sermon, the Pope concluded by saying, 'Tuti homini, et tuti femini' – Blessed be mankind and womankind. The next day, a gay-rights group approached the Pope. They said they had noticed that he had blessed mankind and womankind and asked if he could also bless those who are gay. The Pope said, 'OK.'

The next day, the Pope concluded his sermon with, 'Tuti homini, et tuti femini, et tuti fruiti.'

❋ In Sunday school, they were teaching how God created everything, including human beings.

Little Johnny seemed especially intent when they told him how Eve was created out of one of Adam's ribs.

Later in the week, his mother noticed him lying down as though he were ill, and said, 'Johnny, what is the matter?'

Little Johnny responded, 'I have a pain in my side. I think I'm going to have a wife.'

✳ When cannibals ate a missionary they got a taste of religion.

✳ Definition of fear: a little dark room where negatives are developed.

✳ Did you hear about the man who went to see his guru but he wasn't ommmmm.

✳ An American man has been in business for many, many years and the business is going down the drain. He is seriously contemplating suicide and he doesn't know what to do.

He goes to his rabbi to seek advice. He tells the rabbi about all of his problems in the business and asks the rabbi what he should do.

The rabbi says, 'Take a beach chair and a Bible and put them in your car and drive down to the edge of the ocean. Go to the water's edge. Take the beach chair out of the car, sit on it and take the Bible out and open it up. The wind will riffle the pages for a while and eventually the Bible will stay open at a particular page. Read the first words your eyes fall on and they will tell you what to do.'

The man does as he is told. He places a beach chair and a Bible in his car and drives down to the beach. He sits on the chair at the water's edge and opens the Bible. The wind riffles the pages of the Bible and then stops at a particular page. He looks down at the Bible and his eyes fall on words that tell him what he has to do.

Three months later the man and his family come back to see the rabbi.

The man is wearing an expensive Italian suit. The wife is all decked out with a full-length mink coat and the child is dressed in beautiful silk. The man hands the rabbi a thick envelope full of money and tells him that he wants to donate this money to the synagogue in order to thank the rabbi for his wonderful advice.

The rabbi is delighted. He recognises the man and asks him what words in the Bible brought this good fortune to him.

The man replies: 'Chapter 11.'

✳ A man was brought to Mercy Hospital, and went in for coronary surgery.

The operation went well, and as the groggy man regained consciousness, he was reassured by a Sister of Mercy waiting by his bed.

'Mr Smith, you're going to be just fine,' the nun said while patting his hand. 'We do have to know, however, how you intend to pay for your stay here. Are you covered by insurance?'

'No, I'm not,' the man whispered hoarsely.

'Can you pay in cash?'

'I'm afraid I can't, Sister.'

'Do you have any close relatives, then?'

'Just my sister,' he replied, 'but she's a spinster nun.'

'Nuns are not spinsters, Mr Smith,' the nun replied. 'They are married to God.'

'OK,' the man said with a smile, 'then bill my brother-in-law.'

✳ The new priest is nervous about hearing confessions, so he asks an older priest to sit in on his sessions.

The new priest hears several confessions, then the old priest asks him to step out of the confessional for a few suggestions.

312 MAN WALKS INTO A BAR 3

The old priest suggests, 'Cross your arms over your chest and rub your chin with one hand.'

The new priest tries this.

The old priest then suggests, 'Try saying things like, "I see, yes, go on, and I understand, how did you feel about that?"'

The new priest says those things, trying them out.

The old priest concludes, 'Now, don't you think that's a little better than slapping your knee and saying, "No way! What happened next?"'

✳ The girl knelt in the confessional and said, 'Bless me, Father, for I have sinned.'

'What is it, child?'

'Father, I have committed the sin of vanity. Twice a day I gaze at myself in the mirror and tell myself how beautiful I am.'

The priest turned, took a good look at the girl and said, 'My dear, I have good news. That isn't a sin – it's only a mistake.'

✳ Two priests were going to Hawaii on holiday and decided that they would make this a real break by not wearing anything that would identify them as clergy.

As soon as the plane landed, they headed for a shop and bought some really outrageous shorts, shirts, sandals, sunglasses, etc.

The next morning they went to the beach, dressed in their 'tourist' garb and were sitting on beach chairs, enjoying a drink, the sunshine and the scenery when a drop-dead-gorgeous blonde in a tiny bikini came walking straight towards them. They couldn't help but stare and when she passed them, she smiled and said, 'Good morning, Father,'

'Good morning, Father,' nodding and addressing each of them individually, then passed on by.

They were both stunned. How in the world did she recognise them as priests?

The next day they went back to the shop, bought even more outrageous outfits – these were so loud, you could hear them before you even saw them – and again settled on the beach in their chairs to enjoy the sunshine, etc.

After a while, the same gorgeous blonde, wearing a string bikini this time, came walking towards them again. (They were glad they had sunglasses, because their eyes were about to pop out of their heads.) Again, she approached them and greeted them individually: 'Good morning, Father,''Good morning Father,' and started to walk away.

One of the priests couldn't stand it and said, 'Just a minute, young lady. Yes, we are priests, and proud of it, but I have to know, how in the world did YOU know?'

'Oh, Father, don't you recognise me? I'm Sister Angela!'

✳ A team of archaeologists was excavating in Israel when they came upon a cave.

Across the wall of the cave the following symbols were carved, in this order: a woman, a donkey, a shovel, a fish, and a Star of David. They decided that this was a unique find, and the writings were at least three thousand years old. They chopped out the piece of stone and had it brought to the museum where archaeologists from all over the world came to study the ancient symbols.

They held a huge meeting, after months of conferences, to discuss the meaning of the markings.

The president of the society stood up and pointed at the first drawing and said: 'This looks like a woman. We can judge that this race was family oriented and held women in high esteem. You can also tell that

they were intelligent, as the next symbol resembles a donkey; so they were smart enough to train animals to help them till the soil. The next drawing looks like a shovel of some sort, which means they even had tools to work with. Even further proof of their intelligence is the fish which means that if a famine had hit the earth whereby the crops didn't grow, they would take to the sea for food. The last symbol appears to be the Star of David, which means they were evidently Hebrew.'
The audience applauded enthusiastically.
Suddenly a little old man stood up in the back of the room and said, 'Idiots! Hebrew is read from right to left. This is what it says:
"Holy Mackerel, Dig the Ass on That Woman!!"'

* Mahatma Ghandi walked barefoot everywhere, to the point that his feet became quite thick and hard.
He also was quite a spiritual person.
Even when he was not on a hunger strike, he did not eat much and became quite thin and frail.
Furthermore, due to his diet, he had bad breath.
He came to be known as a super calloused fragile mystic plagued with halitosis.

The following statements about the Bible were written by children and have not been retouched or corrected (i.e., bad spelling has been left in)

- In the first book of the Bible, Guinesses, God got tired of creating the world, so he took the Sabbath off.
- Adam and Eve were created from an apple tree.
- Lot's wife was a pillar of salt by day, but a ball of fire by night.

- Noah's wife was called Joan of Ark because Noah built the ark, which the animals came to in pears.
- The Jews were a proud people and throughout history they had trouble with unsympathetic Genitals.
- Samson was a strong man who let himself be led astray by a Jezebel like Delilah.
- Samson slew the Philistines with the axe of the Apostles.
- Moses led the Hebrews to the Red Sea, where they made unleavened bread, which is bread without any ingredients.
- The Egyptians were all drowned in the dessert.
- Afterwards, Moses went up to Mount Cyanide to find the ten commendments.
- The first commandment was when Eve told Adam to eat the apple.
- The seventh commandment is 'Thou shalt not admit adultery.'
- Moses died before he ever reached Canada.
- The greatest miracle in the Bible is when Joshua told his son to stand still and he obeyed him.
- David was a Hebrew king skilled at playing the liar. He fought with the Finkelsteins, a race of people who lived in biblical times.
- Solomon, one of David's sons, had 300 wives and 700 porcupines.
- When Mary heard that she was the mother of Jesus, she sang the Magna Carta.
- Then the three Wise Guys from the east arrived and found Jesus in the manager.
- Jesus was born because Mary had an Immaculate Contraption.
- St John, the blacksmith, dumped water on his head.
- Jesus enunciated the Golden Rule, which says do one to others before they do one to you.
- He also explained that 'Man does not live by sweat alone.'

- It was a miricle when Jesus rose from the dead and managed to get the tombstone off the entrance.
- The people who followed Jesus were called the 12 decibles.
- The epistles were the wives of the apostles.
- One of the opossums was St Matthew who was also a taxi man.
- St Paul cavorted to Christianity. He preached the holy acrimony, which is another name for marriage.
- A Christian should have only one spouse. This is called monotony.

* A curious fellow died one day and found himself waiting in the long line of judgement. As he stood there he noticed that some souls were allowed to march right through the pearly gates into Heaven. Others, though, were led over to Satan who threw them into the burning pit. But every so often, instead of hurling a poor soul into the fire, Satan would toss a soul off to one side into a small pile. After watching Satan do this several times, the fellow's curiosity got the best of him. So he strolled over and asked Satan what he was doing.
'Excuse me, Prince of Darkness,' he said. 'I'm waiting in line for judgement, but I couldn't help wondering, why are you tossing those people aside instead of flinging them into the fires of Hell with the others?'
'Ah, those … ' Satan said with a groan. 'They're all from Manchester, they're too wet to burn.'

* Scholars have long debated the exact ethnicity and nationality of Jesus. Recently, at a theological meeting in Rome, scholars had a heated debate on this subject. One by one, they offered their evidence …

* There was an old priest who got sick of all the people in his parish who kept confessing to adultery. One Sunday, in the pulpit, he said, 'If I hear

one more person confess to adultery, I'll quit!'

Well, everyone liked him, so they came up with a code word. Someone who had committed adultery would say they had 'fallen'.

This seemed to satisfy the old priest and things went well, until the priest died at a ripe old age.

About a week after the new priest arrived. He visited the mayor of the town and seemed very concerned.

The priest said, 'You have to do something about the sidewalks in town. When people come into the confessional, they keep talking about having fallen.'

The mayor started to laugh, realising that no one had told the new priest about the code word. Before the mayor could explain, the priest shook an accusing finger at the mayor and said, 'I don't know what you're laughing about, your wife fell three times this week.'

✳ A minister told his congregation, 'Next week I plan to preach about the sin of lying. To help you understand my sermon, I want you all to read Mark 17.'

The following Sunday, as he prepared to deliver his sermon, the minister asked for a show of hands. He wanted to know how many had read Mark 17. Every hand went up.

The minister smiled and said, 'Mark has only 16 chapters. I will now proceed with my sermon on the sin of lying.'

Three Proofs That Jesus Was Mexican:

1. His first name was Jesus.
2. He was bilingual.
3. He was always being harassed by the authorities.

But then there were equally good arguments that ...

Jesus Was Black:

1. He called everybody 'brother'.
2. He liked Gospel.
3. He couldn't get a fair trial.

But then there were equally good arguments that ...

Jesus Was Jewish:

1. He went into His Father's business.
2. He lived at home until he was thirty-three.
3. He was sure his mother was a virgin, and his mother was sure he was God.

But then there were equally good arguments that ...

Jesus Was Italian:

1. He talked with his hands.
2. He had wine with every meal.
3. He used olive oil.

But then there were equally good arguments that ...

Jesus Was A Californian:

1. He never cut his hair.
2. He walked around barefoot.
3. He started a new religion.

But then there were equally good arguments that ...

Jesus Was Irish:

1. He never got married.
2. He was always telling stories.
3. He loved green pastures.

✳ There was once a newly ordained priest who joined the staff of a large, well-to-do parish. His boss, the senior priest, had been there for many years and was steeped in wisdom. The young priest was very full of himself, having taken a number of prizes for preaching in seminary. He was particularly proud of his efforts in the pulpit. Indeed, he said to his boss one day, 'Father, there is not a subject in the world that I could not, at the drop of a hat, find a biblical text for and then be able to preach a sermon.' The senior priest decided to put his young charge to the test. 'Well, my boy,' he said, 'don't you be preparing any sermon for mass next Sunday. Instead, when you get into the pulpit you will find a sealed envelope which I will have put there. Inside the envelope there will be a single sheet of paper on which I will have written a one-word topic. I defy you to find any kind of text that will fit.'
The young priest looked forward to the test with relish. The day came. He ascended the stairs into the pulpit. His boss was squirming with

anticipation. The young man opened the envelope, glanced at the sheet of paper on which was written the one word, 'CONSTIPATION', and proclaimed: 'And Moses took the two tablets and went off down the mountain … '

✳ An elderly couple is watching one of those television preachers on TV one night. The preacher faces the camera, and announces, 'My friends, I'd like to share my healing powers with everyone watching this programme. Place one hand on top of your TV and the other hand on the part of your body which ails you and I will heal you.'
The old woman has been having terrible stomach problems, so she places one hand on the television, and her other hand on her stomach. Meanwhile, her husband approaches the television, placing one hand on top of the TV and his other hand on his groin. With a frown his wife says, 'Peter, he's talking about healing the sick, not raising the dead!'

✳ On the outskirts of town, there was a huge nut tree by the cemetery fence. One day two boys filled up a bucketful of nuts and sat down by the tree, out of sight, and began dividing the nuts.
'One for you, one for me. One for you, one for me,' said one boy.
The bucket was so full, several rolled out towards the fence.
Cycling down the road by the cemetery was a third boy. As he passed he thought he heard voices from inside the cemetery. He slowed down to investigate. Sure enough, he heard, 'One for you, one for me. One for you, one for me.'
He knew what it was. 'Oh, my!' he shuddered. 'It's Satan and St Peter dividing the souls at the cemetery!' He cycled down the road as fast as he could and found an old man with a cane, hobbling along.

'Come quick!' said the boy. 'You won't believe what I heard. Satan and St Peter are down at the cemetery dividing the souls.'

After several pleas, the man hobbled to the cemetery with the boy. Standing by the fence he heard, 'One for you, one for me. One for you, one for me ... '

The old man whispered, 'Boy, you've been telling the truth! Let's see if we can see the devil himself.' Shivering with fear, they peered through the fence, yet they were still unable to see anything. The old man and the boy gripped the wrought-iron bars of the fence tighter and tighter as they tried to get a glimpse of Satan. At last they heard, 'One for you, one for me. And one last one for you. That's all. Now let's go get those nuts by the fence, and we'll be done.'

They say the old man made it back to town five minutes before the boy.

✳ There were two evil brothers. They were rich and used their money to keep their ways from the public eye. They even attended the same church and looked to be perfect Christians.

Then, their pastor retired and a new one was hired. Not only could he see right through the brothers' deception, but he also spoke well and true, and the church started to swell in numbers. A fund-raising campaign was started to build a new assembly. All of a sudden, one of the brothers died.

The remaining brother sought out the new pastor the day before the funeral and handed him a cheque for the amount needed to finish paying for the new building.

'I have only one condition,' he said. 'At his funeral, you must say my brother was a saint.'

The pastor gave his word and deposited the cheque.

The next day at the funeral, the pastor did not hold back. 'He was an

evil man,' he said. 'He cheated on his wife and abused his family.'
After going on in this vein for a small time, he concluded with:
'But, compared to his brother, he was a saint.'

✳ A drunken man staggers in to a Catholic church, sits down in a
confession box and says nothing.
The bewildered priest coughs to attract his attention, but still the man
says nothing.
The priest then knocks on the wall three times in a final attempt to get
the man to speak.
Finally, the drunk replies: 'No use knockin' mate, there's no paper in this
one either.'

✳ During a papal audience, a businessman approached the Pope and
made this offer: change the last line of the Lord's prayer from 'give us
this day our daily bread' to 'give us this day our daily chicken' and KFC
will donate ten million dollars to Catholic charities.
The Pope shook his head and said no to the offer. Two weeks later the
businessman approached the Pope again, this time with a fifty-million-
dollar offer. Again the Pope declined.
A month later the man offers a hundred million, and this time the
Pope accepts.
At a meeting of the Cardinals, the Pope announces his decision.
'I have good news and bad news. The good news is, we have a
hundred million dollars for charities. The bad news is, we lost the
Wonder Bread account.'

Genuine church notices

- The Scouts are saving aluminium cans, bottles, and other items to be recycled. Proceeds will be used to cripple children.
- The outreach committee has enlisted twenty-five visitors to make calls on people who are not afflicted with any church.
- Evening Massage – 6 p.m. The pastor would appreciate if the ladies of the congregation would lend him their electric girdles for pancake breakfast next Sunday morning.
- The audience is asked to remain seated until the end of the recession.
- Low Self-Esteem Support Group will meet Thursday at 7 p.m. Please use the back door.
- Ushers will eat latecomers.
- The third verse of Blessed Assurance will be sung without musical accomplishment.
- For those of you who have children and don't know it, we have a nursery downstairs.
- A songfest was hell at the Methodist church Wednesday.
- Due to the rector's illness, Wednesday's healing service will be discontinued until further notice.
- Remember in prayer the many who are sick of our church and community.
- The concert held in Fellowship Hall was a great success. Special thanks are due to the minister's daughter, who laboured the whole evening at the piano, which as usual fell upon her.
- Twenty-two members were present at the church meeting held at the home of Mrs Marsha Crutchfield last evening. Mrs Crutchfield and Mrs Rankin sang a duet, 'The Lord Knows Why'.
- The Revd Merriwether spoke briefly, much to the delight of the audience.

- Don't let worry kill you. Let the Church help.
- Thursday night Potluck Supper. Prayer and medication to follow.
- The rosebud on the altar this morning is to announce the birth of David Alan Belzer, the sin of Revd and Mrs Julius Belzer.
- This afternoon there will be a meeting in the south and north ends of the church. Children will be baptised at both ends.
- Tuesday at 4 p.m there will be an ice-cream social.
  All ladies giving milk will please come early.
- Wednesday, the Ladies Liturgy Society will meet. Mrs Jones will sing 'Put Me In My Little Bed' accompanied by the pastor.
- Thursday at 5 p.m there will be a meeting of the Little Mothers Club. All wishing to become Little Mothers, please see the minister in his private study.
- Sunday, a special collection will be taken to defray the cost of the new carpet. All those wishing to do something on the new carpet will come forward and get a piece of paper.
- The ladies of the church have cast off clothing of every kind and they may be seen in the church basement on Friday.
- A bean supper will be held on Tuesday evening in the church hall. Music will follow.
- At the evening service tonight, the sermon topic will be 'What is Hell?' Come early and listen to our choir practice.
- Weight Watchers will meet at 7 p.m at the First Presbyterian Church. Please use large double door at the side entrance.
- The 1996 Spring Council Retreat will be Hell May 10 and 11. Pastor is on vacation. Massages can be given to church secretary.
- Eight new choir robes are currently needed, due to the addition of several new members and to the deterioration of some older ones.
- Mrs Johnson will be entering the hospital this week for testes.

- The Senior Choir invites any member of the congregation who enjoys sinning to join the choir.
- Please join us as we show our support for Amy and Alan who are preparing for the girth of their first child.
- The Lutheran Men's group will meet at 6 p.m. Steak, mashed potatoes, green beans, bread and dessert will be served for a nominal feel.

* A little boy was walking down a dirt road after church one Sunday afternoon when he came to a crossroads where he met a little girl coming from the other direction.

'Hello,' said the little boy.

'Hi,' replied the little girl.

'Where are you going?' asked the little boy.

'I've been to church this morning and I'm on my way home,' answered the little girl.

'I'm also on my way home from church. Which church do you go to?' asked the little boy.

'I go to the Protestant church back down the road,' replied the little girl. 'What about you?'

'I go to the Catholic church back at the top of the hill,' replied the little boy.

They discover that they are both going the same way so they decided that they'd walk together.

They came to a low spot in the road where spring rains had partially flooded the road, so there was no way that they could get across to the other side without getting wet.

'If I get my new Sunday dress wet, my mum's going to skin me alive,' said the little girl.

'My mum'll tan my hide, too, if I get my new Sunday suit wet,' replied the little boy.

'I tell you what I think I'll do,' said the little girl. 'I'm gonna pull off all my clothes and hold them over my head and wade across.'

'That's a good idea,' replied the little boy. 'I'm going to do the same thing with my suit.'

So they both undressed and waded across to the other side without getting their clothes wet. They were standing there in the sun waiting to drip dry before putting their clothes back on, when the little boy finally remarked: 'You know, I never realised before just how much difference there really is between a Protestant and a Catholic!'

* Don't join dangerous cults: practise safe sects!

* If everyone is weightless in space, would a Catholic astronaut have mass?

* Did you hear about the church janitor who was also the organist? He had to watch his keys and pews!

* I once considered becoming a monk when I was young but I was cloisterphobic.

* Why did Eve swap her fig leaf for a bunch of flowers? She wanted to wear bloomers.

* If a priest is called a white collar worker, is a nun a creature of habit?

* How do you measure an evangelist's effectiveness? In billigrams.

❋ Why did the farmer bring milk to church? So it could be pastorised.

❋ Noah wasn't the first off the ark. He came forth.

❋ A nun was kicked out of the order for inappropriate attire: sheer habit.

❋ Amenities – the Greek goddess of luxury.

❋ What did the arsonist say in confession?
Bless me father, for I have singed.

❋ Did you hear about the medium who no longer believed in ghosts?
He became dispirited.

❋ I used to be able to clap with just one hand. But that was Zen, this is Tao.

❦RESTAURANTS

❋ Did you hear about the restaurant that took lemonade off the menu out of sprite?

❋ What happened to the man who didn't drain the cooked pasta properly? The chef gave him a restraining order.

❋ Man: I'll have the steak and kiddley pie, please.
Waiter: You mean steak and kidney, sir?
Man: That's what I said, diddle I?

﹡ A guy goes into a restaurant wearing a shirt open at the collar and is met by a bouncer who tells him he must wear a necktie to gain admission. So the man goes out to his car and he looks around for a necktie and discovers that he just doesn't have one. He sees a set of jump leads in his boot. In desperation he ties these around his neck, manages to fashion a fairly acceptable-looking knot and lets the ends dangle free.

He goes back to the restaurant and the bouncer carefully looks him over for a few minutes and then says, 'Well, OK, I guess you can come in … Just don't start anything.'

﹡ Why did the chef throw the food out the window? To see the butterfly!

﹡ 'Waiter!' shouted the furious diner. 'How dare you serve me this! There's a TWIG in my soup!'

'My apologies,' said the waiter. 'I'll inform the branch manager.'

﹡ A man asked a hot dog vendor, 'Can I have more onions?' 'No, that's shallot,' he replied.

﹡ A man, looking as if he had lost his last friend, entered a restaurant one morning and sat down at a table. He said to the waitress, 'Bring me two eggs fried hard, a slice of toast burned to a cinder, and a cup of very weak coffee.'

As she set the order in front of him, she asked, 'Anything else, sir?'

'Yes,' he answered, 'now sit down and nag me. I'm homesick.'

﹡ Two lawyers went into a restuarant and ordered two drinks. Then they produced sandwiches from their briefcases and started to eat.

The waiter became concerned and marched over and told them, 'You can't eat your own sandwiches in here!'
The lawyers looked at each other, shrugged their shoulders and then exchanged sandwiches.

✳ A man walks into a Chinese restaurant but is told by the maitre d' that there will be at least a twenty-minute wait. 'Would you like to wait in the bar, sir?' he says. The man goes into the bar and the bartender says, 'What'll it be?' The man replies, 'Give me a Stoli with a twist.' The bartender pauses for a few seconds, then smiles and says, 'Once upon time, there were FOUR little peegs … '

✳ 'What flavours of ice cream do you have?' enquired the customer. 'Vanilla, strawberry, and chocolate,' answered the new waitress in a hoarse whisper. Trying to be sympathetic, the customer asked, 'Do you have laryngitis?' 'No … ' replied the new waitress with some effort, 'just … erm … vanilla, strawberry, and chocolate.'

✳ The head waiter of an elegant restaurant recoiled in disgust as a man in boots, torn jeans and a leather jacket approached him. 'Hey, man,' he said, 'where's the toilet?' 'Go down the hall and turn left,' replied the head waiter. 'When you see the sign marked "Gentlemen" pay no attention to it and go right on in.'

✳ A woman sat down in small French restaurant and a waitress came over to take her order. 'I'll have the steak please.' 'Steak!' she yelled over her shoulder. The woman added, 'Make that well done.' The waitress turned away again. 'Torture it!' she yelled.

✳ Last night I ate Middle Eastern food, and this morning I falafel.

✳ Three couples are dining together.
The American husband says to his wife: 'Pass me the honey, Honey.'
The English husband says to his wife: 'Pass me the sugar, Sugar.'
The Polish husband says to his wife: 'Pass me the steak, Dumb cow.'

✳ I went to a spiritualist restaurant. It's very rare to find a steak this well done by a medium.

✳ A man stood in front of the counter at a fast food restaurant. 'I want two hamburgers,' he said. 'One with onions, and one without.'
'OK. Which one's without the onions?'

✳ I've never gone in for cow-tipping. Mind you, none has ever served me any food worth eating.

✳ Once a man went to a restaurant and ordered an egg. When it was brought he didn't like it so he informed the waiter that the egg was bad. Came the reply: 'I don't lay the eggs, sir, I just lay the table!'

✳ What do they serve at a topless bar? Strip steaks and rice pilaf.

✳ How many McDonald's counter girls does it take to change a light bulb? Two. One to change it and one to put some chips with it.

✳ Why was the restaurant called 'Out of this World'? Because it was full of Unidentified Frying Objects.

✳ Waiter: 'Is your food spicy, sir?'
Diner: 'No, smoke always comes out of my ears!'

✳ The lights were too bright at the Chinese restaurant so the manager
decided to dim sum.

✳ A tourist was lunching in a restaurant in China where the speciality was
duck. The waiter explained each dish as he brought it to the table.
'This is the breast of the duck; this the leg of the duck; this is the wing
of the duck, etc.'
Then came a dish that the visitor knew was chicken. He waited for the
explanation. Silence.
'Well?' he finally asked. 'What's this?'
The waiter replied, 'It's a friend of duck.'

✳ A new chef from India was fired a week after starting the job. He kept
favouring curry.

🍊ROMANCE

✳ Emily Sue passed away and Bubba called 911. The 911 operator told
Bubba that she would send someone out right away.
'Where do you live?' asked the operator.
Bubba replied, 'At the end of Eucalyptus Drive.'
The operator asked, 'Can you spell that for me?'
There was a long pause and finally Bubba said, 'How 'bout if I drag her
over to Oak Street and you pick her up there?'

✳ Did you hear about the girl who stole the policeman's heart? He made a cardiac arrest.

✳ Eight-year-old Johnnie came home from school one day. At the supper table he announced to his mother and father that tomorrow in school they were going to learn about sex education. The next evening at the dinner table Johnnie's mother asked, 'Well, Johnnie, what did you learn about sex education today?' Johnnie said, 'I think the teacher said we should avoid intersections and buy condominiums.'

✳ He told her she looked like Helen of Troy in her glasses. It was a classic optical allusion.

✳ There is a beautiful deserted island in the middle of nowhere where the following people are stranded:
Two Italian men and one Italian woman
Two French men and one French woman
Two German men and one German woman
Two English men and one English woman
Two Irish men and one Irish woman
One month later on the beautiful deserted island in the middle of nowhere:
The first Italian man killed the other for the Italian woman …
The two French men and the French woman are living happily together in a 'ménage à trois' …
The two German men have a rigid weekly schedule of when they alternate with the German woman …
The two English men are waiting for someone to introduce them to the English woman …

The Irish began by dividing their island north-south and setting up a distillery. They don't remember if sex was in the picture, because it got sort of foggy after the first few litres of coconut whisky, but at least they know the English aren't getting any!

* A drunk who smelled like a brewery got on a bus one day. He sat down next to a priest. The drunk's shirt was stained; his face was covered in bright red lipstick and he had a half-bottle of wine sticking out of his pocket.

   He opened the newspaper and started reading. A couple of minutes later he asked the priest, 'Father what causes arthritis?'

   'Mister, it is caused by loose living, being with cheap wicked women, too much alcohol, and contempt for your fellow man.'

   'Well, you don't say!!!' the drunk muttered and returned to reading his newspaper.

   The priest; thinking about what he'd said, turned to the man and apologised. 'I'm sorry, I didn't mean to come on so strong – how long have you had arthritis?'

   'I don't, Father, I was just reading in the paper that the Pope has it.'

* What do you call a forty-year-old on a hot date? A chaperone.

* How can you tell if a woman is really ugly?
   A cannibal takes one look at her and orders a salad.

A bachelor is:

One who never makes the same mistake once.

One who's footloose And fiancé free.

One who never Mrs a girl.

One who believes in life, liberty and the happiness of pursuit.

One who plays the game of love and manages to retain his amateur standing.

One who won't take 'yes' for an answer.

Signs Your Online Relationship Isn't Working Out

* You: Large, hairy man. Your online girlfriend: Large, hairy man.

* Her email programme rejects your messages not as 'undeliverable' but as 'unlikely to get you anywhere'.

* After months of shared experiences and emotional investments, she attacks you in the Mines of Quarn with a +5 Vorpal Sword when she learns you're worth 45,000 points.

* Returned mail: User unknown and never wants to hear from you again.

* Getting perhaps a bit too comfortable, she lets a reference to cutting her chin shaving slip by.

✳ You discover that she has been cutting and pasting her orgasms.

✳ Since her first email, Make.Money.Fast!@cyber-promotions.com has become cold and distant.

✳ She's suddenly changed her address to comingout@lesbian.com.

✳ In an ironic twist of fate, you discover that the object of your affection is a curvaceous eighteen-year-old, rather than the geeky fourteen-year-old boy she'd pretended to be.

🐛 SALESMEN

✳ Will returned to his old home town on a visit. While he was there he looked up his old friend Bob, who had the general hardware shop. He noticed as he went in that the two display windows were jammed full of soap. The two old friends greeted one another. As they did so, Will saw that every shelf in the shop was stacked with soap. 'Gosh! You've certainly got a lot of soap.' 'You think so? Look at this.' He took Will through to the storeroom which was also full of soap. 'I don't think I've ever seen so much soap.'
'Come with me.'
Bob lifted a trapdoor and took him down some steps into a huge cellar, which was jammed with soap from the floor to the roof.
'Wow! You really must sell a lot of soap.'
'No, I don't actually. But the fellow that sold it to me – man, could he sell soap!'

* Did you hear about the used-car salesman who started his own chain of showrooms and thus founded the Auto-man Empire?

* The salesman was shown in to see his customer, Mr Jones, who was staring out the window disconsolately.
'What seems to be the trouble?'
'I promised my wife a Pomeranian and the cheapest one I can get is two hundred pounds. It's too much.'
'You're right. I can sell you one for a hundred and twenty-five pounds.'
'Great! When can you deliver it?'
'I'll let you know.'
Once outside he rushed to a public telephone and rang his sales manager.
'Listen. I've just sold old Jonesy a Pomeranian for a hundred and twenty-five pounds. What the hell is a Pomeranian?'

* A housewife who was hard of hearing answered the door to find a salesman with a large sample case.
'Good morning, madam. I'm representing the Wonderwarm Woollen Works. We're offering discount prices on yarns that didn't come up to our proper standards. The colours ran and the yarns are a bit off-colour. Could I come in and show you my samples?'
'I'm sorry. I'm hard of hearing. What did you say?'
The salesman raised his voice.
'Would you be interested in some off-colour yarns?'
'Sounds like fun. Come in for a cup of coffee and you can tell them to me.'

✳ A rep was flying to a sales conference. It was his first experience in an aircraft, so he was a little nervous, but he tried not to let it show. He was very taken with the air hostess, and particularly flattered when she invited him to sit down the back with her. He asked her:
'Do many passengers get airsick?'
'Not many,' she replied. 'We usually spot them in advance and give them some sweets to suck.'
'What if that doesn't work?'
'Oh, maybe we put a blanket over them, or even give them some oxygen.'
'What if it still doesn't work?'
'Oh, then I bring them down the back to sit with me.'

✳ A rep for McSporran & McHaggis was caught in torrential rain. It came down in sheets. He sent off a telegram to Glasgow:
'MAROONED BY FLOODS, WIRE INSTRUCTIONS.'
Two hours later the reply came back: 'COMMENCE ANNUAL HOLIDAYS IMMEDIATELY.'

✳ Did you hear about the foul-mouthed barbecue salesman?
He was sacked for using inflammatory and propane language!

✳ Asking for directions in the Australian outback is often a chancy business. There was the rep who asked a farmer for directions to Goombungee. 'Take this road here for about two kilometres and turn left at the hollow log. You keep going for about three more kilometres and you'll come to Riley's dam. Turn left again. About four kilometres down the track you'll come to a big sign advertising sheep dip. Turn left there and keep going.' 'And that'll get me to Goombungee, will it?' 'No.

It'll get you back here. If I give you all the directions at once it'll only confuse you.'

❋ Selling used cars is his lot in life.

❋ A notorious used-car salesman wanted to buy a cow, so he approached a local farmer. He inspected the herd closely and picked out a beast. The farmer nodded his approval and told him:
'That there's a hundred pounds of cow.'
'Sounds OK,' said the car dealer, reaching for his wallet. 'I'll take her.'
'Of course that's just the basic price,' went on the farmer. 'There are some extras.' He did some calculations on a piece of paper and handed the result to his customer:

	£
Basic cow	100
Two-tone exterior	35
Additional stomach	85
Storage compartment & dispensing device	70
Four nozzles @	10
Real cowhide upholstery	65
Dual horns @	10
Automatic fly swatter	30
TOTAL	£445

❋ Buying a new lamp often involves a shady deal.

❋ Did you hear about the bogus sales offer? They were giving out dead batteries – free of charge.

* A marketing consultant was brought in by a sales organisation in an effort to boost figures. The sales manager took him into his office and showed him a big wall map with red pins stuck in it.

'That's our sales area. All those red pins represent reps we've got in the field. The figures are just not good enough. I don't know what we're doing wrong.'

'Well, the first thing you've got to do is take all the pins out of the map and stick them into your sales reps.'

* After rushing into a chemist, the nervous young man was obviously embarrassed when a prim, middle-aged woman asked if she could serve him.

'No – no,' he stammered, 'I'd rather see the chemist.'

'I'm the chemist,' she responded cheerfully. 'What can I do for you?'

'Oh … well, uh, it's nothing important,' he said, and turned to leave.

'Young man,' said the woman, 'my sister and I have been running this chemist's for nearly thirty years. There is nothing you can tell us that will embarrass us.'

'Well, all right,' he said. 'I have this awful sexual hunger that nothing will appease. No matter how many times I make love, I still want to make love again. Is there anything you can give me for it?'

'Just a moment,' said the little lady, 'I'll have to discuss this with my sister.'

A few minutes later she returned. 'The best we can offer,' she said, 'is twenty-five pounds a week and a half-interest in the business.'

* Man to salesman: 'Will this PC last five years?'
Salesman: 'Obsoleteley!'

Salespeak

- New: Different colour from previous design.
- Unmatched: Almost as good as the competition.
- Designed simplicity: Manufacturer's cost cut to the bone.
- Advanced design: The advertising agency doesn't understand it.
- Field-tested: Manufacturer lacks test equipment.
- Years of development: We finally got one that works.
- Revolutionary: It's different from our competitors.
- Breakthrough: We finally figured out a way to sell it.
- Improved: Didn't work the first time.
- Futuristic: No other reason why it looks the way it does.
- Redesigned: Previous faults corrected, we hope.
- Hand-crafted: Assembly machines operated without gloves on.
- Performance proven: Will operate through the warranty period.
- Meets all standards: Ours, not yours.
- New generation: Old design failed, maybe this one will work.
- Customer service across the country: You can return it from most airports.
- Unprecedented performance: Nothing we ever had before worked this way.
- Microprocessor controlled: Does things we can't explain.

SCIENCE FICTION

* How many ears has Captain Kirk got? Three: the right ear, the left ear and the final front ear.

✳ Luke Skywalker and Darth Vader are fighting a duel to the death when suddenly Darth says to Luke: 'Not only am I your father, but I also know what you're getting for Christmas!'
Taken aback by the change of subject and suspecting a trap, Luke replies cautiously: 'How could you possibly know what I'm getting for Christmas?'
Darth Vader: 'Because I've felt your presents!'

✳ Why wasn't R2D2 allowed to take part in the Star Wars sports day?
Because he tested positive for droids.

✳ Why did the Jedi trade in his light sabre for a Scottish knife?
He'd gone over to the dirk side.

✳ No one ever wants to babysit a naughty atom, they always have to keep an ion it.

🐦 SciENCE

✳ The astronomer's research project didn't win him the coveted Galaxy Award, but he did receive a constellation prize.

✳ Did you hear about the battery that had an alkaline problem?
It went to AA meetings.

✳ Atheists can't solve exponential equations because they don't believe in higher powers.

✳ Did you hear about the fight at the Copenhagen summit discussing global warming? It was quite a heated debate.

✳ It's hard to get a satellite dish. You have to go through the right channels!

✳ What happens if you drop your mobile in the sea? Call wading!

✿SCOTSMEN AND WOMEN

✳ How many Scotsmen does it take to change a light bulb?
Och! It's no that dark!

✳ A Scotsman walking through a field sees a man drinking water from a pool with his hand.
The Scotsman shouts: 'Awa ye feel hoor that's full o' coos sharn!'
(Don't drink the water, it's full of cow s ** t.)
The man shouts back: 'I'm English, speak English, I don't understand you.'
The Scotsman shouts back: 'Use both hands, you'll get more in.'

✳ When Jock moved to London he constantly annoyed his English acquaintances by boasting about how great Scotland was. Finally, in exasperation, one said, 'Well, if Scotland's so marvellous, how come you didn't stay there?'
'Well,' explained Jock, 'they're all so clever up there I had to come down here to have any chance of making it at all.'

✳ A Scotsman was travelling by train, seated next to a stern-faced clergyman. As the Scot pulled out a bottle of whisky from his pocket the clergyman glared and said reprovingly, 'Look here, I am sixty-five and I have never tasted whisky in my life!'

'Dinna worry, Minister,' smiled the Scotsman, pouring himself a dram. 'There's no risk of you starting now!'

✳ How do you disperse an angry Scottish mob? Nae bother – just take up a collection.

✳ Three guys – one Irish, one English and one Scottish, are walking along the beach one day and come across a lantern and a genie pops out of it.

'I give you each one wish, that's three wishes in total,' says the genie. The Irish guy says, 'I am a fisherman, my dad's a fisherman, his dad was a fisherman and my son will be one too. I want all the oceans full of fish for all eternity.'

So, with a blink of the genie's eye and a quick 'Alakazoom' the oceans were teaming with fish.

The English guy was amazed, so he said, 'I want a wall around England, protecting her, so that nothing will get in for all eternity.'

Again, with a blink of the genie's eye, 'Alakazoom – POOF' there was a huge wall around England.

The Scot asks, 'I'm very curious. Please tell me more about this wall.' The genie explains, 'Well, it's about 150 feet high, 50 feet thick, protecting England so that nothing can get in or out.'

The Scot says, 'Ach, fill it up with water.'

✳ A Scots pessimist is a man who feels badly when he feels good for fear he'll feel worse when he feels better.

✳ Every Scotsman's fantasy is to have two women … one cleaning, the other dusting …

✳ A Scottish football fan told his mate, 'My dog watches all the games. When my team wins it jumps up and doon and claps its wee paws. When we lose it somersaults.'
'Yer kiddin me right? How many somersaults?' asked his impressed friend.
The fan replied, 'Depends how often I kick it … '

✳ Did ye hear about the Scotsman who married a girl born on February the 29th so he'd only have to buy her a birthday present every four years?

✳ Double-glazing is doing great business in Scotland in the hope that the children cannot hear the ice-cream van when it comes round.

✳ A farmer's wife, who was rather stingy with her whisky, was giving a shepherd a drink. As she handed him his glass, she said it was extra good whisky, being fourteen years old. 'Well, missus,' said the shepherd, regarding his glass sorrowfully, 'it's very small for its age.'

✳ A Scotsman's nephew came to him with a problem. 'I have my choice of two women,' he said, 'a beautiful, penniless young girl whom I love dearly, and a rich old widow whom I can't stand.'
'Follow your heart; marry the girl you love.'

'Very well, Uncle,' said the nephew, 'that's sound advice.'
'By the way,' asked the uncle, 'where does the widow live?'

✳ 'I hear your girlfriend and you settled your difficulties and decided to get married after all,' said one Scotsman to another.
'That's right,' the other replied. 'She's put on so much weight that we couldn't get the engagement ring off her finger.'

✳ Have you heard about the lecherous Scotsman who lured a girl up to his attic to see his etchings? He sold her four of them.

✳ A Scottish newspaper ad: 'Lost – a £5 note. Sentimental value.'

✳ There were two Scots who bet a pound on who could stay under water the longest. They both drowned.

✳ Jock was in London wearing his tartan when a curious lady asked if there was anything worn under the kilt.
'No, madam,' he replied with a flourish. 'Everything is in perfect working order.'

✳ The following was seen on a poster in Argyll:
DRINK IS YOUR ENEMY.
Adjacent to this was another poster which said:
LOVE YOUR ENEMY.

✳ Did you hear about the last wish of the henpecked husband of a house-proud Edinburgh wife? He asked to have his ashes scattered on the carpet.

✳ The local train stopped at a station long enough for the passengers to stretch their legs. Sniffing the pure, clean air with appreciation, a passenger said to the guard: 'Invigorating, isn't it?'
'No,' he replied. 'Inverurie.'

✳ A Scotsman went into a shop to buy a pocket knife. 'Here's the very thing,' said the shopkeeper, 'four blades and a corkscrew.
'Tell me,' said the Scot, 'you haven't one with four corkscrews and a blade, have you?'

✳ A Scot was ill with scarlet fever. 'Send for my creditors,' he said.
'I can give them something at last.'

✳ 'I hear you're a great believer in free speech.'
'I am that, Angus.'
'Well, do you mind if I use your phone?'

✳ What if you cross a legendary Scottish monster and a bad egg?
The Loch Ness pongster.

✳ A Scotsman walked into a supermarket with his zipper down. A lady cashier walked up to him and said, 'Your barracks door is open.'
This is not a phrase Scotsmen normally use so he went on his way looking a bit puzzled.
When he was about done shopping, a man came up and said, 'Your fly is open.'
He zipped up and finished his shopping. He then intentionally got in the line to check out where the lady was who told him about his 'barracks door'. He was planning to have a little fun with her. When he reached

her counter he said, 'When you saw my barracks door open did you see a Scottish soldier standing in there at attention?'

The lady thought for a moment and said, 'No, I didn't. All I saw was a disabled veteran sitting on two duffle bags!!!'

* What is the name of the unhappy range of mountains in Scotland?
The Grumpians.

* Did you hear about the Scotsman who washed his kilt?
He couldn't do a fling with it.

* An Englishman, and Irishman and a Scotsman went into a bar.
The Englishman stood a round of drinks, the Irishman stood a round of drinks and the Scotsman stood around.

* How do you know if a Scotsman is left-handed?
He keeps all his money in his right-hand pocket.

* Did you hear about the Scottish kamikaze pilot?
He crashed his plane in his brother's scrap yard.

* Young Jock MacTavish got down on his knees to propose to her when a ten-pence piece dropped out of his pocket and rolled under the sofa. In the twenty minutes it took him to find it she had lost interest.

* A Scotsman went on a week's holiday to England. He took a clean shirt and a five-pound note with him. When he arrived home he hadn't changed either of them.

* It was a bitterly cold day on the golf course and the caddy was expecting a large tip from his rich Scottish client. As they neared the clubhouse, the caddy heard the words he was longing to hear, 'This is for a hot glass of whisky.' He held out his hand and a sugar cube was placed in it.

* What do you call two Scotsmen hanging from a washing line?
A pair of tights.

* A Scotsman bought two tickets for the lottery. He won five million pounds.
'How do you feel about your big win?' asked a newspaper reporter.
'Disappointed,' said the Scot. 'My other ticket didn't win anything.'

* My wife was the last of five Scottish sisters to marry, the confetti was filthy.

* A Scottish gift: 'It's nae use to me, ye're welcome to it.'

* Why is a Scottish boy with a cold like a soldier with seven days' leave?
Because they both have a wee cough.

* The McEwen brothers decided that one of their number would go to America and make his fortune, coming back to share it with the rest of them. The youngest, Ian, was chosen for this task. Off he went, and he worked hard in America, and earned himself a fortune over a few years, and wired his brothers that he'd be returning with it. When he came back to Scotland he got off the boat, and looked around for his brothers, but could not see anyone who looked familiar. Finally, a group

of bearded strangers approached. 'Ho, Ian, are ye not knowing yer own brothers?' asked the first one.

Then Ian realised his brothers had grown beards. 'Fer Heaven's sake, laddies, what would ye be growin' them beards for, now?' he asked.

'We had to, lad, ye took the razor wi' ye!'

✳ Tourist: 'I'm sorry, waiter, but I only have enough money for the bill. I have nothing left for a tip.'

Highland Waiter: 'Let me add up that bill again, sir.'

✳ The Scots have an infallible cure for sea-sickness. They lean over the side of the ship with a ten-pence coin in their teeth.

✳ A Scotsman walked into a fish and chip shop. 'I want ten pence worth of chips, please. I want lots of salt and vinegar on them and two pence worth of pickled onions. And wrap the whole lot in today's newspaper.'

✳ You should be careful about stereotyping the Scots as mean. There was a recent letter to a newspaper from an Edinburgh man which said: 'If you print any more jokes about mean Scotsmen I shall stop borrowing your paper.'

✳ A Scottish prayer – 'Oh Lord, we do not ask you to give us wealth. But show us where it is!'

✳ Did you hear about the Scotsman who got caught making nuisance telephone calls? He kept reversing the charges.

✳ Jimmy took his girlfriend out for the evening. They returned to her flat just before midnight and as she kissed him goodnight she said:

'Be careful on your way home. I'd hate anyone to rob you of all the money you've saved this evening.'

⁕ By mistake, a Scotsman put a fifty-pence coin instead of five pence on the collection plate at church. Despite his entreaties, the minister refused to give it back to him. So for the next nine weeks, when the plate was passed round, he passed it on saying, 'Season ticket.'

⁕ 'Jock suggested a candlelit dinner last night,' his wife reported to her friend the next day. 'That was dead romantic,' said her friend. 'Not really. It just saved him having to fix the fuse.'

⁕ A Scot asked the bus conductor how much it would cost to travel into town. 'Ninety pence,' said the conductor. He thought this was a bit steep so he decided to run after the bus for a few stops. 'How much now?' he asked. 'Still ninety pence.' The Scotsman ran after the bus for another three stops and, panting, he asked, 'How much now?' The conductor replied, 'A quid. You're running in the wrong direction!'

⁕ It is rumoured that the entire population of Glasgow took to the streets with an empty glass in their hands when the weather forecaster said there would be a nip in the air.

⁕ Scottish preacher to his congregation: 'I don't mind you putting buttons in the collection plate, but please provide your own buttons. Stop pulling them off the church cushions.'

⁕ Why are Scotsmen so good at golf? They realise that the fewer times they hit the ball the longer it will last.

Short people

What do you call a short Japanese leader? A sawn off Shogun!

Snakes

It was a sad day for the rattlesnake family. The time had come for the children to strike out on their own.

❧SPORTS

✳ The man was having trouble understanding darts, so his friend explained some of the finer points.

✳ He could play baseball, football, basketball, soccer and tennis. He was a jock of all trades.

✳ Did you hear about the football team who played on gravel?
The lost on aggregate.

✳ Did you hear about the athlete who hated running in lane eight as it made him feel like an outsider?

✳ Two robbers with clubs went golfing, but they didn't play the fairway.

✳ Pool players like to rack and roll.

* A basketball player and a jockey robbed a bank. Police are looking high and low.

* Golf is a lot like taxes – you drive hard to get to the green and end up in the hole.

* Golfers would wear wrinkled clothes if it weren't four irons.

* Did you hear about the man who became a golfer for a living?
He had to earn his bread and putter!

* I couldn't quite remember how to throw a boomerang, but eventually it came back to me.

* Marathon runners with bad footwear suffer the agony of defeat.

* I wanted to exercise last night but it just didn't work out.

* Do the people who climb the world's highest mountain ever rest?

* How do you become a good archer? By understanding arrowdynamics.

* Medical alert: Golf has been linked to risk of strokes due to iron deficiencies.

* Did you hear about the man who shouted so loud at the races he became the hoarse whisperer?

* Swimming can be easy or hard. It deep-ends.

✳ At the tennis equipment sale it's always first come first serve!

✳ Did you hear about the football player who stood in front of his fans?
He was blown away.

✳ Old formula-one drivers never die, they just write their auto biography.

✳ Have you heard about the new Olympic sprint for men who are thinning
on top? It's called the balderdash!

✳ Did you hear about the rifle competition?
The winner was victorious by a long shot.

✳ A high-scoring football match can be very offensive.

✳ What do tiny surfers ride? Microwaves.

✳ If a wrestler calls, don't put them on hold. They don't like it.

✳ What do arrogant cheerleaders have? Pompomposity!

✳ Cricketers are always shouting a catch phrase.

✳ What do prize fighters do before and after work?
Punch in and punch out.

✳ What did the angry sprinter do? He made a mad dash.

✳ What kind of discussions do scuba divers have? In depth ones!

* Cricket in the fog can be a bit hit and miss.

* When bungee-jumping never ask anyone to cut you some slack.

* What do you call a group of Olympic swimmers? A talent pool!

* Why do downhill skiers always change? They don't like to be in a rut.

* Spelunking: a grottofying experience.

* Why did the hurdler put rifles on his hurdles?
  He wanted to jump the gun.

* She played rounders and so did he. They hit it off.

* What sort of diet does a gymnast need? A balanced one.

* The coach didn't let him play all season. The result was a new benchmark.

* Did you hear about the cricket match where they used an orange for a ball? It added zest.

* What sort of diet does a retired boxer go on? Assault free.

* Why is it good sense to employ a 100-metre runner?
  Because they have a good track record.

* If you're addicted to football, you should think about kicking the habit.

✳ How are archery contests usually won? By an arrow margin.

✳ Why did the sprinter decide to go into politics?
He heard that you have to run for office!

✳ Why did the Irishman take a nail to the volleyball game?
He'd heard that you have to spike the ball.

✳ Why can't timid people be bullfighters?
They leave macho to be desired.

✳ How do tennis players insult each other?
They give backhanded compliments.

✳ Did you hear about the man who didn't want to go to the wrestling?
His friends had to twist his arm.

✳ Why was the criminal no good at ten-pin bowling?
His mind was always in the gutter.

✳ What's the Three Musketeers favourite game? Touche football.

✳ Why do boxers never buy a round? Because they're tight-fisted!

✳ What do you get if a jockey's clothes are too small? A tight race.

✳ When do you light an arrow? When you want to fire it.

✳ Surfing: a swell sport.

✴ What did the judges think of the surf contestant?
They gave him wave reviews!

🍎 STUDENTS

✴ A first-year student came running in tears to her father. 'Dad, you gave me some terrible financial advice!' she cried.
'I did? What did I tell you?' said the dad.
'You told me to put my money in that big bank, and now that big bank is in trouble.'
'What are you talking about? That's one of the largest banks in the world,' he said. 'Surely there must be some mistake.'
'I don't think so,' she sniffed. 'They just returned one of my cheques with a note saying, "Insufficient Funds!"'

✴ What's green and takes an hour to drink? A student grant cheque!

✴ If students had written the Bible the ten commandments would have actually only been five, but double-spaced and in a large font to make it look like ten.

✴ If students had written the Bible instead of God creating the world in six days and resting on the seventh, He would have put it off until the night before it was due and then pulled an all-nighter and hoped no one noticed.

✴ If all the students who slept through lectures were laid end to end, they'd all be a lot more comfortable.

✳ Economists report that a college education adds many thousands of pounds to a man's lifetime income – which he then spends sending his children to college.

✳ A college student was delivering pizza to a regular customer's house. The man who answered the door asked him, 'What's the usual tip?'
'Well,' replied the youth, 'this is my first trip here, but the other guys say if I get fifty pence out of you, I'll be doing great.'
'Is that so?' snorted the man. 'Well, just to show them how wrong they are, here's five pounds.'
'Thanks!' replied the youth. 'I'll put this in my college fund.'
'What are you studying?' asked the man.
The lad smiled and said: 'Applied psychology.'

✳ A professor was grading the essay finals he had just given his class and opened the exam book of a failing student to reveal blank pages and a hundred pounds in notes. The only thing written in the book was '£100 = 100% – I get an A.'
A month later, the student approached the professor. 'I don't understand,' he said. 'I failed the course. Didn't you read my final?'
The professor handed the student the exam book.
The student opened it to reveal fifty pounds and the phrase '£50 = 50% –You fail!'

✳ In a primary school classroom, the teacher notices a little puddle underneath Mary's chair.
'Oh Mary,' says the teacher, 'you should have put your hand up.'
'I did,' Mary replied. 'But it still trickled through my fingers.'

✳ While visiting a country school, the chairman of the Board of Education became provoked at the noise the unruly students were making in the next room.

Angrily, he opened the door and grabbed one of the taller boys who seemed to be doing most of the talking. He dragged the boy to the next room and stood him in the corner. A few minutes later, a small boy stuck his head in the room and pleaded, 'Please, sir, may we have our teacher back?'

✳ A pharmacist comes up with a pill which will bestow learning on people who take them. A student, needing some learning, goes to the pharmacy and asks what kind of knowledge pills are available.

The pharmacist says: 'Here's a pill for English literature.' The student takes the pill and swallows it and has new knowledge about English literature.

'What else do you have?' asks the student. 'Well, I have pills for art history, biology, and world history,' replies the pharmacist. The student asks for these, and swallows them and has new knowledge about those subjects.

Then the student asks: 'Do you have a pill for maths?' The pharmacist says, 'Wait just a moment,' goes to the storeroom, brings back a whopper of a pill, and plonks it on the counter.

'I have to take that huge pill for maths?' enquires the student.

The pharmacist replies, 'Well, you know maths always was a little hard to swallow.'

✳ Old teachers never die, they just grade away.

✳ Two students had a week of exams coming up. However, they decided to party instead. So, when they went to the exam, they decided to tell the professor that their car had broken down the night before due to a very flat tyre and they needed a bit more time to study.

The professor told them that they could have another day to study. That evening, both of the boys crammed all night until they were sure that they knew just about everything.

Arriving to class the next morning, each boy was told to go to separate classrooms to take the exam. Each shrugged and went to different parts of the building. As each sat down, they read the first question. 'For five points, explain the contents of an atom.'

At this point, they both thought that this was going to be a piece of cake, and answered the question with ease.

Then, the test continued … 'For 95 points, tell me which tyre it was.'

How university departments mark students

- DEPT OF PSYCHOLOGY: Students are asked to blot ink in their exam books, close them and turn them in. The professor opens the books and assigns the first grade that comes to mind.
- DEPT OF HISTORY: All students get the same grade they got last year.
- DEPT OF RELIGION: Grade is determined by God.
- DEPT OF PHILOSOPHY: What is a grade?
- LAW SCHOOL: Students are asked to defend their position of why they should receive an A.
- DEPT OF MATHEMATICS: Grades are variable.
- DEPT OF LOGIC: If and only if the student is present for the final and the student has accumulated a passing grade then the student will receive an A else the student will not receive an A.

- DEPT OF COMPUTER SCIENCE: Random number generator determines grade.
- DEPT OF PHYSICAL EDUCATION: Everybody gets an A.

TECHNOLOGY - NERDS

※ People who plug their computer keyboards into hi-fi systems aren't idiots. That would be stereotyping.

※ Why do tailors love the internet? For all the threads.

※ I should have been sad when my torch batteries died, but I was delighted.

※ I got a deal on a new computer, and they threw in the operating system to boot.

※ Did you hear about the geek who forgot to pay me for the computer he ordered? Bad cache memory.

※ Years ago, changing TV channels from a sitting position was only a remote possibility.

✳ What do nuclear physicists like to do on holiday? Go on a fission trip.

✳ Did you hear about the wedding of the two nuclear scientists?
  She was radiant, he was glowing.

✳ What IT jobs do descendants of ancient Mexicans favour? As techs.

Time

An hourglass is a waist of time.

When the thief saw two Rolexes he did a double-take.

Did you see the big new clock on the town hall? It's the tock of the town.

TITANIC

✳ What was the last thing the drunken passenger said on the *Titanic*?
  'I know I ordered ice but this is ridiculous!'

✳ What sort of cake do they have for desert on the *Titanic*?
  Upside-down cake!

✳ On the *Titanic* the captain calls a meeting of his officers: 'I have some good news and some bad news. Which do you want to hear first?'
  'The good news', replies an officer.
  'We'll get eleven Oscars.'

✳ What goes down well with ice? The *Titanic*!

✳ The chief designer of the *Titanic* had a lisp. That's unthinkable!

✳ *Titanic* was about to sink. People on the ship were shouting, crying, running and praying. A passenger went up to the captain to ask him a question.
Passenger: How far are we from land?
Captain: Two miles …
Passenger: Only two miles, then why are these fools making so much noise? I can swim that far easily.
Captain: Uh????
Passenger: In which direction should I swim?
Captain: Downward.

✳ According to legend, the last survivor of the *Titantic* was fond of saying: 'If it hadn't been for the ship going down, I'd be an American!'

✳ Sign seen in an office: The difference between this place and the *Titanic* is … they had a band!

✳ A management consultant was aboard the *Titanic* as the ship was listing badly. He stopped a hurrying steward and asked him:
'To confirm, are we short of lifebelts or lifeboats?'
'Both, Sir,' replied the steward.
'Excellent,' replied the consultant, 'we've made savings across the board.'

✳ Overheard as the *Titanic* went down:

So this isn't New York?

So has the all-night buffet been cancelled?

How much hand luggage can I take on the lifeboat?

Do you mind if I hold your baby for a minute?

Ooh my wife's fallen overboard. Hold the lifeboat. I've got to update my Facebook status.

✳ A teacher, a bin man, and a lawyer wound up together at the Pearly Gates. St Peter informed them that in order to get into Heaven, they would each have to answer one question.

St Peter turned to the teacher and asked, 'What was the name of the ship that crashed into the iceberg? They made a film about it.'

The teacher answered quickly, 'That would be the *Titanic*.' St Peter let him through the gate.

St Peter turned to the bin man and decided to make the question a little harder: 'How many people died on the ship?'

Fortunately for him, the bin man had been a big fan of Kate Winslet and answered, '1,228.'

'That's right! You may enter.'

St Peter then turned to the lawyer. 'Name them.'

🌀TOURISM

✳ A bus load of tourists arrives at Runnymede. They gather around the guide who says, 'This is the spot where the barons forced King John to sign the Magna Carta.'

A fellow at the front of the crowd asks, 'When did that happen?'

'1215,' answers the guide.

The man looks at his watch and says, 'Damn! Just missed it by a half hour!'

✳ A frightened tourist at the back of the group raised his hand: 'Are there any bats in this cave?'

'There were, but don't worry, the snakes ate all of them,' replied the guide.

✳ The coach pulled to a halt. One tourist piped up: 'Can you tell me why so many famous Civil War battles were fought on National Park Sites?

✳ 'And will there be anything else, sir?' the bellboy asked after setting out an elaborate dinner for two.

'No thank you,' the gentleman replied. 'That will be all.'

As the young man turned to leave, he noticed a beautiful satin negligee on the bed. 'Anything for your wife?' he asked.

'Yeah! That's a good idea,' the fellow said. 'Please bring up a postcard.'

✳ Walking through Chinatown, a tourist is fascinated with all the Chinese restaurants, shops, signs and banners. He turns a corner and sees a building with the sign, 'Hans Olaffsen's Laundry'.

'Hans Olaffsen?', he muses. 'How in hell does that fit in here?'

So he walks into the shop and sees an old Chinese gentleman behind the counter.

The tourist asks, 'How did this place get a name like Hans Olaffsen's Laundry?'

The old man answers, 'Is name of owner.'

The tourist asks, 'Well, who and where is the owner?'

'Me ... is right here,' replies the old man.

'You? How did you ever get a name like Hans Olaffsen?'

'Is simple,' says the old man. 'Many, many year ago when come to this country, was stand in line at Documentation Centre. Man in front was big blonde Swede. Lady look at him and go, "What your name?" He say, "Hans Olaffsen." Then she look at me and go, "What your name?" I say "Sem Ting."'

TRAFFIC WARDENS

* Two old people were walking along the road. A traffic warden approached them and pointed at a car, and said they were parked in the wrong space. The old couple denied it but the traffic warden wrote out a ticket. The old man protested in a colourful volley of swearwords but the traffic warden simply stuck the ticket on the car. The old man then shrugged and turned to his wife and said, 'lucky for us we came here by bus.'

* Why do traffic wardens have a yellow line round their hat?
So people don't park on their heads.

* As the coffin was being lowered into the ground at a traffic warden's funeral, a voice screamed from inside, 'I'm not dead! I'm not dead!' To which the vicar shouted back, 'Sorry, the paperwork has already been done!'

* I was parking my car up yesterday when a rather angry traffic warden banged on the window and shouted, 'You can't park your car there!' I said, 'I can, the sign says "Fine for Parking"!'

TRAINS

* A man on the northbound 'Night Caledonian' sleeping car train ordered one of the attendants, 'I have to be off at Perth, I'm a heavy sleeper but I must get off there. I want you to put me off, whatever I say.'
The next morning he woke up at Inverness!
Extremely annoyed, he found the attendant and gave him a piece of his mind. After he had left, somebody asked the attendant, 'How could you stand there and take that kind of talk?'
'That's nothing!' replied the attendant, 'you should have heard the man I put off at Perth!'

* Why do steam locos have a sore bottom? Because they have a tender behind!

* Monorail enthusiasts have a one-track mind.

* What's the difference between a teacher and a guard?
One trains the mind, the other minds the train.

* A man and his wife check into a hotel. The husband wants to have a drink at the bar but his wife is extremely tired so she decides to go on up to their room to rest.
She lies down on the bed and just then a train passes by very close to the window and shakes the room so hard she's thrown out of the bed.
Thinking this must be a freak occurrence, she lies down once more.
Again a train shakes the room so violently she's thrown to the floor.
Exasperated, she calls the front desk and asks for the manager.

The manager says, 'I'll be right up.'

The manager is sceptical but the wife insists the story is true.

'Look, lie here on the bed – you'll be thrown right to the floor!'

So he lies down next to the wife.

Just then the husband walks in. 'What do you think you're doing?' he says.

The manager calmly replies, 'Would you believe I'm waiting for a train?'

＊ A passenger train is creeping along, painfully slow. Finally, it creaks to a complete halt. A passenger sees the guard walking by outside. 'What's going on?' she yells out the window.

'Cow on the track!' replies the guard. Ten minutes later, the train resumes its slow pace. Within five minutes, however, it stops again. The woman sees the same guard walking by again. She leans out the window and yells, 'What happened? Did we catch up with the cow again?'

＊ A young English woman decided to visit Germany by train. The German ticket inspector on the train punched her ticket, then chatted cordially for a bit, making gestures like a windmill. The young lady simply nodded from time to time to show him that she was interested. When he had gone, an American woman soldier in the compartment leaned forward and asked if the young lady spoke German.

'No,' she confessed.

'Then that explains it,' she said. 'Explains what?' asked the young woman. 'Why you didn't bat an eyelid when he told you that you were on the wrong train.'

＊ What do you call a train man who steps on a live rail? A conductor!

✳ Did you hear that they're making a new fuel for trains out of grapes in France? They call it 'Vin Diesel'.

✳ There once was a five-year-old boy who enjoyed playing with his train set. One afternoon, his mother happened to be standing by the door listening to the boy play. She was shocked when she heard him saying, 'All right, all of you sons of bitches who want to get on the train, get on the train. And all of you sons of bitches who want to get off the train, get off the train. And all of you sons of bitches who want to change seats, change seats now 'cause the train's getting ready to leave. Whoo whooooo.'
The mother was just devastated, so she scolded her son and said to him, 'Now, son, I want you to go upstairs and take your nap, and when you get up, you can't play with your train set for two hours.' So the boy took his nap and didn't even mention his train set for two hours. After the two hours were up, the boy asked his mum if he could play with his train set again. She said yes, and asked him if he understood why he was punished. He nodded his head yes, and off he went. The mother stood by door to listen to what her son would say.
The boy sat down to his train set and calmly said, 'Whoo whoooooo. All of you ladies and gentlemen, who want to get on the train, get on the train. All of you ladies and gentlemen, who want to get off the train, get off the train. And all you sons of bitches who are pissed 'cos the train is two hours late, go talk to the bitch in the kitchen.'

✳ Did you hear about the man who got a new job with a railway?
He had to keep track of everything.

✳ Why is it dangerous to doze on trains? They run over sleepers!

✳ An elderly gentleman on a train was mumbling to himself, smiling, and then raising his hand. After a moment of silence, he would go through the same process: mumble, smile, raise hand, silence.

Another passenger observed this, and after about an hour, he said, 'Pardon me, sir. Is anything wrong?' 'Oh, no,' replied the pensioner. 'It's just that long trips get boring so I tell myself jokes.'

'But why, sir,' asked the passenger, 'do you keep raising your hand?'

'Well,' said the old man, 'that's to interrupt myself because I've heard that one before.'

✳ A Scotsman left on a long trip taking a train the entire length of the line. Still at each station along the way he insisted that he had to get off the train to buy a new ticket. And he did not buy a ticket for his final destination, but just one to take him to the next stop on the line.

After watching this go on for several hours, another passenger asked, 'Why are ye buying all of these tickets, mon? Why not just save time and money and just get one ticket for the rest of your trip?'

The Scot scowled at the very idea and darkly replied, 'My doctor has told me that I am not long for this world and I don't plan to waste any of my moneys on train tickets I won't use while I am here.'

✳ An elderly lady walked into a Toronto ticket office and asked for a ticket to New York. 'Do you want to go by Buffalo?' enquired the ticket agent. 'Certainly not!' she answered indignantly. 'I want to go by train!'

✳ Why is the railway angry? Because people are always crossing it!

✳ A couple of honeymooners got on the sleeper train to Scotland. The new bride's eyes lit up as they entered their cabin when she saw a sign on the door: 'Notice to all passengers sleeping on board. The berth rate has gone up.'

* Why don't elephants like to ride on railways?
They hate leaving their trunks in the baggage car.

* How many conductors does it take to change a light bulb?
Only one, but to no avail as he always punches a hole in the new bulb.

VICES

* Don't change from alcohol to drugs – it'll leave you high and dry.

* Did you hear about the alcoholic who wasn't sure if he could really give up drink so he had a dry run?

* Why can't you take another polygraph test? They can't be re-lied upon.

* It beats me why anyone would want to be a masochist.

* Did you hear about the man who was arrested for growing marijuana? He said his friends were involved too – it was a joint venture.

* Did you hear about the man who wanted to go to a topless bar? When he arrived they'd gone bust.

 WINTER

٭ The Indians asked their chief in autumn if the winter was going to be cold or not. Not really knowing an answer, the chief replies that the winter was going to be cold and that the members of the village were to collect wood to be prepared.

Being a good leader, he then went to the next phone booth and called the National Weather Service and asked, 'Is this winter to be cold?'

The man on the phone responded, 'This winter is going to be quite cold indeed.'

So the chief went back to speed up his people to collect even more wood to be prepared. A week later he called the National Weather Service again, 'Is it going to be a very cold winter?'

'Yes,' the man replied, 'it's going to be a very cold winter.'

So the chief goes back to his people and orders them to go and find every scrap of wood they can find. Two weeks later he calls the National Weather Service again: 'Are you absolutely sure that the winter is going to be very cold?'

'Absolutely,' the man replies, 'the Indians are collecting wood like crazy!'

✳ Winters were fierce in Scotland, so the owner of the estate felt he was doing a good deed when he bought earmuffs for his gamekeeper. Noticing, however, that the gamekeeper wasn't wearing the earmuffs even on the bitterest day, the owner asked, 'Didn't you like the muffs?'
The gamekeeper said, 'They're a thing of beauty.'
'Why don't you wear them?'
The gamekeeper explained, 'I was wearing them the first day, and somebody offered to buy me lunch, but I didn't hear him! Never again, never again!'

✳ A young couple purchased an old home in north Scotland from two elderly sisters. Winter was fast approaching and the wife was concerned about the house's lack of insulation. 'If they could live here all those years, so can we!' the husband confidently declared, always keen to save a few pounds.
One November night the temperature plunged to below zero, and they woke up to find the interior walls covered with frost. My husband called the sisters to ask how they had kept the house warm. After a rather brief conversation, he hung up.
'For the past thirty years,' he muttered, 'they've gone to Florida for the winter.'

✳ What do chefs call Baked Alaska in Alaska? Baked Here.

✳ Getting a job in the Arctic in the winter is great! Why?
When the days get short, you only have to work a thirty-minute week.

✳ What kind of maths do Snowy Owls like? Owlgebra.

✳ What do you call fifty penguins in the Arctic?
Lost! (Penguins live in Antarctica.)

✳ Arguments about the weather always eventually blow over.

✳ What did the detective in the Arctic say to the suspect?
'Where were you on the night of September to March?'

✳ What should women use to stay young-looking in the wintertime?
Cold cream.

✳ It was so cold hitchhikers were holding up pictures of thumbs!

✳ It was so cold … the optician was giving away free ice scrapers with every new pair of spectacles!

✳ It was so cold … kids were using a new excuse to stay up late:
'But, Mum, my pyjamas haven't thawed out yet!'

✳ It was so cold … the squirrels in the park were throwing themselves at an electric fence!

✳ It was so cold … Grandpa's teeth were chattering – in the glass!

✳ It was so cold … the snowman knocked on the door and asked to sleep on the couch!

✳ It was so cold … I chipped a tooth on my soup!

✳ Knock! Knock!
Who's there?
Blue!
Blue who?
Blue your nose – the cold is making it run!

✳ Knock! Knock!
Who's there?
Alaska!
Alaska who?
Alaska my mum if I can come out and play in the snow.

✳ Knock! Knock!
Who's there?
Eddy!
Eddy who?
Eddy idea how I can cure this cold!

✳ Knock! Knock!
Who's there?
Mammoth!
Mammoth who?
Mammoth is sthuck 'cause I'th been eatin' peanuth buther!

✳ Knock! Knock!
Who's there?
Emma!

Emma who?
Emma bit cold out here – let me in!

✳ Knock! Knock!
Who's there?
Tobias!
Tobias who?
Tobias some nice cold ice cream, you need some money.

✳ Knock! Knock!
Who's there?
Mandy!
Mandy who?
Mandy lifeboats – the ship has hit an iceberg!

✳ Knock! Knock!
Who's there?
Aurora!
Aurora who?
Aurora's just come from a big polar bear!

✳ Knock! Knock!
Who's there?
Howard!
Howard who?
Howard you like to stand out in the cold while some idiot keeps asking
'Who's there?'

✳ Fred and his wife lived in Anchorage, Alaska. One winter morning while listening to the radio, they heard the announcer say, 'We are going to have 8 to 10 inches of snow today. You must park your car on the even-numbered side of the street, so the snow plough can get through.' Fred's wife went out and moved her car.

A week later while they are eating breakfast, the radio announcer said, 'We are expecting 10 to 12 inches of snow today. You must park your car on the odd-numbered side of the street, so the snow plough can get through.'

Fred's wife went out and moved her car again.

The next week they are having breakfast again, when the radio announcer said, 'We are expecting 12 to 14 inches of snow today. You must park … ' then the electric power goes out.

Fred's wife is very upset, and with a worried look on her face she asked, 'Honey, I don't know what to do. Which side of the street do I need to park on so the snow plough can get through?'

Patiently and kindly Fred said, 'Why don't you just leave it in the garage this time?'

✳ An elderly woman lived on a small farm in Canada, just yards away from the North Dakota border.

Their land had been the subject of a minor dispute between the United States and Canada for years. The widowed woman lived on the farm with her son and three grandchildren.

One day, her son came into her room holding a letter. 'I just got some news, Mum,' he said. 'The government has come to an agreement with the people in North Dakota. They've decided that our land is really part of the United States. We have the right to approve or disapprove of the agreement. What do you think?'

'What do I think?' his mother said. 'Sign it! Call them right now and tell them we accept! I don't think I can stand another Canadian winter!'

✳ There were three Inuit in the Arctic, and while drinking at a local bar they got to talking about how cold it was outside, and how cold their igloos were. They couldn't agree on whose igloo was the coldest, so they set out to find out whose was.
They went to the first Inuit's igloo, where he said, 'Watch this!'
He poured a cup of water into the air. The water froze in mid-air and fell onto the floor solid.
'Not bad,' said the other Inuit, but each maintained their igloo was colder.
They went to the second Inuit's igloo and he said, 'Watch this!' He took a big breath, exhaled and his breath froze into a big solid lump of ice and fell to the floor.
'Wow, that's colder than mine!' said the first Inuit.
But the third Inuit believed his igloo was colder. So off they went to his igloo.
'Watch this,' he said.
He went into the bedroom, threw back the thick furs and retrieved one of several small balls of ice lying there. He placed one on a spoon, lit a match and held it under the spoon.
When it heated up enough, the little ball of ice went 'FFFAAAARRRRTTT!'

WORK AND JOBS

* Resolving to surprise her husband, an executive's wife called at his office. She found him with his secretary sitting in his lap. Without hesitating, he dictated, ' … and in conclusion, gentlemen, shortage or no shortage, I cannot continue to operate this office with just one chair.'

* Did you hear about the rubbish cobbler? He was given the boot!

* The man who worked at the watch factory was very funny. He stood about all day making faces.

* Why do blacksmiths have loyal customers?
Because they forge strong links.

* Did you hear about the man who qualified to be a carpenter?
He nailed his woodwork test.

* What happened when the electrician made a mistake?
He was grounded.

* Why are dry-cleaners often in a rush? They are pressed for time.

* Why was the marine biologist sacked? He made a mistake on porpoise.

* Why do builders carry see-through lunchboxes?
So they can tell if they are going to or coming home from work.

* A construction worker goes to the doctor and says, 'Doc … I'm constipated, could you help me?'

  The doctor examines him, and after a minute tells him to lean over the table.

  The construction worker leans over the table and the doctor hits him square on his bottom as hard as he can with a baseball bat!!

  Then he sends him into the bathroom to do his business.

  The construction worker comes out a few minutes later and says, 'Doc … I feel great!! What should I do so this doesn't happen again?'

  With that the doctor replies, 'Stop wiping with cement bags.'

* What is a South African lumberjack's favourite month? Septimber!

* A worker was killed on a building site – the circumstances were suspicious.

* Did you hear about the speaker at the firearms convention who lost his place and had to rifle through his notes?

* The police began questioning the workers. Many had criminal records. Here are some past offences …

  The plumber leaked these stories because he felt he was trapped.

  The roofer had fallen on some bad times and went to the hospital with shingles. Everything was dropped because they felt his third story was OK.

  The electrician was once suspected of wiretapping … though was never charged.

  The carpenter was almost nailed for trying to frame another man, who thought he was a stud.

The painter has had several brushes with the law ... many times he tried to run; his alibis were thin.

The HVAC man was known to pack heat, he was arrested but duct the charges.

The mason was suspected because he gets stoned regularly.

The cabinetmaker was an accomplished counter fitter.

﹡ If a lawyer can be disbarred can a musician be denoted or a model deposed?

﹡ Did you hear about the woman who became a lifeguard to keep the buoys in line?

﹡ Why is being a litter collector a great job? It's always picking up!

﹡ Why couldn't the woman get a job at the post office?
It was a mail-dominated profession.

﹡ Why are weather forecasters no good at taking decisions?
Their thinking is often clouded.

﹡ Did you hear about the redundant shepherd? He felt ewes less.

﹡ Roofers are OK, but they can be a bit shingle-minded.

﹡ Why did the stripper quit her job? She couldn't bare it.

﹡ Massagers always knead new clients.

✷ What happened when the glassblower inhaled?
He got a pane in the stomach!

✷ Why couldn't the lumberjack cut down the tree? He was stumped!

✷ I want to work in a sleep clinic. It's my dream job.

✷ Finally, the carpenter confessed. The autopsy confirmed the person was hammered when they died.

✷ Rebuilding a kitchen is counter-intuitive.

✷ Why do engineers enjoy fixing steelwork together? Because it's riveting.

✷ Why do roofers hate to lie to you?
Because afterwards they have to fascia.

✷ How do you build with wood that you don't want polished?
Use timber with a clear lacq of varnish.

✷ Did you hear about the nosy roofer who got sacked?
He couldn't stop the eavesdropping.

✷ There was a terrible body count when customers fell through the mezzanine at the new shopping centre. Apparently it was due to a fatal floor.

✷ Why did the toilet paper go to the job centre? Two-ply for a job.

✳ Why are brickies always getting into fights? Because it's rude to point.

✳ Did you hear about the lazy rodent-catcher was always trying to weasel his way out of work?

✳ Why did the cabinetmaker get sacked?
He was always looking for the catch.

✳ Over the years lift-makers have had their fair share of ups and downs but thankfully none of them has been shafted.

✳ Who at discos is in charge of staring at bricks? The Party Wall Surveyor.

✳ Why was the chimney thrown out of art classes?
Because it wasn't drawing very well.

✳ I used worry about plumbing problems, but now that's just water under the fridge.

✳ Where do timber merchants hold rock concerts? Woodstock.

✳ Why did the bricklayer have trouble getting up in the morning?
Because he'd been bedded in mortar.

✳ Do lawyers refer to their homes as legal pads?

✳ I asked the removal men if they could quickly move some donkeys.
They said they could haul some ass.

✳ Two blonde builders were working on a house. One blonde was on a ladder doing some nailing. She'd reach into her nail pouch, pull out a nail, look at it, and either toss it over her shoulder or proceed to nail it into the wood.

The other blonde couldn't stand it any longer and yelled up, 'Why are you throwing some of the nails away?'

The first blonde explained, 'When I pull it out of my nail pouch, if it's pointed towards me I throw it away. If it's pointed towards the house, then I can use it!'

The second blonde got real excited and called her all kinds of names, explaining, 'Don't throw away those nails that are pointed towards you! They're for the other side of the house!'

✳ Did you hear about the prospector who gave it up? He didn't think it would pan out.

✳ I'm in ore of steelworkers.

🍎WRITERS AND WRITING

✳ How many publishers does it take to screw in a light bulb?
Three. One to screw it in. Two to hold down the author.

✳ Back when papers were written on clay tablets there was a lot of breaking news.

✳ I don't like rhymes. Poetry is averse to me.

✳ Why is communism complicated? You have to consider all Engels.

✳ Last night, I kept dreaming that I had written *Lord of the Rings*. The wife said I'd been Tolkien in my sleep.

✳ Why did the young man visit the lady librarian every day?
He wanted to get into her good books.

✳ A backwards poet writes inverse.

✳ Why are grammarians never late? They are always punctual.

✳ Did you hear about the writer who left his notes on a new book about the American Civil War outside? One gust and suddenly it was all gone with the wind.

✳ How many screenwriters does it take to change a light bulb?
Answer: Ten.
First draft. Hero changes light bulb.
Second draft. Villain changes light bulb.
Third draft. Hero stops villain from changing light bulb. Villain falls to death.
Fourth draft. Lose the light bulb.
Fifth draft. Light bulb back in. Fluorescent instead of tungsten.
Sixth draft. Villain breaks bulb, uses it to kill hero's mentor.
Seventh draft. Fluorescent not working. Back to tungsten.
Eighth draft. Hero forces villain to eat light bulb.
Ninth draft. Hero laments loss of light bulb. Doesn't change it.
Tenth draft. Hero changes light bulb.

✳ How many cover blurb writers does it take to screw in a light bulb? A VAST AND TEEMING HORDE STRETCHING FROM SEA TO SHINING SEA!!!!

✳ Poets are often big. They stanza tall.

✳ What's another name for writer's cramp? Authoritis!

✳ Jokes about writer's block aren't funny because of … you know … stuff … and things.

✳ Writing programmes for prisoners have their prose and cons.

✳ Did you hear about the author who worked in his basement? He wrote a best cellar!

✳ The book about Teflon contained no frictional characters.

✳ Why did the baby bird get such a small advance from his publisher? He was just a fledgling author.